# LIVING
## AT THE
# EDGE
## OF THE
# WORLD

ALSO BY JAMIE PASTOR BOLNICK

*Winnie: My Life in an Institution*

# LIVING
## AT THE
# EDGE
## OF THE
# WORLD

A TEENAGER'S SURVIVAL IN THE
TUNNELS OF GRAND CENTRAL STATION

TINA S.
AND JAMIE PASTOR BOLNICK

ST. MARTIN'S PRESS ⚹ NEW YORK

www.stmartins.com

Book design by Clair Moritz

Library of Congress Cataloging-in-Publication Data

Pastor Bolnick, Jamie.
    Living at the edge of the world: a teenager's survival in the tunnels of Grand Central Station / Tina S. and Jamie Pastor Bolnick—1st ed.
        p. cm.
    ISBN 0-312-20047-1
    1. Homeless teenagers—New York (State)—New York. 2. Teenage girls—New York (State)—New York. 3. Runaway teenagers—New York (State)—New York. 4. Grand Central Terminal (New York, N.Y.)—Social conditions. I. S., Tina. II Title.

HV4506.N7 P37 2000
362.74—dc21

00-040238

First Edition: September 2000

10  9  8  7  6  5  4  3  2  1

To Ann Marie: who has held my hand and never lost her grip. To my family and friends who loved and supported me. In loving memory of April, who I believe is my guardian angel, and who will always be alive in my heart. And to my mom, for although she never got to read my story, I'm grateful I had the chance to spend her last days at her side as her friend and daughter.

—T.S.

To Ron, for practically everything

—J.P.B.

# ACKNOWLEDGMENTS

Thanks to:
George and Harriet McDonald, for giving me a new lease on life.
Jamie and her family, for believing in me when there were days I didn't.
Everyone at Ready, Willing & Able, who helped me through the tough days.
The people at Samaritan Village, who gave me the tools to start rebuilding my life.
And Pollie, for her help and support.

—T.S.

Thanks to:
Thomas Antenen, Deputy Commissioner for Public Information, New York City Department of Corrections, for allowing me to visit Rikers Island, and Assistant Deputy Joseph Patrissi, also of the New York City Department of Corrections, who was an informative and patient guide.
Dave Kreuter, Program Director, and Lil Helthaler, Assistant Director of Operations, at Samaritan Village in Ellenville, New York, as well as all the residents who made me feel welcome when I visited.
Attorney Nancy Lee Ennis, for her considerable time, trouble, and expertise.
Mike McGrady, for reading an early draft and offering astute advice, and also Geraldine Medina, Bernadette Medina-Nieves, and Samantha Pomerance, who read portions of the work and supplied helpful feedback.
My agent, Clyde Taylor, who believed in this project from day one; my editor at St. Martin's Press, Michael Denneny, whose insightful editing helped shape this book; and Christina Prestia, who smoothed the way.
The late Katherine Baugh, for sharing her grace, wisdom, and strength.
My family: Ron, Britt, and Piers, for their enduring love and support.
And all the people of Grand Central Terminal who trusted me enough to share their lives, and left an indelible imprint upon my own.

—J.P.B.

# Author's Note

All personal names, including street aliases, have been changed with the exception of George, Harriet, and Abigail McDonald; Harold Dow and Dan Rather of CBS; April; Ron (author Jamie Pastor Bolnick's husband); and Tina. In addition, certain identifying characteristics such as physical descriptions and locations have been altered.

Tina sometimes had difficulty placing an event in time, especially when it occurred during the chaos of her years in Grand Central Station. In such instances, the chronology of events was reconstructed by relying on Tina's best recollections, as well as on objective data from hospital and police records, and diaries Tina kept in rehab and on probation.

Obviously, Tina could not have remembered all the conversations that took place during the more than ten years this book spans. When necessary, dialogue has been re-created to reflect the essence of her various interactions.

Every prominent character is portrayed faithfully; a few characters who were, at best, peripheral to Tina's story are composites. Much of the book, after all, takes place in Grand Central Station, and the number of people who drifted in and out of Tina's daily life during her four years in residence most certainly was in the hundreds. Similarly, while the majority of events depicted took place exactly as reported, a few that occurred over a period of time have been condensed for the sake of brevity and readability. However, each and every scene in this story represents our best efforts to accurately recount Tina's experiences.

—J.P.B.

# INTRODUCTION

"YOU WANT TO TALK TO someone who really knew April?" Brian asks. He nods in the direction of the second row of benches. "There she is. Over yonder. Scarf on her head."

It would be easy to spot her, scarf or no scarf. She is the only white person besides me in this part of the waiting room, and one of the few females. She seems very young; although I later learn she is eighteen, she doesn't look much older than my fourteen-year-old daughter. She is wearing bleached-out jeans, a T-shirt, and scruffy sneakers. A red cowboy bandanna holds back her dark hair and she has a butter-cookie face, round and sweet and innocent.

"She knew April better than anyone," Brian continues. "They were best friends."

"What's her name?"

"Tina. She'll talk to you. I'll tell her you're okay." Although just as homeless as everyone else who hangs out in Grand Central Terminal, Brian is highly respected, a definite leader. I made friends with him early on. Having Brian's okay carries weight.

But it's not that easy with Tina. When Brian introduces us she hangs back, when she speaks it's sometimes so soft I can't hear, and I have the feeling that at any moment she's going to bolt. It's like trying to make friends with a fawn.

I explain I'm researching a book about April, have been interviewing people who knew her, and Brian has just informed me she was April's closest friend. Tina was in jail when April died last month, serving thirty days for probation violation, and she learned of April's death while in jail. This is her first time back in Grand Central since, and the reality is just now sinking in. She seems shell-shocked. "I don't want to talk about her," she tells me. "Let April rest in peace."

I tell her that from what I know about April, resting in peace might not really appeal to her.


I barely knew April when she was alive. Occasionally I saw her darting around the station, always in a hurry to get wherever she was going. Sometimes she'd come outside to the Coalition for the Homeless food van, where I worked as a volunteer on weekend nights, to get a sandwich and a pint of milk for someone who was too sick, too old, or too stoned to come out and wait on line. Everybody knew April, not just the homeless who lived with her in and around Grand Central but the station workers, vendors, police, and homeless advocates. She was young and pretty, smart, funny, and articulate—and a favorite of the media. She was interviewed by numerous reporters when they came to do stories on the homeless, and early in 1986, when CBS brought their cameras to Grand Central Terminal to film a story on the homeless for Dan Rather's nightly news program, their interview with April was a main feature.

I was there the night it was filmed and I remember how Harold Dow, the anchorperson, and his crew went with April into a stairwell off the station's main concourse so they could shoot in relative privacy. In the piece, April is sitting on the stairs talking of her resolve to someday leave Grand Central. She wants to marry a rich man and live in a big house, even bigger than Grand Central, but, she explains, she knows her Prince Charming will never find her here.

She looks especially glowing and vibrant: her skin is luminous under the white television lights, her dark hair glistens, and her eyes shine with spirit.

Dan Rather used portions of that footage again a year and a half later, when he did a follow-up after April killed herself.


It was April I set out to write about but, ultimately, Tina who hooked me and pulled me in. That first day, when Brian introduced us, Tina had recently finished serving her thirty days on Rikers Island and had been assigned to a residential drug rehabilitation program in Harlem—she was battling addictions to alcohol and crack. I was able to persuade her to talk to me briefly about April and to describe for me on tape how they'd met two and a half years earlier, when both girls were just sixteen, and how Tina subsequently left home to join April in Grand Central.

We've been sitting on one of the worn wooden benches in the waiting room, and after a few minutes of conversation Tina abruptly stands and says, "Well, I'm outta here."

"Wait," I say. "Can we set up another interview for the next time you're around?"

"I don't know," she replies. "They make me follow this tight schedule at the rehab place." She gazes restlessly around the room, pulls a pack of Newports from her jeans, takes out a cigarette and lights it. Despite the cigarette, she doesn't look much older than twelve.

"Anyways," she adds, "there's not much reason to come around now that April's gone." She gives a small, sad shrug, and for a second I think she's going to cry. Instead, she turns on her heel and is gone.


During the next two years, I spent three or four days a week around Grand Central Terminal. By the end of that period I had collected hundreds of taped interviews with the people who lived in and around the station. And I had found it impossible to spend so much time with a group of people, even one as large and transient as the population of Grand Central, without becoming intrinsically involved in many of their lives.

Rio was a handsome and intelligent man in his late twenties—the love of April's short life—who came from a large, close-knit Hispanic family. He was still very attached to his family and suffered considerable guilt for the shame his lifestyle brought upon them. Several times he asked me to call them, to feel them out and see if the door was still open. It always was, and on at least two occasions, determined to kick his drug habit and build an honest life, he returned home to his mother's house in rural Sullivan County. Both times he was back at Grand Central within three months. The city was in his blood and he was almost as addicted to the rush and danger of street life as he was to crack and heroin. Not long after his second visit home he was caught robbing an apartment on the Upper East Side and sentenced to three to seven years in an upstate prison that is, coincidentally, a short distance from where his family lives.

I also made a phone call home for a seventeen-year-old boy named Jackie. He was a good friend of both April's and Tina's, and one of the few other white kids among the station regulars. Jackie was so strung out on crack that he'd sit around the waiting room some days crying and sobbing because he was terrified by the way he was deteriorating. He'd lost twenty pounds, his hair was falling out in great patches, and he couldn't remember things that had happened to him the day before (like how he'd gotten two black eyes and a lacerated jaw). He wanted to go home. Unfortunately, Jackie's family wasn't as receptive as Rio's. When I called them at their Long Island home, at Jackie's request, his parents refused to talk with me. Instead, his grandfather got on and explained that Jackie had repeatedly sold off valued family possessions for drug money and that his parents did not care to hear from him anymore. Eventually Jackie dropped out of sight. I have no idea what happened to him, but I hope he was somehow able to save himself.

Once in a while somebody left Grand Central. They picked themselves up by their bootstraps and, with Herculean effort and usually some help from someone in an outreach organization, entered a residential program, moved upstate to work at one of the farms that employed the city's more motivated disenfranchised, enrolled in a long-term drug treatment program, or just plain went back home. I rooted for them all. But in the years I was around, I knew of only one person who got out and stayed out—by means other than jail or death. And that was Tina.

Tina was back at Grand Central full-time. Shortly after I met her she left the rehab program and resumed her old life, this time with a vengeance. She seemed bent on self-destruction, drinking and drugging as if she had to take in April's share, too.

I had asked Tina to call me if she was able to find some notebooks of April's that she thought might still be down in the tunnels, or just to let me know when she was around Grand Central and available to be interviewed. I wrote down my number on a page of yellow legal tablet I carried in my backpack along with the tape recorder. She thanked me offhandedly, then crumpled it up and jammed it into the back pocket of her jeans. I didn't think she'd keep it, let alone ever use it.

But one night about a month later she calls.

"It's Tina," she says, as soon as I pick up the phone.

"Tina. Are you okay?"

"I gotta talk to someone. I'm going crazy and there's no one I can talk to."

"I'm listening," I tell her.

"Because the others, they don't wanna hear your problems. They don't care. Unless you got crack they don't give a shit about you. Nobody gives a shit about anybody in this place."

"So maybe it's time to think about getting out."

"Yeah, yeah. I do. I do think about getting out."

"So why don't you?"

"Where would I go?"

"Your family, maybe?"

"My mom's in a welfare hotel with my little brother and sister. They got no room for me. And they don't need my problems."

"What about a good rehab program?"

"The thing is, I'm feeling so goddamn alone, you know?"

"Where are you now, Tina?"

"In a phone booth in the waiting room. I'm drinking. I been drinking a lot today. And I'm wondering sometimes what my life would be like now if I never met April. Maybe I wouldn't be living here, maybe I wouldn't be into drugs. I miss April so much I want to die, but maybe meeting her was the worst thing that ever happened to me, because I followed her here. And now I'm so alone. You know? You know that feeling you get when you're so alone?"

"I think."

"It's like, it's like nobody in the whole fucking world cares. Because you're worthless." I can hear tears in her voice; I can hear her fighting to hold them back. "I mean, I want a better life. But I don't know if it's possible. I only see two choices, wind up in jail or kill myself like April did."

I want to reach down into the phone and grab this kid and shake some life and love into her. "Oh, Tina, one thing you're not is worthless."

"I'm just a fucking runaway. I do bad things."

"You're not a runaway, you're a kid who ran away. You try to hide it, but you're a good person, Tina, smart and pretty and caring. You've got so much good stuff inside you, but you just haven't realized it yet."

There's a silence, long enough for me to wonder if she's hung up and I've been talking to myself. Then I hear a harsh, choking sound, and I realize she's sobbing convulsively.

"I need to hear that from someone," she says when she is able to speak again, "I need to hear that from someone."


Tina did get out, and she is now in the process of building a better life. It's been an uphill struggle, ten years of it at this writing, sometimes two steps forward and one step back. She's got a way to go but she's definitely on course.

Throughout, she's had help and support from several dedicated homeless advocates, a few close friends, and me and my family. She has said on several occasions that she couldn't have made it "without you guys," but she's only partially right. She clawed her way out of the tunnels with her own strength—we just grabbed on to a grubby little hand and helped her along.

Recently Tina expressed the need to tell her story as a way of examining her past, making some sense of it, and, ultimately, putting it to rest. She and

I began working together with a tape recorder, reliving her memories and setting them down. Because I became involved in her life when she was eighteen, I was able to help her fill in some of the blanks. This is, however, Tina's story, in Tina's own words. We offer it with the hope that its telling will help Tina and, perhaps, a few others, too.

—James Pastor Bolnick
New York City
February 2000

"BUT IF I AM TO HEAL I MUST FIRST LEARN TO FEEL."

—*from the song "Ruins" by Melissa Etheridge*

# LIVING
## AT THE
# EDGE
## OF THE
# WORLD

*I have to get to April.*

*I'm running through dark tunnels, running and stumbling over train tracks, my face wet from tears, my jeans wet because I peed in them while he was choking me. But the tunnels are endless, and even though I know this place like the back of my hand, because it's where I live, somehow I keep getting lost.*

*Footsteps behind me. Maybe it's him. Maybe he's still in the tunnels and he's coming after me. I want to scream for help, but there's no one to hear me and the cops would just arrest me anyhow. Because I'm homeless. Because I'm underage. Because they can charge me with trespassing for being down here.*

*The footsteps are coming closer. Slamming into the gravel between the tracks. I try to go faster. My sneaker comes down on something soft and slippery and I slide, have to fight to keep my balance so I don't fall down. The soft, slippery thing, it's a dead rat. Lying mashed across the track, all pinkish brown and red. If I weren't crying so hard I'd puke.*

*I have to get to April. I know she's down here somewhere. But he's right behind me now. I don't need to turn my head to know he's close enough to reach out and grab me. He's going to do it to me again. It's going to happen all over again.*

*Where is April?*

———— • ————

Sinead is shaking me, shaking me by the shoulders. "Stop," I tell her. I try to push her away so I can sit up in bed. The little light is on; it's the middle of the night. "Why did you wake me up?"

"You were having another nightmare."

Then I remember about running through the tunnels. The man. And trying to find April.

"You need a tissue," Sinead says. She hands me one from the little packet on the bed stand and points to her cheeks. That's when I realize mine are wet. I've been crying in my sleep. "Are you okay, Tina? You want some hot tea?"

I rub at my cheeks, my eyes, shake my head no.

She asks me, "Do you want to talk about it?"

I do. I want to talk about everything. But I don't know if anybody in the world can really understand. Or if it's even fair to Sinead to tell her everything.

"No." I scrunch down in the bed. Sinead looks tired and we both have to be up for work at six. "Just leave the light on."

"Okay," she says. "Are you sure you're all right?"

"Fine. Go to sleep."


Some of the dreams are so real. Especially the ones about April. When I dream about April it's like she's really alive and I'm really with her. One funny thing I've been noticing recently: the older I get, the younger she seems. I'm getting older but she never will.

When I think Sinead is sleeping I get out of bed real quietly. The dogs are asleep, Einstein on the floor near the foot of the bed, Minnie on the La-Z-Boy. Rubbish, the cat, is up on the windowsill ledge, curled in a ball on her pillow.

Then I do what I always do after a nightmare. I tiptoe into the living room, switch on the lamp. Sinead's blue canvas tote bag is on the table where she puts it at night. On one of the futons there's a copy of *Pet Sematary* by Stephen King, which I'm reading for the second time. Also on the futon is a rubber chew toy in the shape of a fire hydrant that Einstein and Minnie always fight over. The futon, it's kind of a funky color—lavender and silver. The other one is deep purple.

Up against the wall near the futons is a brand-new twenty-seven-inch TV and a VCR that Sinead bought. The rest of the furniture is from our old apartment. Some of the stuff is a little chewed from the time when Einstein and Minnie were puppies, but we're saving up little by little to replace it. One day everything will be new.

The room looks quiet and clean and peaceful, except for the little red words SET CLOCK on the VCR that keep blinking off and on because we haven't been able to program it. I flick off the lamp.

The kitchen is ready for morning: sink and counter clean, a couple of pots drying in the drain, coffeemaker full and timer set for 5:50 A.M. I scrubbed the floor over the weekend and it still looks shiny.

I go down the hall, past the room where my sister, Jessica, is sleeping, unlock the front door, and crack it open just enough so I can see the street out front. It's dead quiet now. Third car from the corner is ours. A second-hand Dodge. It's there, right there where I parked it when I came home last night. It's still there.

Everything is still there. Everything is real.

In the bedroom I pat Einstein and Minnie on the head, scratch Rubbish behind her ears. Einstein stands up, does a couple of turns, and lies back down on the floor. I crawl into bed. I'm feeling safe again.

I lean over and turn out the light.

# PART ONE

THE COPS ARE FOLLOWING ME. I can hear their walkie-talkies somewhere behind me, I can hear that crackling static sound they make, I can hear one of the cops saying, "Okay, we got a tail on her now."

Or maybe they're not following me. You get real paranoid when you're smoking crack.

I'm walking up Lexington Avenue and I need more smoke real bad, so I duck into a doorway, light up, and then I have to start walking because I'm getting paranoid again. Keep moving, keep running to stay safe. Because I can hear those cops behind me with their walkie-talkies.

Three, four, five hours I've been doing this. Maybe all day. I'm so high now I don't even know where I am anymore.

These are the clothes I've been wearing for at least a week: jeans, sneakers, two layers of T-shirts, over them a plaid flannel shirt and a sweatshirt. Over all that is a man's blue down jacket I took from the backseat of a car that me and Jackie broke into. And under that is grime and soot that doesn't come off when I wash anymore. Built-in dirt, I call it.

When I get tired I sleep where I am. A doorway, a park bench, a stair landing in the subway, wherever I happen to be when I can't keep on going. I don't even bother, a lot of the time, to go back to Grand Central Station.

It's like I'm running away from running away.

If I'm not too stoned, I'm sometimes looking at other people lately, people I'm passing on the street. People going to work or coming from work, people going home to wherever they live. I wonder what it's like to be them. And how did they manage to do it, to just be so right and ordinary and safe?

Probably they're thinking I'm dirt. Probably they're thinking I'm shit, just a piece of garbage.

That makes me want to sink even lower, get so far down no one can see me anymore. To where I have nothing left to lose. Or maybe to where I just plain stop existing. Because I know as long as I continue to exist there's a choice I'm making: staying like this, or getting better.

But I don't want to do either one. It hurts too much.


The baby I'm carrying, it's Harley's. I know that. Because I wasn't messing around with anyone else. Harley wants me to keep it. He started making all these promises, he gave me the "It'll Be Okay" story: "I'll change, I'll stop dealing drugs, I'll get a job, you'll see, we'll get an apartment, we'll get married."

I told him, "Yeah, right, Harley. Forget it. It's my body, it's my choice." Hey, I'm not stupid, you know? I just looked at him like he was crazy. Like who the hell do you think you're kidding? I'm not going to do this for you. I don't love you enough to do this for you.


When I've had a lot to smoke I talk to myself. Only I don't realize what I'm doing until I see people staring at me when I pass them on the street. Then I notice my lips are moving and words are coming out.

I'm having all these little conversations with myself when I'm stoned. I feel like nobody else in the world can understand what I'm trying to say anymore.


Harley spots me dozing on the steps of St. Agnes Church, half a block from Grand Central. He bugs out.

"I told you to leave that fucking shit alone and go home," he yells. He's talking about crack, but while he's yelling this at me, he has his stem in his hand, ready to fill it up and take a blast.

"Sure, Harley. While you sit there getting high."

"I'm not fuckin' pregnant."

"I wouldn't be neither if you didn't lie to me. You said you were being careful."

Harley is a big guy, black, he wears his hair in clumpy dreadlocks. He can be sweet, which is why I stay with him, but when he gets mad you better duck fast. He's mad now. Grabs me around the neck with his big hands and squeezes. I'm trying to push him away, but he just squeezes tighter until I start choking. "You don't belong on the streets when you got a baby inside you. Go on home to your mama, girl."

He lets me go so suddenly I fall against the railing of the steps. My throat hurts too much to yell back at him.


My mom is surprised to see me at the door because usually I call first. Also, I'm dirty and crying. She's seen me dirty before, but I almost never cry in front of people unless I'm drunk.

All I tell her is some guy was strangling me. By now there's bruises coming up on my neck. She says, "I'll call the cops."

"No," I tell her, "I'll be all right. I just need to rest."

My mom lives in a welfare hotel, the Prince George. Her and my little brother and sister, and my mom's boyfriend, Robert, who is the father of my little brother. All in one room, like sardines. My other brother, Frankie, who is almost my age, doesn't live with them anymore. This is my mom's second time in a welfare hotel. When I was twelve we had to move from our house in Astoria, Queens, because of a fire and we wound up spending a year in the Martinique Hotel.

I run home to my mom once in a while. I don't go there because she can protect me, I'm just running to someplace where I know no one can hurt me. My mom, she has her own troubles. Plus she and Robert are always fighting and screaming at each other. He gets his welfare check, runs off to Forty-second Street, comes back broke, breaks down the door to get in, then they fight all night long. He wants more money, and she doesn't have it because she spent it on food or clothes for the kids. And if it isn't about big stuff like money it's about something little, like my mom turning the TV off, him turning it back on. It's insanity. I feel sorry for my sister and brother, who are stuck there.

When I'm at my mom's I can take a shower, I can eat, and if they're not fighting I can get some sleep. There are two sets of bunk beds in the hotel room. I sleep in with Robby on the bottom or up top with Jessica. But Jessica moves around a lot while she sleeps, and she kicks. Sometimes I wake up in the morning with bruises.

When I'm leaving, my mom always says something like, "I worry about you all the time. Every time I see something on the news I'm wondering if it's you."

I tell her, "I'm fine, Ma. I can take care of myself."

I never stay more than a couple days.

About a week later I call my mom again. I'm coming down from a three-day binge and I don't want to bump into Harley again. I ask her could I come spend the night and she says, "No, no, I don't think so."

She never said no before.

That really knocks the wind out of me. I can't answer. Can't even ask her why not.

Then she says, "Robert told me he sees you sometimes on Forty-second Street. He says you go there to buy crack."

I tell her, "Yeah. Sometimes I do."

"Well, Tina, if you're smoking crack I don't think I want you around the kids. Jessie is almost ten now and you could be a very bad influence."

I'm standing at a pay phone on Madison Avenue and the tears start pouring down my cheeks. Crack is the worst thing in the world and it's killing me. How could she think I would turn my own little sister on? How totally disgusting does she think I am, anyway? I hang up the phone and stand there for five or ten minutes because I'm crying too hard to see.

I know it had to be Robert, putting ideas into her head about how she should handle me. And she listens to him like she has no brain of her own. What the hell does she think *Robert* is doing on Forty-second Street all the time? She knows damn well he's dealing. She's with a guy she knows is doing drugs and selling drugs and yet I'm her daughter, flesh and blood, and she tells me to stay away.

She chose him over me.


That night I sleep in Central Park. On the ground near a big bush is all I remember. And it is very cold. I put all four sections of *The New York Times* on top of me.

You've got to be crazy to sleep in Central Park because you can get killed there after dark, but I don't care. I'm just so tired. I must have a guardian angel watching over me because nobody bothers me the whole night long.

People I know at Grand Central, they're all saying I'm getting more and more like April. And that makes me glad. That's one way of getting back to her so that she will always be inside me and we will always be together.


I'm back at Grand Central, hanging out but doing my best to avoid Harley. My head is still cloudy from bingeing, it takes three or four days to get it out of your system. And I get in a fight with this girl, Michelle. She's a black girl about my age, twenty, who lives in the tunnels with a guy who sometimes sells drugs with Harley.

I can't remember what we're fighting about or who started it, me or Michelle. I have a lot of blanks like this. But we're on the stairs near the delicatessen, the stairs going down to the lower level of the station, and I'd taken off my jacket and sweatshirt, so I'm down to the T-shirt layer. I've got her in a headlock, trying to get her down on the ground. I think I probably wanted her head to hit the stairs, but my elbow hits instead. There's a shot of pain up my arm and I let go.

Afterwards I notice the cut on my elbow. Jerry, the guy who owns the delicatessen, gives me a Band-Aid. "Tina," he says, "you're looking bad. I'm worried about you."

"It's just a little cut."

"I'm not talking about the cut."

"Don't worry, okay? When people start worrying about me, they always wind up making trouble."

Jerry gives me a sour dill from the pickle barrel and tells me to go into the ladies' room and wash the cut good before I put on the Band-Aid. But I don't bother washing, because the cut is so small.


Me and Harley made up and I spend two or three days in the tunnels, in his spot under the platform of Track 103, sleeping off my latest binge. Harley comes a few times a day to bring me McDonald's Quarter Pounders or containers of hot soup Jerry sends from his deli. And always, he brings crack. Usually crack perks you up, way up, but I take a couple of hits and go right back to sleep. So that's how I know I'm really out of it.

The spot is warm and dark and it smells musty, like old clothes and damp concrete. I'm lying in an army blanket on a big piece of flattened cardboard. Sometimes I wake up because a train is pulling into the station. They turn the engine off and it goes *chhhhhh!* and when it pulls out again there's that *chug chug chug* noise. Also, when a train is in, I can hear people's footsteps on the platform above me. These noises, they comfort me. They make me feel that out there the world is still going on okay.

Once I wake up and see April sitting near me on a pile of old clothes, taking hits off her stem. She's wearing her Yankees baseball cap turned backwards and looking off into the distance somewhere, kind of dreamy and peaceful. She looks so real I want to say something. There's so much to tell her. But I have the feeling if I make a sound she'll disappear. So I watch her as long as I can, until finally my eyes won't stay open anymore and I doze off again.

THE FIRST TIME I WAS ever down in the tunnels was with April. She took me there because I thought she was joking when she said she lived in Grand Central Station.

I was sixteen and so was she, and I met her when she was staying with Vince, my ex-stepfather. He's a cabdriver and he picked April up one day when she was panhandling near Grand Central. When he found out she was homeless, April wound up staying with him part-time in Queens. Vince was always letting people crash. In fact, that's where my younger brother Frankie was living. He couldn't stand my mom's boyfriend anymore, so Vince said he could move in with him. And Vince wasn't even Frankie's father. Just the father of my little sister, Jessica. Our father, Frankie's and mine, is dead.

My family and I were living in an apartment on Fordham Road in the Bronx, and I cut school one day, came home, and saw Vince's cab out front. He didn't come around often because he and Robert didn't get along. I knew Vince didn't come to visit Jessica, because she was in school, but it turned out he was looking for my mom. Only she wasn't home. So he said, "Come on, we'll go to Burger King for lunch." He never even asked why I wasn't in school.

In Burger King he told me he had this runaway staying with him, a girl from California. "She's about your age, she's even half Italian like you. You want to meet her?"

I said, "Yeah. Sure."

So we drove over to Vince's. It took my eyes a few minutes to get used to the dimness inside, because it was a basement apartment with just a few high-up windows, but then I could make out two people sleeping in the living room. The one on the couch was my brother Frankie. April was on the futon, tangled up in a sheet. She was barefoot, wearing jeans and a Garfield sweatshirt, and she had shiny brown curls all rumpled around her face. She looked so pretty sleeping that way, almost like somebody had posed her. I think I worshiped her from that first minute.

Later I found out she wasn't really from California. She had lived there with her father when she was little, but she was actually from Queens and had run away from a group home in Westchester. But it didn't make her any less glamorous to me.

Vince went into his bedroom to make some phone calls. I sat down in one of the chairs, and finally Frankie woke up and asked how come I wasn't in school. I said, "The same right back to you," and he didn't ask again. Then April woke up and Frankie introduced us. April said, "I'm hungry," and they went into the kitchen, ate some cereal, and left. They didn't say where they were going and I was too shy to ask if I could come.

When Vince was finished on the phone, he drove me home again. He said, "Did you meet her?" and I said yes.

I don't think April said a word to me that first day.

About two weeks later I was in the Thirty-fourth Street subway station, riding the up escalator to the street level, and I looked over and saw Frankie and April on the down one. I got so excited I forgot to be shy. Started yelling, "Hey, Frankie, hey, April!" I got off at the top and rode back down to them.

They told me they were going to Grand Central Station. I thought they meant they were catching a train, but April said, "No, that's where I live when I'm not at Vince's."

"Oh, right," I said. I was pissed because I thought she was making fun of me. Maybe she thought I was some kind of jerk.

She told me, "Come on and I'll show you. Or are you in a big hurry to get someplace?" She had kind of a froggy voice, husky. I liked how it sounded.

"Nah, I'm in no hurry."

So I went over to Grand Central with them and we took the elevator by the Oyster Bar two levels down to Track 111. At the back there was one door that April said was a workers' bathroom and another door with a sign that said DO NOT ENTER. AUTHORIZED PERSONNEL ONLY.

She pulled a fold-up knife from her jeans pocket, slid it between the door and the doorway, and the lock clicked open. "See?" she said. "I'm authorized." Inside was an enormous room a couple of stories high. There were pipes all over the walls and ceiling, and thick wires and air ducts hanging down everywhere.

"What is this place?" I asked her.

"It's the boiler room. Come on, I'll show you." You had to go down fire-escape-type stairs to the floor. She got halfway down and saw I wasn't coming. "Scared?" she asked.

"Hell no," I said, and followed her.

When we got to the main level I could see there were other rooms leading off the big one. All with pipes and air ducts, also ladders and stairs going up to catwalks that crisscrossed the top. In the second room, in a corner behind a bunch of pipes, were some pieces of flattened cardboard covered with blankets, a bunch of candles stuck in empty cans, a few beer and Coke bottles, and a *Seventeen* magazine.

"Home, sweet home," April said.


Frankie had gone off somewhere, but he was supposed to meet April back at Grand Central later so they could take the subway out to Vince's together. April told me I could come with them if I didn't have anything better to do. "We'll get some reefer and hang out," she said.

I told her, "Sure, why not?" She asked if I had any money, but all I had was a couple of subway tokens.

I went with her to Bryant Park, which is a block from Grand Central, to get the reefer, and there were a couple of guys sitting on a bench near the back of the public library who she seemed to know. They were black and Hispanic, and skeezy-looking.

April said, "Wait here." She and one of the men disappeared behind a big bush, and I sat on the grass for five or ten minutes waiting for her and trying to make up other stories for what was happening, instead of the one I knew was true.

But when she came back she had a nickel bag.


We didn't get to Vince's until real late because there is a huge cemetery a few stops before his, and Frankie wanted to get off the train and go see our father's grave. We had the reefer and a pint of blackberry brandy and Frankie had a Walkman, and after we gave up looking for my father's grave, which we did after fifteen minutes because we weren't even sure we had the right cemetery, April said we should stay and party.

That was the first time Frankie smoked pot. I think he smoked it just to impress April. I could tell he had a big crush on her.

After we finished the reefer and the brandy we spent an hour taking flowers off people's graves and putting them on graves that didn't have any. April said, "We've gotta spread them around fairly so everyone has some." She said she had a soft spot in her heart for dead people because her brother was dead and he was her favorite person in the world.

We got to Vince's about three A.M., a little drunk, a little stoned, with flowers in our hair. What happened in Bryant Park, it was like that didn't count. I told April, "I never met anyone like you before."

"And you never will again," she said.

Then we all crashed in Vince's living room. I didn't wake up until noon, so I had to play hooky again.

FOR DAYS I'M LYING THERE, down in the tunnels in Harley's spot. Three days, four days, five days, I don't know how many. Once in a while I think about being pregnant. How I'm going to get rid of it. Because I know there is no way I can take care of any baby. I can't even take care of myself.

No way can I tell Harley I want an abortion either. And I have to get an abortion soon, because it's a few months by now. Somehow I have to. But it all seems too complicated. When I even try to think about it my mind gets tangled up.

One of the girls told me if you drink a whole bottle of castor oil it could make you have a miscarriage, and if that doesn't work you can get someone to kick you in the stomach.


Beverly, one of the girls who also lives in Grand Central, comes down to see me because Harley told her I was sick. She brings coffee and a little bottle of Anacin. "Man," she says, "Harley's got a nice spot."

"Nice? This is nice?"

"You know. Roomy. And it's got electricity."

"It's a shit house. It's for rats, not people."

"Well, I don't notice no key to a room at the Plaza hanging from your pocket," she tells me.

Then I shut up, because I get her point. People like me and Beverly and all the others who hang out in Grand Central, we don't have too many other choices.

One of the bag ladies who hangs around the station is named Edna. She sits on a milk crate by the entrance every day, panhandling. She's maybe fifty or sixty years old, fat, always wears dirty dresses and a heavy coat, even in summer, and torn stockings. Her legs are so swollen they look like elephant legs. Sometimes I give her quarters. I always feel sorry for the bag ladies. To me, they're the saddest thing in Grand Central because at their age you know there's no hope for them.

Once I was leaving the station with a couple of guys on a crack mission, and as we passed Edna one of them grabbed her shopping bag and started running. When he got to the next block, he just dropped it in a trash can. Edna stood up and started yelling and cursing us. I guess she thought I was in on it because she screamed at me, "You little snot-nosed girl, you won't think it's so funny when you get to my age! I hope they do worse to you!"

I'm thinking about Edna while I'm lying there in Harley's spot in the tunnels. I'm thinking about how I could wind up just like her. I'd kill myself before I'd be a bag lady.

The second or third day my arm starts waking me up because it hurts. First I don't know why, but later I remember the fight with Michelle, and the cut on my elbow. I can't see it because I'm wearing long sleeves, but I know it's swelled up because it doesn't bend right. My whole arm is throbbing.

Another day or two and I can't move my arm at all. And not even crack takes the pain away. So that's when I know I have to do something.

I get myself upstairs to the waiting room and call this writer I know, collect. When I tell her about my arm, she says get right to the hospital, to the emergency room. She's sick in bed but she calls George McDonald, a homeless advocate who spends a lot of time around Grand Central, and about an hour later he meets me at Bellevue Hospital.

IN BELLEVUE I SLEEP ON clean sheets. Someone comes and changes them every morning. Breakfast-, lunch-, and dinnertime, ladies in green dresses wheel meal carts down the hall and bring everyone a tray of food. I never ate so good in my life, except for the other time I was there, when I was seventeen. That was when my mom decided she couldn't control me because I was living in Grand Central. She made me a ward of the court and the court put me in the psycho ward in Bellevue for a month, until they decided I wasn't crazy.

The infection in my arm is so bad they have to give me intravenous antibiotics. Also, they say I'm malnourished. They tell me they can do the abortion for me, but not until my arm is better.

George McDonald's wife, Harriet, comes to visit the second day. She brings me a bathrobe and a pair of slippers. I'm too tired to talk much, so she doesn't stay long. Before she leaves, she tells me the doctors say they're going to do the abortion in a week or ten days.

To tell you the truth, the idea of staying in the hospital a week or two is a relief. You wake up at a certain time, have meals at a certain time, get your medicine. You're not just wandering around all day thinking, Well, what am I going to do next?

There are three beds on one side of the room, three on the other. My bed is right near the windows and all I have to do is turn my head to see the East River.

Only one of the other women is young, around my age. She has a broken leg, which she got falling off a fence. She's from England. She talks like that, too, with an English accent, so I know she's not just bullshitting about it.

After a few days in Bellevue I'm starting to feel really good. My arm still hurts and I still have the infection, but my stomach is getting used to being full again, I'm rested, my mind is clear of drugs. It's kind of enlightening. Because when you're living with crack you're oblivious to everything but crack and how to get it. And when you've been off it three or four days, you start seeing things around you, taking in everything that's happening. Things that other people take for granted. Eggs and toast in the morning, and how good ice water tastes when you're thirsty. A funny show on TV that makes you laugh. Something nice a nurse says. Hot showers and feeling clean all over.

It's like somebody's pulled off your blinders. You see the sun come up, you see the sun go down. You know there are days and then nights and then days again, it's not all one long day until you come down off your binge.

You look around and think, Wow. There's so much more than crack. That drug is really such a tiny little thing if you hold it up against the whole world.

Seven stories below my window, on the river, is the biggest boat I've ever seen. It's huge and white and it sparkles in the sunshine. Definitely the kind of boat that people like Donald Trump ride on.

The English girl with the broken leg was telling me how she took an airplane to France, a train to Spain, then a freight boat to America. So I tell her the yacht down there is mine, parked and waiting for me to get better so it can take me around the world, too.

Harriet makes me cry.

She comes back a few days later. I'm sitting up in bed watching *All My Children*. She's looking really nice, she has on a long skirt and cowboy boots, and her hair is up in a ponytail. She's got a little box of chocolates for me. She asks, "So where are you going when you get out of here?"

I turn down the TV. "Grand Central. Where else?"

"Is that what you really want?"

"What's my choice?"

"You could always give rehab a try."

I tell her I already did and it didn't work. After I was in jail the first time, for probation violation, they sent me to a residential rehab facility. First of all, I was a mess, because it was right after April died and I was going through my mourning thing. And the residence was right in the middle of Harlem. You go to see your probation officer every day and then you have to walk home right through all the dealers, the crack, the heroin. On one hand they're telling you to get away from people, places, and things that have anything to do with drugs, but yet they put you right in the middle of *Harlem,* you know? I didn't last long. Maybe a month, tops, and I was right back at Grand Central. Getting high, feeling no pain.

"Maybe," Harriet says, "it wasn't the right place or the right time. There's a place called Samaritan Village, they have a residence upstate, in the mountains. There's a waiting list but I think George can speed things along for you. You want to give it a try?"

Mountains.

I think of green. Trees and grass and things like meadows and forests. Flowers, growing wild.

"No way," I say.

"Give me one good reason."

"Maybe I like my life the way it is."

Then she starts the "You Have So Much Potential" lecture. I've heard it a million times before. From my probation officer, the cops around Grand Central, some of the conductors and train workers, Jerry at the deli, my "regulars"—the commuters who'll give you a dollar every day and want to hear your life story. All of them tell you, "Oh, what are you doing here, you have so much potential, you're young, you're pretty, you're bright, you could do anything you want with your life."

So Harriet goes through the "You Have So Much Potential" routine while I eat a bunch of chocolates. Once she takes a break from telling me how wonderful I am to ask, "Tina, are you listening?" and I say, "Yeah, yeah, yeah, you want a candy?"

She says, "Where are you going to be five years from now?"

"I don't know."

"Ten years?"

"How should I know?" I think of Edna. I think of her swollen elephant legs.

"If this is all in the name of April, I don't think it's what she would have wanted for you."

I just shrug. Harriet has no right talking about what April would have wanted. She knows nothing about April.

"There's a whole world waiting for you, Tina. Just love yourself a little, will you? Just love yourself enough to want something better."

I have my head down low, pretending I'm checking out the rest of the candy, but she sees the tears running down my cheeks. She hands me a tissue from the table. Watches while I wipe my eyes. "I'll be back in a couple of days, honey. Do some thinking."

I can hear her boot heels clacking all the way down the hall to the elevators. "Fuck off, Harriet," I say, even though I know she can't hear.


Corey comes to see me, with Beverly. Corey was my first boyfriend at Grand Central. He looks good. He doesn't do a lot of drugs, some angel dust and pot but no crack or heroin.

Beverly, she's a skinny little black thing, on the street about ten years. We've shared a bunch of spots, Beverly and me, spots and drugs. I'm glad to see her. But God, she looks bad. Face all sunk in and wrinkly, toothpick arms and legs. Clothes kind of raggedy and way too big, probably because she got them from a church charity like most of the rest of us. She looks like a dressed-up raisin.

When she goes to the bathroom, I say to Corey, "Wow, she's looking bad."

He says, "Like how?"

"Did she lose some weight, or what?"

"You've only been here four days, Tina. She looks the same as she did four days ago."

"Yeah," I say, "I guess so."

"She's just all cracked out. Like everyone else."

I figure I never noticed how bad Beverly looked because like Corey said, nearly everyone I know looks that way. Skinny and dirty and sick and drugged out. I'm just used to it.


Daphne is the name of the English girl. I like the way she talks, with that accent. She says we're the ones with accents. Daphne tells me about the different cities and countries she's seen and the people she's met. When her leg is better she plans to hitch around the country, to New Orleans and Florida and Hollywood, and then she wants to go to Hawaii. She's got it all mapped out, exactly what she wants to do.

I don't tell her much about my life. The little I do tell her, she doesn't understand. She just says, "But why would you want to live in a railroad station, for heaven's sake?"

Hᴀɴɢɪɴɢ ᴏᴜᴛ ᴡɪᴛʜ Aᴘʀɪʟ ᴡᴀꜱ like nothing I'd ever done before, and the world she lived in was like nothing I'd ever experienced. We'd go to Grand Central, smoke reefer, drink Mr. Boston's Blackberry Brandy, which was her favorite drink, hang around with some of her friends. Grand Central Terminal is a huge place, but April seemed to know every inch.

And it's beautiful, the high ceilings and the double staircase in the main concourse, and the balconies, everything in marble. The ceiling over the main concourse is dome shaped and blue like the sky, and there are constellations painted on it that look so real they almost twinkle. April told me some of their names and that's how I learned the constellations, from Grand Central's ceiling. It wasn't until a long time later that I found out the constellations on the Grand Central ceiling aren't in the right order. There wasn't enough space to put them up right, so whoever painted it had to cram them in the best they could.

April knew a lot of people because she'd been living in Grand Central for about a year. They lived in Grand Central too, these people, in hiding places under the train platforms or down in the tunnels. Whenever I'd go there with April, they'd all be sitting on the benches in the waiting room, on the side where the men's room was. The younger ones, anyway.

The older ones hung out on the benches on the other end of the waiting room. They were mostly alcoholics, and some were on the street because they were a little crazy. Most of the older people didn't stay in the station overnight, because you had to be pretty young to go crawling and climbing through the tunnels and into the hiding places. So when the station closed every night at one-thirty and the cops came through kicking people out, it was mostly only the older people who got put on the street. The others had already disappeared into the tunnels.

April really liked the old ones. She gave them cigarettes and sometimes bought them cheap booze, but she also brought them food and tried to make them eat if she saw all they were doing was drinking. She introduced me to Benny, a little black guy who must have been ninety years old. He had a white beard and he was always sucking on a bottle of Thunderbird. April told everyone they were getting married and going to Bermuda on their honeymoon and Benny played along. He called her sweetheart and honey bunny and he gave her a cigar band for an engagement ring. He got so excited when she put it on her finger and kissed him, I thought he was going to drop dead from a heart attack. I think Benny really loved her.

Another one that April was close friends with was an old lady called Mama. Mama always wore a purple coat and couldn't speak much English. Nobody knew anything about her, not even her name. April was the only person she would talk to, but her English was so bad April never understood what she was saying. April brought her hot soup from the Salvation Army truck, and whenever April had money, she bought her a pack of Lucky Strikes. Mama didn't drink much, but she loved her cigarettes.

April really cared about some of those people, but mostly she hung out with the younger group. She introduced me to Maria and Francisco, the couple she was living with in the boiler room. Maria was Dominican, about eighteen, short and chubby, always joking. Francisco was a little older, good-looking. He had tattoos on both arms and a thick Afro.

There were others: Bonnie, a cute dark-skinned girl, she was real fat, but it turned out it was because she was pregnant, and R.J., who Bonnie was going with, and these guys Jabba and Chewie, who were cousins. Also Flash, who was kind of April's boyfriend.

Everybody was happy, laughing and goofing off. I was shy and didn't talk much, but they all liked me because April did. In school I had a few friends, but I always felt like everyone was better than me. Here, for the first time, I felt like I fit in. Every time I went back to Grand Central, it was easier and easier for me to stay longer and longer. Time flew by when I was there.

If it was nice we'd spend the day smoking and drinking and playing Frisbee in Bryant Park. When we got hungry April would steal some fruit from a grocery store, or we'd go into a deli and I'd buy a pack of gum while she'd steal things like cupcakes and Doritos and Pepsis. Or she'd stand on a corner and panhandle, ask everyone going by, " 'Scuse me, can you spare a quarter?" She had so much nerve, she amazed me. And the people, they would stop for her. Give her a quarter, a dollar, sometimes even five dollars. Guys, especially, would give her money because she was so pretty. She had high cheekbones and sleepy eyes, and her teeth shone when she smiled. That smile, she could stop traffic with it. I wished I could be just like her, but I knew I never could, so the next best thing was to be with her.

April did the kinds of things I could never do: There was a group, the Grand Central Gospel Trio, who sang around the station every day, and they kept a box by their feet for donations. They were singing "Swing Low, Sweet Chariot" one night at rush hour, and when they saw us go by, the leader, Hershey, interrupted his singing to holler, "Yo, April!" She just jumped right in with them, like she'd done this before.

They switched to "Under the Boardwalk," because April knew all the words. She stood in front of them singing and imitating their arm gestures and their little dance steps. She didn't have a great voice but you could see how much fun she was having. She looked so cute in her jeans and baseball cap, waving her arms around and singing with the guys, "Under the board-walk, down by the sea-eeee," stretching out that last word until she was red in the face. By the time they finished, the crowd around them was twice as big. Everyone clapped and April took a big bow, then at least half the people dropped money in Hershey's box.

"Works every time," Hershey told the other guys. "She comes and sings, we get paid double."

April said, "Someday I'm gonna be a star."

"Little girl," Hershey said, "you already are."

"Just don't forget my cut," she told him, and Hershey counted out some bills and change. April walked away with almost nine dollars. She bought us a small pepperoni pizza and spent what was left on a pack of Luckies for Mama.

At night sometimes I went to Vince's, but mostly I went home to my mom's. We were still living in the Bronx then, in the apartment on Fordham Road. My mom was getting on my case about playing hooky, because the school had told her about me being absent so much. She knew I had this new friend, April, and she knew April was staying at Vince's a lot, but I don't think she knew I was going into the city and hanging out at Grand Central.

One night we were sitting around in the waiting room and April decided she wanted to go to Queens to see her mom.

It was a long subway ride, and then we had to walk about ten blocks, so it was late when we got there. April's mom had a beauty parlor and she lived in the back. But it was all dark and locked up, so April banged on the door until we saw a light go on, and then April's mother came out. We could see her through the glass door, walking through the beauty parlor wearing a bathrobe and slippers. She was pretty, with long blond hair, and she looked half sleepy and half scared, like who the hell is coming around at this hour? She turned on the outside light and saw us, then opened the door. She didn't even say hi to April. The first thing she said was, "Who's this?" Meaning me.

"This is my best friend, Tina," April said.

"Well," her mom said, "you can come in, but she stays outside." She didn't seem real glad to see April, or maybe it was because she was so sleepy.

So I waited outside, by a little gate, while April went in. A few minutes later she came out again and said, "Let's go."

We started walking the long way back to the train. The streets were dark and empty because it was so late. I said, "Well, that's a long way to go for such a short visit."

April dug her hand into her jeans and pulled out a ten-dollar bill. "This is all I came for," she said. "She paid me to go away."


I went over to Vince's after school one day and April's boyfriend, Flash, was there. He hung out with a gang at the Port Authority Bus Terminal, across town from Grand Central. He had a bunch of girls and it was obvious he didn't care that much about April.

I tried to tell her that, but April never listened to anybody. Whenever Flash came around, April got all flustered and flirty, like a little girl in love.

On this day she was sitting out front in Vince's taxicab with Flash, and they were fighting. She jumped out of the cab and walked away. Flash left, too. I don't know where he went, but I didn't see him again that day.

I sat in the taxi waiting for April to come back, and after half an hour I gave up and went inside to Vince's. There was April, lying on the futon, crying, and Vince was standing there saying, "What's wrong? What's wrong?"

"My stomach," she said.

Vince saw me. "What the hell is wrong with her?"

"She had a fight with her boyfriend," I told him. "She's upset."

April said, "My stomach," again. It was strange to see April cry. She didn't seem like that type of person.

Vince went into the bathroom and came out waving an empty bottle. "April," he said. "Did you take these?" She just went on crying and holding her stomach. "April, dammit," he practically shouted, "answer me, did you take these? Because I just bought this goddamn bottle a few weeks ago and there were a hundred then!"

When April finally told him yes, she did take them, he called 911, told them to send an ambulance to his address right away because he had a sixteen-year-old girl here who'd just swallowed about eighty Tylenols.

They took April to Elmhurst Hospital in Queens. I went over to Vince's later that week, and he told me that at first the doctors thought they were going to have to send April to a special hospital in Pittsburgh for a kidney transplant, but she pulled through without it. He said she'd have to stay at Elmhurst a long time and he'd take me to see her, but he never got around to it. I tried to call her once, but a nurse told me April couldn't get phone calls.

Now that April was away, everything went back to the way it was before. My mom and Robert were still fighting every day, there was never enough money, and there was always something new to worry about. Like the baby was sick or Robert was drunk or how was my mom going to pay the rent this month. And on top of it, my mom was picking on me about school. I used to be an honor student, but my grades were shot to hell because of all I'd been missing.

Over Memorial Day weekend my mom and I had a huge fight and I walked out of the house, got on a train, and went to Grand Central. I felt shy and self-conscious without April, but the minute I walked into the waiting room I saw Maria and Francisco and Bonnie and R.J. and Chewie on the bench, and they started hollering, "Hey, here's Tina! Tina, where you been keeping yourself?" Like I was a big deal, like I was someone they were really glad to see.

And they told me they'd been talking to April. She called on one of the pay phones in the waiting room a couple times a week, told them she was in the psychiatric ward at Elmhurst now and they wanted to keep her there for a couple of months. She wasn't allowed to have any visitors except her family. They said she always asked about me: "Where's Tina? Where the hell is Tina?"

Next time she called I was there. I told her about all the shit that was going on at home and she said, "Stay there in Grand Central. Maria and Francisco will let you sleep in the boiler room. Tell them I said so."

"Okay."

"So you wait there for me, right? Until I get out. Swear to God?"

I told her, "Swear to God."

After I've been in Bellevue a week, one of the nurses tells me that in a few days I'll be finished with the intravenous antibiotics and then they're going to transfer me to another floor for the abortion. She explains they can't just scrape the baby out, because I'm almost five months pregnant. They have to induce labor, give me injections of something to make the baby come out.

I ask if it'll hurt or if they could put me to sleep. She just pats my arm and says, "Oh, honey, don't you worry about it."

So that makes me worry about it.


That same day, Ron comes with a bag of paperback books. He's the husband of the writer I called from Grand Central when my arm got so bad. Her name is Jamie and she used to hang around Grand Central interviewing people who knew April. And when she found out I was April's best friend, she spent a lot of time talking to me with a tape recorder. That was about two years ago, right after April died, and over that time Jamie and I got to be friends.

So Jamie sent the books to the hospital with her husband, Ron, because she's still sick. The books are scary books or mysteries, like Stephen King, which she knows I like, plus a couple by S. E. Hinton. She bought me some before, but I don't think I ever actually got to finish a whole book. I'd lose it somewhere whenever I was bingeing.

By this time I'm allowed to walk around pulling my IV hookup, and Ron and I go sit in the visitors' lounge so we can smoke. I thank him for the books and ask how Jamie is. He explains she had a bad allergic reaction to penicillin but she's almost better now, and then we make small talk, but it's awkward because I only met him once before. So I go over to the window and tell him, "You want to see something?"

He whistles when he sees the white boat down in the river. "That's some huge boat," he says.

"It's mine, you know. I got it parked there waiting for me. When I get out I'm going to spend a year traveling around the world."

Ron reaches out and ruffles my hair. He says, "Hey, kid, at your age anything's possible."

And that really touches me. Because my friends would be saying, "Yeah, right, dream on," or telling me how crazy I am instead of saying, Yeah, Tina, maybe you can do it.


Harley never comes to see me in the hospital. Which is okay. He probably planned to but just never actually got to do it, because I guess he figures I won't mind too much. Me and Harley, I don't know how you'd describe our relationship. For me, it's being able to think, Okay, I guess I'll go look for Harley now, and knowing if I find him he is going to want me there. It's a kind of love, in a way.

So Harley never makes it to the hospital, but he told Dwayne and Dwayne does come. Dwayne is one of the few white guys around Grand Central. The left side of his face is all scarred. When he's panhandling, he says he's a vet and it was a war injury because then people give more, but he told me how it really happened. He used to shoot up heroin, and he did some next to a radiator once and his head dropped onto the radiator when he nodded off. The dope was so strong he didn't even realize his skin was burning up. He had to go to the hospital and everything.

Now Dwayne has a bad crack habit. He stopped eating except for ice cream. He has seizures brought on by the crack and he says ice cream helps him have less seizures.

So he shows up just a few days before I'm scheduled for the abortion and we sit in the visitors' lounge. He says, first thing, "I got a present for you," and takes a vial of crack out of his jeans pocket.

It's funny, but I haven't seen crack in ten or eleven days and for a second I just stare at it, because that's how long it takes for me to register what's in that little vial.

"Jesus, Tina, take it," Dwayne says, shaking it at me. He's scared someone is going to walk in and see it.

I reach out and take it, but I don't know where to put it. My hospital nightgown has no pocket and neither does the bathrobe Harriet gave me.

"Put it in your slippers," Dwayne says, so I stick it down in there.

"Well, thanks," I say.

"You want me to leave you a lighter too?"

"Nah, that's okay. I can borrow one."

"Well, you better take my stem at least, because I'm sure you don't have one." And he takes it out of the lining of his jeans zipper and gives it to me. What a stem is, is a glass pipe with the bowl part broken off. I stick that in my other slipper.

"I bet you've been dying for a smoke."

I tell Dwayne yes, but really I haven't been thinking much about crack lately.

He doesn't stay long. Tells me I look good, probably because he's never seen me without my customary grime. Then he starts looking around, getting jumpy, says he has to go. I thank him again for the crack and go back to my room.


My lunch tray is there on the table, still with its cover on. And Harriet is there, too, sitting in the chair by my bed.

"I saw you in the lounge with your friend," she says. "I didn't want to interrupt."

"No, no, that's okay, you could've come in."

"You're looking good. You've filled out a little."

"Gained too much weight," I tell her.

"But you look healthy now. And your hair is so shiny."

"So how's George?"

"He's fine. We've been in touch with your doctor and they're going to do the abortion on Tuesday. You'll be able to leave afterwards."

"You mean, they're not going to keep me a couple of days after they do it?"

"No. Not necessary." She looks at me a minute, then says, "Are you looking forward to getting out of the hospital?"

"Sure. Of course I am. I'm sick of this lousy place."

"And have you thought about where you're going?"

"Nothing to think about."

"It's Grand Central, huh?"

"Well, where else?"

"I hoped you might have given Samaritan Village some thought. George called them yesterday and they'd be able to take you in two weeks."

I lift the lid off my lunch plate. Spaghetti, two pieces of white bread, a pat of butter. A little cup of red Jell-O. Coffee. Apple juice.

"Tina," she says, "you're not a kid anymore. You're twenty years old and this is real life now. You're playing for keeps."

"I know," I say. "I'm not stupid."

"Think about what you're going back to."

I think about Harley not coming to see me. He really could have if he wanted to.

"My friends," I say. "I'm going back to my friends. They're like my family and Grand Central is like my home."

"Tina, maybe you didn't make it in rehab the first time, but I want you to try again. While you're still young. And you won't stay young much longer on the streets. When you get out of the hospital, you can come stay with us. There's an extra bed in Abby's room and she's got her own TV and VCR, too. You'll have two weeks to take it easy, get your strength back, and then we'll take you to Samaritan. It's a two-year program and they have a very high success rate."

That really floors me. That Harriet and George would be willing to let me come live with them for two weeks. That they would let me sleep in their daughter's room. There is so much I want to say that I can't say anything at all.

"We'll get you some summer clothes to take upstate," Harriet says. "You and me and Abby will go to the Gap."

I want, I want, I want, I want. That's what keeps running through my head, I want, I want, I want, rushing and whooshing around in there like the wind.

When I'm still not answering, Harriet asks, "What is it, Tina?"

"Changes, you know? They're really scary."

Harriet says, "Not as scary as some of the other stuff you've been through."


After Harriet leaves I try to eat my lunch. Then I remember the crack Dwayne gave me, the vial stuck down in my slipper, smooth against my bare foot.

That crack feeling starts coming up in me. It's a nervous, electric feeling running all through your body. I'm starting to ache for a hit, just one little hit. I've got that old taste in my mouth, that taste they call being thirsty.

I go into the bathroom, into one of the stalls, and close the door. Pull the vial out of one slipper, Dwayne's stem out of the other.

And then remember I don't have anything to light up with.


I didn't have any feelings about the abortion either way. It was just another obstacle, something I had to get through before I could go on with my life. But it turns out to be a nightmare.

I was pregnant once before, when I was seventeen, but I didn't know it until I had a miscarriage in the stockroom of Jerry's deli in Grand Central. Jerry called an ambulance to take me to Bellevue and he called my mom too. That's when she decided she couldn't handle me anymore and made me a ward of the court and I wound up in Bellevue's psycho ward for a month.

Having a miscarriage wasn't any fun, but it was a picnic compared to the abortion.

They give me a bed in a room with a couple of other girls who are also waiting to get abortions. The nurse keeps coming in to give me shots every hour or two. I ask her what the shots are for and she tells me, "To make the baby turn, because it has to turn to come out."

Then she comes back again, minutes or hours later, I can't tell, and I say, "When is it going to be over?" and she says, "Oh, not yet, you're not ready," and gives me another shot.

After a while it's hurting so bad I'm screaming, and she gives me another kind of shot for the pain. It seems like this goes on all night. I fall asleep whenever she gives me something for the pain, then wake up with even more pain. I'm screaming and crying, "Ma, make it stop! Please, Ma, make it stop!"

Finally they wheel me into this operating room with a couple of nurses and a doctor all wearing masks, and it's cold and the lights are very bright. They're telling me, "Push, honey, push hard!" and I push so hard I shit on myself, do number two all over everything. Maybe it's because they gave me an epidural. If you're numb and they tell you to push hard, I guess you just push everything. Once it pops, it all comes out.

They clean me up and one of the nurses says, "Aaah, don't worry, it happens." But you still feel dirty afterwards.

The rest of it, maybe I'm hallucinating. I'm real groggy, but I could swear one of the nurses brought it to me. The baby. And I'm looking at it. It's just a big bloody mess wrapped in a long umbilical cord. She says it was a boy. It doesn't look like a baby to me. Maybe it's deformed or something because of all the drugs.

Then she takes it away. I hear a flushing. And I think it's over but she says, "No, it's not over because there's the afterbirth." Then there's more pain and I'm crying and screaming for my mom again.

I don't know, maybe it didn't all happen. Maybe I'm imagining the part about seeing the baby and the nurse telling me it was a boy. Maybe I'm imagining the toilet flushing. I fall asleep again and when I wake up I'm in the recovery room.

And that's when it hits me. That it had been a living thing.


Harriet comes for me later that day. She brings me jeans and a sweatshirt of Abigail's and some new underwear and socks. My own clothes were so filthy they threw them away in the emergency room. The only thing they kept were my Reeboks.

When I was a kid we moved around a lot, so there were lots of changes, but at least my mom and brothers and sister were always there. And when I left home to live in Grand Central, April was with me. Now here I am, going to George and Harriet's and then upstate to live at Samaritan Village, and nobody is with me. Nobody will really know me, nobody will know who I am or where I came from or how important I was to somebody.

For the first time in my life I'm doing something on my own. And I'm terrified.

I'D ONLY MET HARRIET a couple times before the hospital, but I knew George McDonald ever since I came to Grand Central. George was a homeless advocate and he was always around the station—a tall, thin guy, kind of floppy, like his arms and legs were too long for him. He had started an organization called the Doe Fund to help homeless people.

Of everybody in the station, April was one of his favorites. He was always trying to get her into drug rehab, but she wouldn't go. Once he even threatened to drag her. She said, "You do and I'll yell rape all the way."

Whenever George got reporters to come by and do stories on the people who lived in Grand Central, he would try to get April to let them interview her because she was so smart and pretty. She would do it, but she always charged him a fee. Ten dollars for newspaper interviews and once, when it was for a TV news show, she asked for thirty. He gave it to her, too, because he wanted to be on TV as much as possible so he could get publicity for the Doe Fund, but he said he felt uncomfortable about giving her money she might spend on drugs. So she told him, "Look at it this way, George, you're saving me from prostitution."

After April died, George sometimes asked me to do interviews. I know I wasn't as good as April, but I charged the same amount. Then I'd go blow it on crack like she used to. One day he came and found me and said, "Listen, I've got a TV crew here from *48 Hours* and they're doing a story on the homeless. So I want you to give them an interview."

Me and Harley and two other guys were sitting up in the balcony. They were bullshitting about some deal and I was drinking a can of Coke, watching the herds of people down below on the main concourse running to catch trains.

"You mean, for TV?"

"Yeah, it's a newsmagazine show. You'll be seen all over the country."

I didn't know if I wanted to be seen all over the country. I didn't know if I wanted to be on TV at all.

"We won't use your last name," George said.

"I don't know . . ."

"Okay, kid, so what's your price?"

Well, then Harley's ears pricked up. Without George seeing he gave me a quick elbow in the ribs. Kept on talking to the other guys, but now I knew he was listening.

"Thirty," I said. Because that's what April got.

So I wound up getting interviewed by this guy Harold Dow in the coffee shop off the main concourse. I made George give me the money first, and I slipped it to Harley. The crew set up their cameras and lights, and me and Harold Dow sat at a table and he asked me questions. But he didn't ask about my family. I told George to tell him I wouldn't talk about my family or about drugs.

At first I was nervous. But then I started thinking about what Harley and I were going to do with the money and that loosened me up. When Harold Dow asked if I wanted a better life, I said yeah, and when he asked what kind, I told him I'd like to live on a farm with lots of horses. I had to say something, and that was all that came to mind.

The interview went on a bit longer, and I'm talking and looking out the door and here comes Harley. Just kind of walked by slowly to let me know he'd gotten the stuff. I told Harold Dow, "I'm through talking to you." Got up from the table and left. I figured George got his money's worth.

Harley already had twenty dollars, and now we had fifty altogether. You can get a real deal buying fifty dollars' worth of crack. Harley got about thirty vials and the two of us went through it in half the night. Just slam-dunked it all.

The TV show wasn't on for about a month. I didn't see it until later, on tape. But I heard that on the show George talked about me to Harold Dow, and he kept saying, "Tina's just waiting to die." That got me furious because it made me sound like I was someone you should pity. And it wasn't true. I knew deep down that I wasn't waiting to die, I was waiting to live.

Next time George came around the station I bugged out. Started throwing bottles at him from a trash can, yelling, "How could you say that about me, you fucking bastard! How could you say that on *television!*"

And he's got his arms in front of his face, trying to block himself, he's saying, "Tina, Tina, okay, calm down a minute, will you?"

I didn't really hurt him. I made sure all the bottles I threw were plastic.

The funny thing was, the TV station got lots of calls, all these people who saw me on *48 Hours* and wanted me to come live with them. The TV station put them in touch with George, and George had me call some of the people back. A few of them even had horse farms.

I thanked them all for inviting me and told them I wanted to think it over.

George wasn't a threatening kind of guy in Grand Central. He'd yell at us or joke with us, and we'd yell or joke right back. But living in his house was different. For the first time, I felt uncomfortable around him. Before he was in my territory, but now I was in his.

George and Harriet own a brownstone, but Harriet's parents live on the second floor and the third and fourth floors are rented out. So George and Harriet have the first floor and basement, with the garden in back.

The whole place is kind of elegant, just what I would have imagined. I grew up in the slums and in welfare hotels with just the bare necessities, and here I am in this town house on the Upper East Side with big-screen cable TV, a laundry room with a washer and dryer, and an oversized refrigerator packed with food.

The living room and George and Harriet's bedroom are on the first floor, and also the entrance to the back garden. There's a fancy spiral staircase going downstairs to where the kitchen and dining area are, plus Abigail's bedroom and another room that she uses as her own living room. That's where the TV is. Actually, the downstairs is like Abigail's own little territory. Harriet comes down to cook, and we all eat there, but Harriet and George stay mostly upstairs.

The first afternoon I spend lying on the sectional in front of the TV with a bottle of Coke and some chips. I'm not feeling great and also I'm nervous about meeting Abigail. When she gets home from school, Harriet brings her downstairs. Abigail is only eleven and in sixth grade, but she's tall. She looks more like a teenager. "This is Tina," Harriet says, "and she's going to be staying here for a while."

Abigail just says something like, "Oh, good." Harriet must have told her about me because she doesn't seem surprised. She puts her books down on the kitchen counter and says she'll show me where to put my stuff.

"I don't have any stuff," I tell her, and for a minute she looks at the sweatshirt I'm wearing, which is hers, and I wonder if Harriet had asked before loaning me her clothes.

Abigail says, "You like MTV?" and thinks I'm kidding when I ask her what MTV is. So she takes the remote, plops down on the couch, and switches the channel. I've had a couple of Walkmans in Grand Central and I really like music, so this is kind of neat, the MTV. For the first time I can see my music instead of just hearing it.

"I've got five pairs of sneakers," she tells me, "so you're welcome to borrow a pair if you want."

I think Abigail likes it that I'm here. She's an only child and I'm going to be someone to hang out with. She makes me feel really comfortable.


My first night I wake up at two-thirty and think I'm in Grand Central, down in Harley's spot, then realize I'm in a bed with sheets. So then I think I'm still in the hospital, until I look over and see Abigail sleeping in the other bed.

It's kind of scary. Here I am in George and Harriet's house, sleeping in their daughter's room and wearing her pajamas, and in two weeks I'm going away to a rehab place in the country. I don't feel like me. I get out of bed and go to the mirror, but there isn't enough light in the room to see more than just my outline. That's not enough to prove I'm still me.

I sit outside on the front stoop, smoking. It's May and it's a warm night, but my hands are shaking. I have trouble keeping them steady enough to light my cigarettes.

There are almost no people around and hardly any traffic, and it feels good and free to be out in the night again. The city is all around me like an old friend.

Then I start thinking how rested I feel. I start thinking it's time to go. Time to go to Grand Central and get high.

I smash out my cigarette and go back into the house.


If you saw us the next morning, you would think we're a regular television family, sitting around the table over our eggs and juice and talking about what we're going to do today. Then George rushes out, and while me and Abigail are clearing, her girlfriend comes so they can walk to school together. Then it's just me and Harriet. She's on her second cup of cappuccino.

She tells me she's been in touch with my mom. She tells me they aren't in the welfare hotel anymore, the city found them an apartment in Coney Island.

The last time I talked to my mom was over the phone when she told me not to come there. I don't ask how Harriet found her. Maybe it was George.

"I have her new phone number," Harriet says.

I carry it around in my pocket a week before I get up the nerve to call.


My mom, when I call her, is real nice. She says Robby and Jessica miss me a lot. She tells me, "Harriet had nice things to say about you. I'm glad you're finally getting yourself together."

"Well, maybe I could come by and see you before I leave. Say good-bye and all."

My mom says sure.

When I tell Harriet about the phone call, and that I want to see my mom before I go, she says, "We'll make an occasion of it for Mother's Day."

It's weird. When I'm home, it's just a place to get away from. But when I get away, I always wind up missing my family really bad.

WHAT I FOUND WITH APRIL, and with Grand Central, was another home and family, one that I didn't want to get away from. During the months April was in the hospital from trying to kill herself, I kept my promise and stayed there waiting for her to come back. Because April was the only person I really cared about. And the way I saw it then, April was the only person who really cared about me.

Living in Grand Central, I felt free. Nobody was going to boss me around or tell me what to do. We spent most of the days hanging out in Bryant Park, and at night I stayed in the boiler room with Maria and Francisco. Maria was real friendly and Francisco was nice, too. He belonged to a gang on the West Side, but he had done something to piss them off, so that's why he started hanging out here.

My second night in the boiler room, Francisco woke me up. He was lying on my cardboard next to me, trying to unbutton my shirt. I said, "Hey, what're you doing?"

He just kept saying, "Shhhh."

"Francisco," I said, "don't."

"Maria said okay. She doesn't mind."

But I minded.

I looked over at Maria. It was too dark to see if she was really sleeping, but she was very still. I couldn't say no to Francisco and I didn't know what else to do. So I tried to be very still, too.

The boiler room was where I got arrested for the first time. That night it was just me and Francisco and two of his friends, because Francisco and Maria had a fight. She told me she was fed up and she was going home for a couple days.

It was the middle of the night, we were sound asleep, and at first I thought I was having a dream. Then I woke up and saw it was real: three cops were standing over us, yelling that we were under arrest for criminal trespassing.

It never dawned on me I could go to jail for being in the boiler room, because all the cops knew we were there. They joked about it. Only later, when crack started taking over everyone, did they see us as a real problem. But we got arrested that night probably because they had a quota to make. They always did a sweep when they needed to fill a quota.

They handcuffed us and took us to the Metro North precinct, which is upstairs in the station's balcony. And from there we were sent downtown to Central Booking. That's when I got separated from the guys and I was really alone.

In Central Booking they took me down to the basement, where the cells are, and lined me and some other women up and made us take off our shoelaces, belts, any hair stuff like bobby pins and barrettes. Then they marched everyone but me into a big cell that was already full of women. Me, they put in one of the two smaller, empty cells down the hall. They said it was because I was under eighteen.

My cell had a bench and a sink and a toilet. And that's where I stayed for three days while I was waiting to see the judge. Three days of sleeping on that bench. Three days of bologna sandwiches and cold tea, because that's all they gave you for meals. Three days of going through nicotine withdrawal, because if you didn't happen to have a pack of cigarettes on you when you were busted, there was no way of getting any. And three days of going to the bathroom on that toilet in the middle of the cell, in front of anyone passing by.

I couldn't see the other women but I could hear them. From what I heard, and from what I saw when they brought us all in, most of them were prostitutes. It was easy to tell by their skimpy clothes and their makeup and the fact that most of them seemed to know each other. I could hear them laughing and joking, talking about the different pimps, who was cool and who was a bastard, and bitching about being locked up. Which they called "down time."

My charge, criminal trespassing, wasn't a bad one, and the judge gave me time served, which means the three days I spent already were enough of a sentence and now I could go.

On the train back to Grand Central I told myself, Okay, I had my initiation. Now I know what's going to happen if I get arrested again and it's nothing I can't handle. In a funny way I felt almost proud. I couldn't wait to tell April.

We couldn't go back to sleeping in the boiler room, but some of April's other friends, like Jabba and Chewie and Bonnie and R.J., were living in an abandoned train way down on the tracks and they said we could stay with them.

How you got to the train was through Gate 45. Way at the end of that platform was a long grating you walk through, then you go over a couple of tracks and through an opening in the tunnel wall, which is where workers stand when the trains go by. On the other side of that wall is another section of tunnels, underneath Park Avenue, where there's a small freight yard with some old trains.

Our train had three cars. All the seats had been taken out and a couple of the guys spray-painted the windows so you couldn't see inside. We used candles and flashlights for light. The first night I was there we sat around drinking beer by candlelight, and Jabba's cousin Chewie passed around some reefer. Bonnie asked if I was going to be staying with them now and I told her yeah, I guess so.

"Her family sucks," Maria said. "She's waiting here for April to come back."

"Man," Bonnie said, "at least you got a family. If I had a real family, I'd be at Great Adventure right now instead of sitting here in this stinky train puffing reefer." Bonnie said she was raised in foster homes because her mom was a junkie and she was born addicted. She had an uncle who put her out on the street when she was ten years old, had her hooking to help pay for his habit.

I said, "Wow, ten years old until now? You lived that long on the streets?"

"Yeah," she said, "I lived that long." She crumpled her empty beer can and threw it at one of the train windows. "I'd like to get out of New York. New York is one helluva ugly town."

I couldn't understand how anyone would want to get out of New York. For me, it was a big adventure that was just beginning. I didn't have the view of it yet that Bonnie did.

I HANG OUT WITH ABIGAIL after school, sometimes with her girlfriend, too. If it's rainy we sit around the house and eat popcorn and watch MTV, but on nice days we go to the park or the pizza store or maybe window-shop.

Abigail and her friend like to roller skate. I'm happy just sitting on a park bench watching them. It's like being a kid. No worries, no nothing, just relaxing.

Abigail knows about me and where I come from, but it's no big deal to her because George and Harriet work with homeless people all the time. She'll make comments about it sometimes, like if we pass a bum lying on the sidewalk she'll say, "Gee, is that anyone you know?" But she says it as a joke. I never feel embarrassed. Like I said, she really makes me feel comfortable.

But for some reason I don't feel so comfortable around George. Which is funny, because he's the one I know best.


George is sometimes hard on me. I guess it's his way of making sure I don't back out of going to rehab, but it makes me mad. He's always reminding me that this is my last chance and I better make it work.

A few days before I'm supposed to go to Samaritan I'm watching Harriet make dinner, and she says something about how I was a little sarcastic to George at breakfast and she hopes I'll apologize when he comes home.

I tell her, "He's not my father, so it really doesn't matter."

"Look, Tina," she says, "I don't like it when you talk that way. We're trying to help you."

"I don't remember asking for help."

Harriet just shakes her head and keeps stirring the spaghetti sauce. I go into the other room, sit next to Abigail, who is glued to MTV. And I'm thinking, I don't want to put up with this shit. I'm going to walk the hell out of here.

But I don't.

It's hard to admit, but it's such a relief to let Harriet tell me, "This is what you're going to do." My body and mind are totally worn out and I'm ready to stop fighting with myself and the world. April isn't out there anymore, so what's the point?

But a lot of times I wake up in the middle of the night with bad dreams. My heart is pounding and I'm sweating. So I sit outside on the stoop and smoke, try to calm down a little. Some nights, I'll be thinking I'm the luckiest person in the world because I have a place to sleep and a real bed, and every morning when I wake up I can take a shower or a bath. But other nights I get that ache, that ache for crack. In a way it seems like Grand Central is in another world but, really, it's so close. Just a few minutes on the subway.

Sometimes I got so excited on my way to buy crack I had to go to the bathroom. Not number one, number two. That's how worked up you can get just thinking about it. Now when the crack thoughts come, I have to try to focus my mind on something else. It's a constant struggle, because you're always fighting your own thoughts and memories.

Some nights when George comes home he has a drink, also when there is company. Once in a while Harriet has a drink with him. One night I'm sitting out on the stoop smoking, fighting that crack ache, and I remember that they keep their liquor in a cabinet under the sink. I don't think it would be so bad to just have a tiny drink. Not like doing drugs again.

I put on the little stove light, pour a big glass of orange juice, then get out George's vodka and pour a couple shots into the juice. Vodka is what I used to drink most of, next to Mr. Boston's Blackberry Brandy. If you drink it when you're getting high, it eases the crash coming down.

I sit there on the stoop sipping it, feeling more and more relaxed. And after that I have a drink every night or two, sometimes more if George and Harriet are out. George's vodka helps me through a lot of nights.


Harriet takes pictures of us on Mother's Day. Of me and my mom and Robby and Jessica at Coney Island.

It's a gloomy day, kind of gray. I'm wearing new clothes Harriet bought me: jeans and a denim jacket, a green striped shirt and a white Gap hat. Jessica's got eyeglasses. I never saw her before with glasses. Robby is five, but small even for five, and he can't wait to go on the motorcycle ride. I have a picture of him sitting on one of those motorcycles, hanging on to the handlebars and looking like the happiest kid in the world.

When my mom told me she was pregnant with him, I wanted her to get an abortion, anything to stop her from having Robert's baby, because I figured then Robert would definitely be around forever. But she wouldn't do it. I told her I'd always hate that kid and I really thought I would, until the first time I saw him. He started to cry, he was all mouth and toothless little gums, and my mom put him in my arms and he stopped. I looked down at him, teeny red face, big eyes, perfect fingers and toes, and from that second on I loved him.

I have a picture of my mom from Mother's Day, too, with me and Robby in front of the Tilt-a-Whirl. Her face is blank, expressionless. I have no idea how she's feeling that day, I can never tell how she's feeling. Looking at that picture now is almost like looking in the mirror. I have the same blank look because I try never to let my feelings show either.

I spend most of the time with the kids, and my mom hangs mostly with George and Harriet. The kids want me to go on the rides with them, so we go on the Tilt-a-Whirl, the Ferris wheel, the little roller coaster. They play some games, throw balls at bottles, things like that. They don't win anything but I don't think they care. Just to spend the day at Coney Island, that's magical enough for them.

Sometimes when I had a little extra money, like from panhandling or robbing somebody, I used to put it in an envelope and go over to their hotel and leave it at the front desk. Five or ten dollars, a few times twenty. If it was Jessica's birthday, I'd put it in a birthday card, or if it was the holidays, I'd put it in a Merry Christmas or Easter card, whatever it was. They never said anything about it to me and I never asked. But if Robert got the mail first, he probably opened it and took the money. That's the only thing I was ever able to do for them, but I'll never know how much of it they actually got.

Saying good-bye that day is so hard. I hug my mom, I hug Jessica and Robby real tight. It hurts to know they're going to have to go through the same things that made me leave home, it hurts that I have no power to make their lives better.

Once I turn away I don't look back.


My last night at George and Harriet's I don't sleep at all. Tomorrow I'm going to start a new life. I'll be going away to a strange place and meeting all new people.

The only thing that keeps me from running is thinking about Grand Central. That it's still there, and so are Harley and Corey and Francisco and Beverly and Dwayne and all the others. They're still there and most of them will stay there, except for the ones who die or go to jail, and I can always go back if I want to.

# PART TWO

SAMARITAN VILLAGE IS IN A plain brick building on the Van Wyck Expressway in Queens. There's no sign outside, so you'd never know it's a drug rehab place. They have two groups of people there, the new ones like me and the old ones who are on Re-Entry. That means they went through the program upstate and now they're back, living at Samaritan but working at regular jobs. For them Samaritan is like a halfway house.

I thought I'd be going to the country right away, but when I get there they tell me I have to stay at the Queens place a month to detox. I tell the woman, her name is Wendy Kaplan, that I'm detoxed already but she says that's the rules. They don't just take someone and send them right upstate. Their theory is, you're still thinking about drugs, so you can be a bad influence on the other people.

Harriet stays in the office with Wendy while I go with the nurse to get my medical exam done. When I come back Wendy says, "I've got to get a little information from you, history and stuff. Would you like Harriet to wait in another room?"

I tell her no, Harriet can stay. I have nothing to hide.

Wendy wants to know about my family and childhood, but most of the questions have to do with my drug use. I tell her about the first time I tried marijuana, when I was twelve. There was a candy store down the street from where I lived in Astoria, it was a front. There was one of those racks with potato chip bags clipped on, there was some candy in the window, and the rest of the store was empty except for a window with Plexiglas and the guy who stood behind it selling marijuana.

One of the boys at school started talking about pot and I said, "Oh yeah, well, I know where to get some." He gave me money and I brought a bag to school the next day. We tried it together. I think it was his first time too.

And it started from there. Me and one of my friends, Pamela, we'd buy a bag every morning from the guy behind the Plexiglas. It was three dollars and we'd use my allowance money or hers, whoever had it, then go behind this apartment building where no one could see us and smoke. We'd be laughing and giggling. Getting dry mouth. Getting the munchies. At one point when I was twelve we were smoking reefer before school just about every day.

I tell Wendy Kaplan that when I met April all I was really doing was smoking reefer, and also drinking a little. It was in Grand Central that I started branching out to other stuff. She wants to know about that. In fact, she wants to know all about what it was like, living in Grand Central.

FOR ME, LIVING IN GRAND Central Station was an adventure, the kind of crazy adventure kids have in library books.

Hunger was never a problem. A lot of churches had soup kitchens and you just had to know the schedules. On weekdays St. Michael's served breakfast and St. Joseph's served lunch and on Sundays they both also served dinner. During the week you could get dinner at the Salvation Army headquarters, or St. Catherine's on Lexington Avenue, or, on Fridays and Saturdays, at St. Andrew's. The Salvation Army also served holiday meals and so did some of the churches.

Also, seven nights a week both the Salvation Army and the Coalition for the Homeless sent food vans to Grand Central. At the Salvation Army van you could get a sandwich and hot soup, sometimes chili, and at the Coalition's you could get a sandwich and a pint of milk.

We'd hang out in Bryant Park all day. Play Frisbee, lie around on blankets in the sun, drink beer. Then when it was getting night we'd go back down to the abandoned train, drink beer, smoke reefer, and party half the night. Bonnie left in the middle of the summer because she was having R.J.'s baby, but she was back again a few weeks later. She had the baby, it was a boy, and she said some relative was taking care of it for her.

———— • ————

The only bad part was, living on a train you get kind of dirty. You could go wash your hands and face in the ladies' room sometimes, depending on which matron was on duty. Some were really bitchy, chased us out whenever they saw us.

Even when I did get to wash in the ladies' room, the rest of me was getting pretty ripe. The weather was warm and we were out running around Bryant Park getting sweaty and grubby. Then you'd go down to the train and you'd get dirty and sooty from climbing around the tracks. I was looking like a ragamuffin. I was smelling. Getting to the point where even washing my face and hands didn't help much.

The third week I was there, Bonnie took me down to the back of one of the tracks and showed me where she washed. It was a big old silver washbasin, and it was for the workers, but once in a while you could sneak in there if they weren't around. Take off all your clothes and climb in the sink. It was almost as good as taking a real bath. By the time I got out the water was all black.

There was a shower, too, that we used once in a while. It was down in one of the work areas on the lower level, and Francisco took me there. It was just a pipe with running water, but it was high up, so you could stand under it like a real shower. The workmen stored stuff down there, pipes and barrels and big bags of concrete, and that's also where they kept their forklift carts. You had to be careful nobody was around. Usually you could only go on a Sunday. We didn't have soap or towels or even clean clothes, we'd just put our dirty stuff back on afterwards. Or maybe throw away the top layers, like the sweatshirts or flannel shirts. It was the top layers that got the dirtiest, anyway.

Chewie, the cousin of Jabba, took me to his home in the South Bronx one night. It was mostly abandoned buildings there, and the house where his family lived was the only house still in one piece. Chewie told me to wait outside and he came out about half an hour later with a pair of jeans, a denim shirt, and some socks that belonged to one of his brothers. Chewie also had a bag of food: chicken wings and a jar of pickles and a couple apples.

Chewie was really good-looking, dark-skinned, curly hair, maybe eighteen years old. He's the guy I liked most when I first came. He was the type who would hold the door open for a girl.

I was starting to itch a lot. Sometimes I'd be scratching so much it was hard to sleep, and I noticed I was getting little pink bumps, like bites, on my arms.

One Sunday I was stripping down to take a shower and feeling really itchy under my bra, and when I took it off I saw teeny little bugs crawling around the band. I picked one off, pinched it between my fingers, and it popped. I hollered, "Aaaagh!" and Francisco, who was standing guard by one of the forklifts, said, "What happened?"

I just said, "Oh, shit," because I realized my whole bra was infested. I threw it behind a stack of barrels and never wore a bra again, the whole time I was at Grand Central.

Only that didn't get rid of the bugs. It turned out they were all over me. Even showering didn't get them off. Francisco told Maria, because I was too ashamed, and she stole me some stuff from a drugstore that you put all over yourself to kill them. She said, "Don't feel bad, we all get bugs."

Even after that, I still had some left. Mostly in my hair. I just kept plucking them out whenever I felt them on my scalp. That's how I finally got rid of them all.

The whole time April was in Elmhurst, I lived on the abandoned train. I spoke to her almost every day on the phone, and she'd tell me funny stuff about some of the crazies on her ward. Always before we hung up she'd say, "Now, you're going to stay there until I come back, right?" I was so flattered she wanted me to wait for her, the station could have burned down and I wouldn't have budged.

Corey showed up around the end of summer. How we all met is when Chewie's cousin Jabba stole his wallet. Corey was in the men's room and he laid his wallet down on the sink, and Jabba, who was hanging out in there looking for something to steal, pocketed it. Corey was a good-looking, light-skinned black, and sweet, but he wasn't too bright or he never would have left his wallet on the sink.

I didn't even know at that time what Jabba had done, but I saw this cute young guy wandering around the waiting room and, maybe because we were all about the same age, he came over and told us his wallet was just stolen off the sink in the men's room.

He said, "Any of you guys know who could've taken it?" He was mostly asking Jabba, I guess, because he had seen him in there.

Jabba said, "No, man, but you ought to know better than to leave your valuables lying around when you're in New York City. I can tell you're an out-of-towner."

Corey said yeah, he was just up from Georgia and he wanted to go back because he tried New York and he didn't like it. Only now he couldn't leave because all his money was gone. So Maria and Francisco told him to go out on the main concourse and panhandle and he'd have enough money in no time.

Corey did make some money, because a few hours later he came back and asked, "Where do I buy the ticket?"

"What do you want a ticket for?" Jabba said. "Let's go get some beers."

Corey said okay, and we also got some reefer, and that night when we went down to the train we took Corey with us because now he had no money left for a ticket home and no place to sleep. The next day Jabba gave him back his wallet, without the money, of course. Said he found it in a trash can in front of the station. Corey was really grateful, he kept saying over and over, "Oh, wow, you found my wallet, man, thank you!"

That's how Corey started hanging out with us, and pretty soon he was mostly sticking around me. First it was me and Chewie and Corey and then it was just me and Corey, and after a while Corey got to be my boyfriend. You know that cartoon dog, Marmaduke? Corey was a little like that. Kind of clumsy and sweet at the same time. He would do whatever I wanted, and his feet were real big, so that made him awkward. Corey and me, we got to be a team. If we weren't together, we always knew where the other one was.

He wanted us to have sex but I told him, "Well, Corey, I'm not ready, I want to wait until I get to know you better." Corey was always gentlemanly and he let it be my decision.


Corey introduced me to angel dust. He did a lot of it down in Georgia. It's green, it looks like leaves and smells like mint and it comes in a little bag, like pot. You roll it like pot, you take just two smokes and you're floating.

I thought it was great. When you smoke dust you feel like you can be anything or do anything. Corey told me about this one guy who jumped off a garage because he thought he could fly. Corey also told me you have to be careful because it can be very dangerous. On a dust high you could do something and not realize you did it, you could even kill somebody and not know it. And if you smoke too much, Corey said, you can forget who or where you are forever.


They say there are seven levels below Grand Central, but no one I know has been that far down. Most people stay on the first level, right below the station's lower level. You just walk along the tracks until you find a place where you can crawl under the platform.

It's not too hard to get to the second level either, because if you know where to look, there are some old stairs and passages that the workmen use. But I went down to the third level with Corey and I'll never forget it.

He was telling me one day how he went exploring way deep, around the third or fourth level, and came across some guys living in boxes in a big cave. They even had a campfire. I heard that the deeper down you go, the weirder the people are. I heard stories about people who live so deep in the dark tunnels that skin has grown over their eyes, and about a man who'd lived down there for thirty years who cooks and eats the bodies of other bums he's murdered.

But I didn't think any of that stuff was true and I didn't believe what Corey said, either. I told him, "You're full of shit about those guys."

"No, I swear. I watched them. They don't talk, they make train noises. And one of them saw me, so I had to run."

"What'd he do? Toot his whistle?"

"You don't believe me, I'll show you. I can find that cave again."

I told him no way was I going down there. "Ten bucks," he said. "I pay you ten if I'm lying, you pay me ten if I prove it's true." Well, hell. For ten dollars.

I followed him down the tracks, and we crawled under the platform and through a big hole where the bricks had been moved away. I could hear steam hissing somewhere, from hot pipes, but it was totally dark. This was way below the boiler room, a place I'd never been. I said, "Wait, Corey, because I can't see," but he told me in a couple of minutes my eyes would adjust, and they did.

I think we were on the second level now. Corey had found a back way to get to it, without using the stairs. I followed him down a passage that was so low in some spots we had to crawl, and then we came to an even bigger hole in the side of the passage. It was weird because this hole was not supposed to be there, it was like somebody chipped it away or busted it out with a sledgehammer.

Corey climbed through and I followed, and we came into a huge empty space full of rocks and boulders. It was like a big cavern. Except I could hear trains. No matter where we went, I could hear the trains above us through all those layers of rock and concrete, blowing their whistles and roaring up and down the tracks like monsters.

In order to get into the next passage, we had to walk along a high ledge, then climb down a rock and drop about eight feet. After we'd been walking and crawling for a while, I noticed a pile of rocks that I was sure I saw before.

I said, "Hey, Corey, I think we're going in circles."

He said, "No we're not, trust me."

When we passed the same pile of rocks again fifteen minutes later, I told him, "See? See? This is where we just were."

I was getting creeped out. We doubled back all the way to the cavern and got into a different passage, with little lights in the wall every hundred yards or so. I wondered, Do these bulbs ever burn out? And if they do, who keeps changing them?

At the end was a big hunk of flattened cardboard and a blanket, some clothes, beer cans, old newspapers, candles. Somebody's spot. That's when I really got scared. Because who knows what kind of nut was living here, and if the guy happened to come along and see us, he'd probably think we were there to steal his stuff. People like that, there's no way of knowing what they're going to do.

I grabbed Corey's sleeve, told him, "Listen, you won the bet, okay? Let's just get out of here."

I think he was relieved; he didn't know where the hell he was going, anyway. It took us over an hour to find our way back up to the first level. I heard stories of people getting lost down there. Most find their way back, but a few never do.

I never went below the first level again and I don't think Corey ever did, either.

One day around the end of August, me and Corey were on the lower level smoking dust when Chewie came running down. "Yo, Tina," he said, "guess what, April's back!"

There was a big commotion when I got up to the waiting room. April was running around hugging everybody, hollering, "I'm home! I'm home!" I was so happy I almost couldn't believe she was real. She gave me a big hug and said, "Well, I'm glad to see you waited like I told you to!"

Turned out the hospital didn't let her go, she escaped. Her mom took her out to a restaurant and April told her she was going to the bathroom. Her mom said, "I know you're leaving. Just do it when I'm not looking." April said, "Okay. Bye," and walked out.

I took her down to the lower level and introduced her to Corey and he gave her some dust. We all got high together. She loved the dust, thought it was the best thing she ever had. So after that we were on a dust mission for months.

Sometimes, on dust, you can pretend you're in a different part of the world and it works. One time April, Corey, and me went to China, because it was April's turn to pick and that was the one place she said she really wanted to see.

AFTER WENDY KAPLAN AND I finish the intake, she explains about the program, how it's two years in all—about a year or year and a half upstate, depending on how well you do, and the rest back here in Queens on Re-Entry. Also, there are things for me to sign. I don't really understand what the papers are, but Harriet does, and that's good enough for me.

Then Wendy calls in one of the Re-Entry people and tells her to take me up to my room. Harriet tells me to write, and we hug each other. I don't want to let go.

Being in Samaritan Village in Queens isn't anything exciting. Watching TV, eating, hanging out in the dayroom, mostly just waiting to go upstate. That's where all the programs and groups and activities are.

Lights out is at nine, except for the Re-Entry people who can stay up later, and everyone has to be up by six. The best times are when one of the Re-Entry people takes us to the park. We aren't allowed to go alone. The park has swings and basketball hoops, and we can play punchball too. Going to the park is the most excitement I get that month.

The doors to the building are always guarded. You can walk out if you want, but if you do, you're not allowed back in. Every time I go by one of the doors, I think of walking out. The two things that stop me are the idea of going back to Grand Central, knowing what I'm going to face there—nothing—and not wanting to be a disappointment to Harriet.

I don't make any real friends, just keep to myself. Because maybe, if people get to know you, they'll see past the tough facade and you can't let that happen because then there's nothing left to protect you.

So I watch TV a lot and read. I have a couple of books by S. E. Hinton that I started in the hospital—*The Outsiders* and *That Was Then, This Is Now*. I used to read a lot when I was younger. It was my main escape next to TV. Especially the year we were living in the Martinique Hotel, because even the halls were dangerous, drunk people fighting and junkies shooting up. My mom made us stay in the room except to go to school or when we went out for food. So I spent half my time reading. I didn't have any books of my own, but I was always taking them out of the library.

In seventh grade we read *Tom Sawyer* and *Huckleberry Finn* and I especially liked those books. I dreamed about doing what those boys did, running away and going on adventures. I used to try to imagine what it would be like, being free, doing just what you wanted. It sounded like a great way to live.


The night before I go upstate I can't sleep. I was so anxious to get up there but now I'm terrified. Because what's it going to be like? Suppose I don't fit in? It's so far away. It's too far away. I keep telling myself, Look, you don't have to go, you don't have to do anything you don't want to do. The doors are unlocked, you can walk right out of here anytime you want. Get on a subway. Go to . . . go to . . .

The van leaves early in the morning. I'm bleary-eyed from being awake all night, but I try to watch the route we're taking so I'll know how to find my way back if I need to. Like in the fairy tale, Hansel and Gretel dropping bread crumbs through the woods. But it's a two-hour trip and I sleep through most of it.


Samaritan Village upstate has four or five buildings, all painted white. And around them just grass and trees, more than I ever saw in my life except in Central Park. Plus there is a swimming pool, a basketball court, and a handball court. If you're over twenty-one, you get put in the Adult House, otherwise they put you in the YDA Building. I asked my roommates what "YDA" means but they didn't know. One girl said she heard it stands for "young drug addicts" and someone else told me "young dumb assholes."

My first day there one of the YDA counselors, Nancy Cruz, takes me into her office and tells me about the place. First you're in Orientation for a couple of months. That's where you learn the rules and philosophy and get to know the people. Then you graduate to Lower Peer. If you do okay there, you go to Middle Peer, then to Upper Peer. After that they send you back to Queens on Re-Entry.

I guess my closest friend at the beginning is Jacinta. She is who they give me for a Big Sister. Everyone in Orientation has a Big Sister. They tell me, "You go to Jacinta if you have any questions." But mostly I just try to keep to myself and not get close to anybody.


They put me in a room with three other girls. There are two sets of bunk beds, and two bureaus, and you have to share with someone. Three drawers apiece. Some rooms have their own bathroom, but ours connects with another room so eight of us are sharing.

Well, I'm up here. Made it this far and trying to take one day at a time like the counselor, Nancy, told me.


When you're in Orientation you have a buddy and you're not supposed to go anywhere alone. That first night everyone is sitting around on the grass behind YDA, smoking and talking and joking. There's a big flat rock nearby and I stretch out on that. It's so beautiful and peaceful. The grass and trees smell good even at night.

I light a cigarette and look up at the stars, and I can see the Little Dipper. It looks exactly like the one on the ceiling in Grand Central, but it's harder to find because the real sky is so much bigger than the one in Grand Central. Here there is so much sky it covers the whole world. I feel safe and protected, like nothing bad can ever happen with that big sky hanging over me.

It makes me think of April. It makes me hope she can look down and see me here.

APRIL AND I WENT OVER to Port Authority one night because she wanted to see if Flash was still hanging out there, but one of his friends told her Flash left town. He was in hiding or something. I didn't say anything, but I was relieved.

We were walking back along Forty-second Street when I bumped into Robert, my mom's boyfriend. He was standing in front of one of the movie theaters. Looking real innocent, but I knew why he was there. He saw me, said, "Yo, Tina."

So I stopped, said hi, and introduced him to April. "This is my friend April. April, this is my mom's boyfriend, Robert."

I could tell by the look on April's face that she thought he looked awful young to be the boyfriend of my mom. Robert was only twenty-five then, just a few years younger than Vince. They were both ten or twelve years younger than my mom. In fact, Vince was only twenty-one when he and my mom had my sister, Jessica.

"This is your friend?" Robert asked me, like I just introduced him to a snake. He told April, "I've seen you hanging around here before."

"Is there something I should know?" April asked. "Like maybe you own this whole block?"

"Let's go," I told her.

Robert grabbed my jacket sleeve. He asked me, "What are you doing, hanging out with her?" I yanked my arm away and started walking. I told April, "You just met one of my reasons for leaving home."

Corey could be a pain in the ass. There were times I didn't want to have anything to do with him because he'd get drunk and be all over me, acting sticky and yukky, telling me he loved me. I'd tell him, "Corey, leave me alone!"

Also, April was bugged when she first came back from Elmhurst because Corey and I were so tight. She'd tell me, "If you're going to hang out with him, then you can't hang out with me." So I'd tell Corey to get lost. Then he'd get hurt and I'd feel bad, and by then April would have forgotten what she said and the three of us would be taking dust trips together again and getting along fine.

April's grandma, the mother of April's father, lived in Coney Island and late one night we went to see her. I figured April wanted to get money from her, like when we went to her mom's. It didn't matter to me. For me it was just another place I could go with April.

So we rode the D train all the way out to Coney Island, April and me and Corey. April's grandma lived in a tall building across from the beach, and since it was four A.M. by the time we got there, April said we should wait on the beach until her grandma got up. "It won't be long," April told us. "She's a very early riser."

We all fell asleep. April woke us at about eleven because she was wearing shorts and her legs were burned. "Come on," she said, "I gotta get out of this damn sun."

But Corey started digging in the sand. He had buried his bag of angel dust because he didn't want to have it on him if we got caught sleeping on the beach. "Help me, will you?" he said, so for half an hour we dug up the beach all around where we were sleeping. But all we found was a yellow plastic shovel and a used condom. Corey was pissed. Kept saying, "Goddamn son of a bitch, that bag cost me ten dollars!"

April's grandma was surprised to see her. She told April that her mom had called to tell her April ran away from the hospital. "Your mother is very upset," she said.

"My mom is full of shit if she told you that," April said, "because she let me."

I thought the grandma was going to get mad at April for saying that, but she didn't. April told me later that her grandma and her mother never liked each other much.

The grandma tried to make April take a cool bath because her legs were so burned, but April wouldn't do it. So the grandma gave her a bottle of special lotion and made her put it all over her legs. She was a nice lady. And her apartment was furnished really pretty, with dark blue carpets everywhere. She lived on the twentieth floor, and from the windows you could see the ocean.

She gave us sandwiches and soda and cookies and fruit, and what we didn't eat she put in a bag for us to take. She said, "I'm half Italian and half Jewish, so I've gotta feed you." April had some clothes in the spare bedroom, and before we left she packed some shirts and jeans in a ShopRite bag the grandma gave her.

"You're not going back to that Grand Central Station, are you?" the grandma asked April. April said yeah, she was, and the grandma said, "You could stay here."

"We already tried that, Gram," April said.

The grandma gave us the bag of cookies and fruit and said it was real nice meeting us. Then she hugged April. The hug went on so long April had to push her away.

We walked down the hall to the elevators and the grandma called after us, "I put the lotion bottle in with the cookies in a little Ziploc. Tina and Corey, you make sure she keeps putting it on her legs every couple hours! Because I know April, she'll forget!"

"Wow, you got a nice grandma," Corey said when we were in the elevator.

"Did she give you any money?" I asked.

"Shut up," said April.


We got off the train on the West Side, because Corey was looking for someone who owed him ten dollars so he could buy another bag of dust. Only we couldn't find the guy and April's legs were starting to get swollen. She was having trouble walking.

We were about to go back to Grand Central when I bumped into my mom. I mean, I really bumped into her. I was trying to help April step down the curb and I walked smack into this lady and the lady was my mom. She was waiting for the green light, with Robby in the stroller. I guess she must have been coming from seeing Robert.

I was so surprised I didn't run, and she was so surprised she didn't seem mad at me for staying away from home so long. I introduced her to April and Corey. She let me lift Robby out of his stroller and give him a big hug. He smelled of lollipop and baby sweat.

My mom said April should see a doctor about her sunburn. "Got no money," April told her, and then my mom did something really nice. She said April could come to our house, take cold soaks in our tub, and stay off her feet until she was better. At that time she was living in the Bronx, in the apartment on Fordham Road that the city found for us after the Martinique Hotel.

We went with my mom, and that's how I wound up moving back again. My mom said if I'd promise to live at home and start school in September, April could stay with us too. April seemed to like the idea, but I wondered how long she'd stay. April was jumpy. She'd do something for a little while and then move on to the next thing.

Everything was different at home with April there. My screwed-up family didn't bother me as much, because I felt like I was with April now, not them. Robert and April hardly talked to each other, but if my mom noticed, she never said anything. She never asked much about where April's parents were, either, and why April wasn't with them. My mom is good at ignoring stuff she doesn't want to know about.

One night Robert was out and my mom took the little kids to my aunt's for dinner. There wasn't much food, but April found a box of elbow macaroni in the cupboard, boiled it up, and put it in bowls with clumps of vanilla ice cream on top.

"I used to do this when I was a kid," she said. "When my mom was out, I'd make up all these weird combinations."

She told me her parents got divorced when she and her brother were little. The brother, he lived mostly in California with their father. When April was twelve, her mom let her go visit for two weeks. She had a great time, they all went to Big Sur and San Francisco, and when April went back to her mom she acted real snotty because she wanted to stay with her father and brother. Her mom finally got fed up and put April on a plane, called her father, and said, "You better get to the airport and pick your daughter up again." So her father did, but he sent her right back to New York.

"They were playing cross-country Ping-Pong," she told me while we ate our macaroni and ice cream, "and I was the ball."

"So your mom had to keep you?"

"No. See, she was so pissed off she sent me to *her* mother, in Germany. It sucked. I couldn't understand a word anybody was saying and my grandmother made me eat pizza with a fork."

April's brother, Travis, got killed in a car crash when he was seventeen and April was fourteen. She was in a group home in Westchester and she practically went nuts when she heard. They had to put her in some private little mental hospital for a month and keep her on medication. She told me Travis was the only one in her family she truly cared about, or who truly cared about her. She told me, "My ambition is to die at the same age."

I asked her why the hell she would want to die, and she said it was the only way she could be close to her brother again.

Robby was walking now and getting into everything. Somebody always had to be watching him and usually I didn't mind doing it. In fact that was one of the best things about being home again, spending time with Jessica and Robby.

On weekends April and I hung around the park in my neighborhood. We'd meet some guys, smoke reefer, nothing major. School days, April stayed home with my mom, and at night, after my homework, we'd watch TV, play checkers and cards. It wasn't too bad being home, at least not with April there. So when my mom kicked her out, it was like the end of the world.

It wasn't a school night, so we'd gone to the park, and we got home around midnight, which was the curfew. My mom had gone to bed, but she left a note on the kitchen table that said, "Your room is a mess and April drinks too much milk. So April has to leave."

April went right to our room and started stuffing clothes into her ShopRite bag. I kept begging her to stay, but she said, "I don't stay where I'm not wanted," and walked out the door.

I woke my mom and Robert up. I was so mad I was waving the note around in my hand, yelling, "What's this? What's this? What the hell do you mean, she's got to leave because she drinks too much milk?" That's the first time I ever cussed my mother.

"She has to leave and that's that," is all my mom would say. Robert just put his pillow over his head. Probably he was enjoying this.

I lay in bed and cried. After a while I got up, put on a couple layers of clothes—jeans and sweatpants, a T-shirt and sweatshirt—took all the money I had, which was only a couple of dollars, and tiptoed out of the apartment. When I was a little kid in Astoria, I'd sneak downstairs at night to the foyer between the double doors and sleep there. I thought that was running away and, anyway, I was too afraid to actually go out the door. In the morning my mom would come down and get me for breakfast. She always knew where to find me.

This time I went through the door. And who did I find on the front stoop but April, just sitting there, her bag on her lap, puffing on a cigarette.

"I knew you would come," she said.

I sat down next to her. "I'm nothing here. I'm leaving too."

She threw her cigarette into the street, took out a little plastic compact from her bag and a tube of lipstick. Opened up the compact and started putting on the lipstick. It was plum colored. "I was thinking we could go to Florida," she told me. "It's a good place to start over."

"I always wanted to see Florida."

She put back the compact and lipstick, took a fold-up knife out of her pocket, and made a quick cut across the tip of her finger. Squeezed it so the blood came out, like a little red bead, and passed the knife to me. For a minute I just sat there, looking at her.

"Do it," she said. "Do it."

I had to force myself, shut my eyes and pull the blade fast across my finger.

"Our blood is mixing," April whispered while we pressed our fingers together. "This makes us blood sisters. We are part of each other now and we will always be together in spirit if not in body."

And she leaned over and she kissed me.


The first ride we got took us as far as Elizabeth, New Jersey. We were walking around a truck stop trying to find a driver who was going to Florida when the state troopers picked us up. They said no way did we look eighteen.

We wound up in a shelter for runaway kids, but we got out the back entrance before they even processed us, found a PATH train back to Manhattan and took it to Thirty-fourth Street. Before we went back to Grand Central we stopped at Macy's because April needed clean underwear. We picked out a couple pairs of panties, went to the ladies' room, put them on, and then we just walked out. We chose Christian Dior because April said they were the most expensive.

THERE ARE LOTS OF TIMES after I first get to Samaritan that I dream about Grand Central. And April. Sometimes the dreams are nightmares. Once in a while it'll be about the man in the tunnels, but usually it's about crack. I'll dream I'm out there on a mission, roaming the streets looking for crack. Or I wake from a dream where I'm actually smoking it and getting high. My heart's racing and I can smell the smell and taste that burnt-peanut taste. It always seems so real, like it hasn't been a dream at all.

This is what you do in Orientation: Get up at six-thirty. Go to breakfast in the cafeteria in the Adult House. Then Morning Meeting. Then Orientation Class, in the living room of the YDA House, before and after lunch. That's where they teach you the rules, and also you have to know the names of all the counselors and staff. Plus you have to learn the Samaritan Village Philosophy by heart, because everyone recites it each day at the Morning Meeting. The Philosophy goes like this:

We, the brothers and sisters of Samaritan Village, have based our philosophy on the concept of reality. We must keep our trust in each other to have concern in order to build up the bricks of our broken-down lives. Just like a builder uses special tools to build a house, we must use special tools to build our lives.

The foundation of this building that we call our lives is honesty. If you are honest with yourself, it will follow that you will be honest with others.

We must become aware of our problems, and have the strength of our convictions, to fight and eventually win over all of them. We must also have consistency, and be sure to stay on the road that leads to our goals. This road is a long one, but together, all of us as one will win back our identity and self-respect, and begin walking our new road to this beautiful thing called life.

I said that thing every day, along with everyone else in Morning Meeting, the whole year I was at Samaritan. It got to be like a song that you sing all the time, where after a while the words start to sound like noise without meaning. It wasn't until after I left that it started to mean something to me.

Besides Morning Meeting, the other meetings you go to in Orientation are the House Meeting, which is a general meeting each night after dinner, and Caseload. Caseload groups are once a week, with about twenty other people from different peers. Caseload is like group therapy and it's run by one of the counselors. You're supposed to talk about personal stuff, like your past and what got you here. But for a long time, in Caseload, I can't say anything. I don't feel like spilling my guts to a roomful of strangers.

The counselor that I have for Caseload is a guy named Todd. We have a private session first, to go over my treatment plan. Talking about what I need to do, how I have all these unresolved family issues I have to work on. Also, Todd arranges for me to start GED classes when I get out of Orientation so I can study for my high school diploma equivalency test.

You don't have a lot of privileges in Orientation. We can't use the pool or handball court, and we can't write letters or make phone calls except to let family or friends know what we need. So I write to Harriet and Jamie to ask them to please send shampoo and deodorant and insect repellent and suntan oil, things like that. And they always stick in extras: potato chips, candy, cigarettes, playing cards. Also, Harriet sends me a teddy bear from Bloomingdale's and Jamie sends me a spotted Pound Puppy. I put them both on my bed. It's comforting to have them there when I wake up from a crack nightmare.

The other thing you have to do in Orientation is memorize the Concepts. Those are sayings, like: "One day at a time." "The longest journey starts with a single step." "Listen to learn, learn to listen." "Progress, not perfection." "Resiliency: the ability to bounce back." "Hang tough."

And in Orientation we also have to learn the vocabulary. Because Samaritan Village has its own language. Like, a "haircut" is when one of the counselors or an Upper or Middle Peer yells at you for doing something wrong. And when you do something really wrong you're "on Contract," which means you lose your privileges and have to spend all your time cleaning and doing chores.

But the one that really hangs me up is what they call "dropping guilt." That means that if you break one of the three cardinal rules—which are no drugs, no violence, no sexually acting out—you have to drop your guilt and tell on yourself. Or if you know someone else who did it, you have to tell on them.

And I could never in a million years rat on somebody, and I'm sure as hell not going to rat on myself. So that's one of the things that keeps getting me in trouble. In Grand Central, where I spent a lot more years than Samaritan Village, they have their own Concepts, and one of them is "Snitches get stitches."

I DIDN'T KNOW ANYBODY WHO snitched in Grand Central. And I didn't know anyone in Grand Central who wasn't doing something illegal. Even if they weren't robbing or dealing drugs, they had a scam going, like Dwayne giving out this bullshit story when he panhandled about how his face got burned in Vietnam. Everyone had their own little specialty. Some had a lot. It was something you did to survive, and when it's part of the world you're living in, you just accept it. Maybe you know it's wrong. But so is everything else in your life. So, big deal.

First time I ever robbed anyone was a couple of months after April got out of Elmhurst.

April had this friend, Lorenzo, he came from El Salvador in a tire. He knew some guy who owned an abandoned building in Harlem, and he gave the guy two hundred dollars to use one of the apartments. Lorenzo told April and me that we could come, too. We stayed there a month, until November, when someone padlocked all the entrances.

The building was old and crumbly, with smashed windows and boards and beams hanging down inside. A lot of the steps were missing, so you had to be careful going upstairs. We had gone there in early October with Lorenzo and picked out the apartment we wanted, and put our own lock and chain through the door. The apartment had three rooms, but no furniture except a couple of lumpy mattresses, and no electricity, water, or heat, either. We hardly ever had food. Me and April would curl up on the mattress under the blankets, smoke dust, and wait for Lorenzo to come home with sandwiches or fried chicken or hamburgers so we could eat.

Lorenzo was an older guy, maybe in his thirties. He was secretive, always watching his back. He told us he'd been involved in a plot to kill Castro and that's why he had to come to this country, but I don't know if that was true.

Lorenzo is the guy who started April on crack. At this point we were mainly into dust, but Lorenzo was a crackhead and he gave April a woolly to smoke. That's a cigarette with crack in it, crushed and rolled in with the tobacco. It seemed like one day April was puffing on woollies, telling me, "Don't worry, you can't get addicted this way," and next thing, she was taking real hits off her own stem and telling me, "I better never catch *you* smoking this shit."

So now both Lorenzo and April were smoking crack, and always needing money. Nothing to do but steal it.

The first time we waited until late at night. April sat on a stoop near our building while me and Lorenzo hung out on the corner, trying not to look suspicious. When she saw a guy who she thought might have some cash, she flicked her lighter twice.

He was young, black, dressed like a college student or an office worker. We ran up behind him and Lorenzo wrapped his arm around the guy's neck and yoked him up while I went through his pockets. I was so nervous my knees were shaking. But what surprised me was how fast it went, and how easy. The guy was very cooperative, probably wanted to get it over with even more than we did. We got about twenty bucks and a lottery ticket. I couldn't believe we got away with it.

After that, most nights we'd go out and rob people and each time I was a little less scared. We'd sleep in the abandoned building all day, hit the streets at night. April was always the lookout. She'd pick a spot near our building and sit there, scraping the resin that was left in her stem and smoking it. The res—that's what it's called, "the res"—she said that's the best part because it's really concentrated. But April was always telling me, "Stay away from crack because if I ever catch you smoking, I won't be your friend anymore."

And I'd promise to stay away from it. I'd smoke a little reefer, do a little dust, drink some beer or a pint of blackberry brandy. But the more I saw her getting high off crack, the more I wanted to try it too.


I woke up in the middle of the night. Something was wrong. Me and April and Lorenzo had been sleeping together on the same mattress so we could share body heat, because it was near the end of October and it was getting so cold that one night my Coke froze in the can. Lorenzo was snoring on one side of me, but on the other side there was nothing but empty mattress.

April was in the living room, sitting on the floor in front of a burning candle. Her head was bent over, she was very busy doing something and at first I couldn't tell what it was. When I got closer I could see she was making cuts in her wrist with a razor. There was a little line of blood running down onto her hand.

I must have yelled, because she jerked her head up and saw me. She said, "Leave me alone," but I ran over and grabbed her arm so hard she dropped the razor. I got the razor before she did and threw it into a hole in the floor.

I think I was shaking. The blood freaked me out. April was wearing her jacket and a fuzzy scarf that she got from some church volunteers and I pulled the scarf off and wrapped it around her wrist to stop the bleeding. She said, "Leave me alone," again, but she wasn't trying to stop me. I wondered if she would really have killed herself or if she was just playing at it. I asked her, "Why did you do that?"

She told me, "Today is Travis's birthday. I was celebrating."

I tried to get her to come back to bed. I was sleepy and I didn't want to leave her alone. But she wouldn't move. We sat there watching the candle burn down until dawn.


On Halloween night April said, "Let's go trick-or-treating."

"That's stupid," I said. "That's for babies. What do you want to go trick-or-treating for?"

"Because," April said, "I'm hungry."

There was no food and no crack, and no money to buy either. Lorenzo had been gone since yesterday and I wasn't going to try robbing someone alone, without a guy.

"Anyway," April said, "it'll be fun."

"But we don't even have costumes."

"Yeah we do. We're wearing them."

So we went as bums. We exchanged clothes first, just so we'd feel like we were wearing something special and not our same old stuff. I wore April's torn sweatshirt and baggy jeans and she wore my flannel shirt and corduroy pants. We switched jackets, too. They were both stained with soot from the train tunnels.

We took the subway downtown and hit all the places along Forty-second Street, the movie theaters and girlie joints and delis and all-night pizzerias. We went to all the crack dealers, too.

We knew most of the people who ran the stores and fast-food places, so we'd just walk in and holler, "Trick or treat!" and April would hold out her plastic bag, decorated with pumpkins and black cats, that she stole from an all-night drugstore. A couple times the store people asked where our costumes were and we said, "We're wearing them. We're bums!"

They thought that was pretty funny, and they loaded us up with candy. The guy at the pizza place gave us each a slice of pizza and a Coke. The dealers all gave us crack and April put that in the pumpkin bag too.

By the time we got back to the apartment in Harlem, at about five A.M., the bag was overflowing. Orange candy corn and little Nestlé bars and Snickers bars and M&M's and Peppermint Patties and peanut butter cups and even some Gummy Bears.

We lit candles, plunked down on the floor, spilled out all the candy, and divvied it up. "Twelve M&M's for you, twelve M&M's for me. Three Snickers for you, three Snickers for me. Six Gummy Bears for you, six Gummy Bears for me . . ."

And we ate it all too. The crack, April split with Lorenzo.

IN THE MIDDLE OF AUGUST I pass the tests in Orientation and graduate to Lower Peer.

That's where you start getting privileges. Like you get WAM, which is Walking Around Money, and every Friday night they take you into town. You start at four dollars and work up to seven by the time you're in Upper Peer, which is enough to go to McDonald's and maybe buy chips or candy and extra cigarettes to take back.

When you're out of Orientation you can use the pool, the handball and basketball courts, watch videos on Friday nights, write letters and get them, plus you don't need a buddy anymore. You also have a job. The first job they give me is in the dining room, carrying trays to the tables. It's kind of like being a waitress but without the tips.

Samaritan, so far, is mostly a breeze. A lot easier than Grand Central because you don't have to think about surviving. Survival is guaranteed, it comes with the bed and food and all the meetings. I'm already detoxed physically, so I don't have that problem. The newness of everything and being with strange people is the worst part. But there isn't anything I'm going to come up against at Samaritan that's as tough as Grand Central.

I figure to get by at Samaritan you just keep your mouth shut, do what they tell you as much as possible, but if you can't, make sure they don't find out, and relax and enjoy the scenery. Club Med for ex-junkies.

In warm weather I spend my free time outside. We play handball in teams, or if nobody's around, I just play by myself. I go swimming every day too, and take lots of walks around the property.

My favorite place is the big rock behind YDA that I found my first night, the night I saw the Little Dipper. Sometimes I lie down on the rock and study the stars. Pick one and stare at it for ten or fifteen minutes until the star seems a lot realer than me and my little life.

In September I start classes to study for my general equivalency diploma. I took GED classes two years ago when I was on probation and did okay, even took the first half of the test. I probably would have passed, too, but I went and got high and didn't make it back the next day to take the second half.

Samaritan Village has a school building, with four classrooms, right next to YDA. The classes are Monday through Friday from nine until twelve and then from two to three. In between we have lunch from twelve to one, and then there is Seminar every day from one to two. Seminars, oh my God. Seminars are given by different staff members and they can be about anything. Mostly they're serious, like they'll talk to you about relapse prevention or important stuff happening in the news, but some of those Seminars are the most boring things in the world.

If you fall asleep, the person next to you is supposed to nudge you, because he's not supposed to allow you to do that negative behavior. But if he doesn't, one of the monitors will catch you and you'll get a "haircut," a scolding, by someone in Upper Peer. And they can scream. So you try to stay awake as much as you can, but some days, when Seminar is really, really boring, I'll be thinking, You know what? Forget it. I'll fall asleep and just take the damn haircut.

The other group you go to when you get out of Orientation is the Encounter group, which is also once a week like Caseload. If you have a beef with someone during the week, you're not supposed to fight or argue, you drop a slip on them. That means you write down on the slip that you want to see them in Encounter group, and that's where you're supposed to confront them and work it out. Which doesn't make a lot of sense to me. Somebody pushes in front of you in line or says something disrespectful, you want to let them have it *now*.

At Samaritan they want to change everything about you, even your way of talking and expressing yourself. They're telling you all the time, "It's your stinking thinking that got you here." Your way of thinking isn't working, so you have to try a different way. *Their* way. And as far as I'm concerned, that's brainwashing. Because they can be wrong, too. Who's to say they're right?

I've always had problems with authority, anyway.

Five weeks after I get to Lower Peer, I get demoted for sexually acting out. That's one of the three cardinal rules, and they said I broke it when I was in Orientation.

In Orientation you always had to have either your buddy or someone else go with you wherever you went, so during the summer this one girl always asked me. If she wanted to get a hairpin from her room, I had to go with her. If she left her sunglasses out in the yard, I'd have to go back there with her to find them. And I could tell she was flirting with me, just by the way she said things, like, "Oh, you look nice today," or she'd compliment something I was wearing.

We wound up doing a little messing around, like kissing. I didn't think we were breaking any rules because I didn't consider that to be sexually acting out.

So in October, when we're both in Lower Peer, this girl leaves the program. Later that week at Morning Meeting, one of the Upper Peer guys who is running the meeting on this day calls my name and tells me, "Tina, you have to take the Chair."

Oh shit. The Chair. That's a special chair in the Adult House where you wait when you've done something wrong until the staff can get together and decide what to do with you.

All morning, I'm on the Chair. You can sit there for hours, you can sit there the whole day. And once you're on the Chair, everyone in the place knows. When they pass by they say things like, "Oh, you're in trouble!" I want to crawl underneath it and hide. And all this time I'm sweating it out, wondering what the hell did I do, anyway?

Finally I get called into one of the staff offices, and there are three counselors there. I sit where they tell me. I ask them, "Could you please tell me what I'm here for?"

"You tell us, Tina," this counselor, Jim, says. "Do you have any guilt to drop?"

"I didn't do anything wrong."

"Are you sure?"

"Yeah, I'm sure."

"Positive?"

"Positive." Only now I'm not. I keep trying to think, Christ, *did* I do something?

"Okay," Sherrelle, one of the lady counselors, says. "Go back to the Chair."

"But why?"

"Looks like you need to think a little more, that's why."

I sit on the Chair for two more goddamn hours, miss lunch, until Jim comes and takes me back into the office. "So," he says, "do you have any guilt to drop?"

"Is it about the cigarette?" I ask.

"This isn't Twenty Questions, Tina."

"Well, maybe it was the cigarette I smoked in my room even though I know you can't smoke up there. But that was a couple weeks ago and I only did it once."

"That's it?" the other lady counselor asks.

"Yes."

"Back to the Chair, please."

Oh, no. I'm going to miss dinner too, and my stomach is already growling so loud they can hear it across the room. "Look," I say, "whatever I did, I'm sorry, but you can make me sit on that Chair until Christmas and I'm not going to remember. Would you just tell me?"

Jim and Sherrelle and the other counselor look at each other, and then Jim says to me, "You broke one of the cardinal rules."

"I did? Which one did I break?"

"You're saying you still don't know?"

"No. Honest."

So then they tell me it was the sexually-acting-out rule. "When Allison left the program she dropped all her guilt. She told us what happened between you two."

"But that wasn't *sex*," I say. "Kissing is not *sex*. Kissing is messing around."

Nope, they say, kissing is a form of intimate contact, and any kind of intimate contact comes under the heading of sex. Jim says, "When you get close with someone you take the focus off yourself and your issues, and that gets in the way of recovery."

"Plus, if you can't uphold the cardinal rules," Sherrelle says, "you don't belong in Lower Peer. So it's been decided you need to go back to Orientation until you can show you're ready to try Lower Peer again."

And Jim tells me, "Also, you're on a two-week work Contract."

"For kissing? All that for kissing? That's not fair."

"The meeting is over. You can go now, Tina."

I wind up back in Orientation and on Contract too. Lose all my privileges. Every spare minute I'm not in class or a meeting I'm sweeping and mopping floors, washing dishes, raking leaves, and scrubbing out toilets.

So maybe this place isn't going to be such a piece of cake after all.

Todd, my Caseload counselor, left in October and I get put in Nancy Cruz's Caseload, which is good because she's my favorite. She's young, in her twenties, and when it's her turn to be counselor on duty over the weekend, she'll always drive us into town to get videos. Some of the other counselors do that, too, but Nancy, she'll sit and watch the movie with us. She's the kind of person who really gets involved. You never feel like she's there just because it's her job.

I finally got up the courage to write to my mom, and she writes a very friendly letter back. So I call her. And she tells me she has a job, earning a hundred seventy-five a week, as a matron on a school bus for disabled kids. I think the city got her the job so she can finally get off welfare. I tell her, "Ma, I'm so glad for you."

Also, she says my brother Frankie called her from Florida. He moved there with our stepfather, Vince, but my mom hadn't heard from him in a long time. Frankie said he had a job now, doing landscaping. My mom told him where I am and Frankie said he's going to call me.

I didn't see him or talk to him in four years. I miss my family a lot.

"I think it's time we heard from Tina," Nancy says one night in Caseload. Everyone looks over at me. Caseload meets in the living room of YDA and there are about eighteen of us in the group. I'm sitting on the floor, leaning up against a footstool, and everybody turns to look at me. A roomful of eyes. I feel so uncomfortable my skin itches.

I know I have to open up sometime. That's one of the criteria for moving up in the program, that you're working on your issues. So far, I haven't been.

"How do you feel about getting bumped back to Orientation?" Nancy asks me. "That's something you could talk about."

I say, "How do you think I feel?"

Nancy doesn't answer right away. And she doesn't act like I'm just trying to give her a smart answer, which I am. After a minute she says, "Well, what I think is that you feel pissed off about it. And maybe a little embarrassed. But that's just what I think. So are you going to tell me if I'm close or not?"

"Yeah, you're close, I guess."

Then she asks me to talk about why I got kicked out of Lower Peer and I tell her it's because that fucking bitch Allison ratted on herself and on me before she left. Nancy says that isn't why I got kicked out. She says why I got kicked out was for breaking one of the cardinal rules.

One of the other girls in Caseload, Loretta, who is new at Samaritan, asks, "So are you like gay or what?"

I tell her, "I'm like me. That's what I'm like."

"No, but I just wanted to know, do you like men too, or is it just girls? I mean, no offense, but I never talked to somebody who was a homosexual, so I was just curious about that."

Nancy jumps in then. She says, "Tina, you don't have to get into this if you don't feel okay with it."

"I'm okay with it," I tell her. The truth is, I'm not. I'm not okay with talking about anything. But I have to start somewhere, so I figure, might as well be here. "I like guys," I tell Loretta. "I just don't trust them like I trust females."

"Well, how much sense does that make?" someone else asks. "Because, look, you trusted Allison, but then she went and got you in trouble once her ass was out of here and safe."

Then Nancy points out that Allison wasn't trying to get anyone in trouble, she was just following a rule she promised to obey. Nancy says Allison wasn't being untrustworthy, she was being honorable.

"Whatever," I say. "I just don't think men are as trustworthy as women."

"Bad experiences with men, huh?" Nancy says.

"Maybe." I think of my father, how him and my mom used to fight all the time. I think of Robert and some of her other boyfriends, and I think of some of the guys I've known. "But I'm through talking for today," I tell her.

THE GUY CAME UP TO me in the waiting room while I was hanging out, asked me do I have a stem and do I smoke crack. He was black, youngish, clean clothes. I never saw him around Grand Central before. I told him no, I don't have a stem and I never smoked crack. I told him I smoked just about everything else, though.

He took a vial out of his jacket pocket and I could see the white stuff in the vial so I knew it was crack. He asked me, do I want to try it now, because he'll share his with me.

April had been smoking crack for a month or two, but she said she'd kill me if she ever caught me doing it. Only April wasn't around right now and I was curious, and still dumb enough to go off alone with this guy when he said, "You know someplace out of the way where we can smoke?"

I took him down to our spot in the tunnels, under the platform of Track 100. He was never in the tunnels before, I could tell from the way he looked around, checking the whole place out. The cardboard and blankets on the floor where we slept, the piles of old clothes, empty bottles, and trash. He saw the TV in the corner. "That thing really work?"

"Yeah it works. We got it wired."

He looked around again and whistled through his teeth. "Quite a place, quite a place," he said, and I couldn't tell if he was putting me on or he really was impressed. "You living here?"

"Me and some others," I said.

"And the rats too, huh?"

"The rats won't bother you unless you're dead."

Then he looked me up and down, real hard. The kind of once-over he just gave the spot. He told me, "You're cute, for a white gal."

I tried to act casual and tough but he was making me uneasy. "So come on, let's get high."

"In due time, in due time," he said. "First you gotta fuck."

"Hell, no. No way," I told him, and turned to leave. And just like that, he had me in a headlock. I tried to fight him but he was behind me, and he was a big guy and I was just a kid, five feet tall give or take an inch. His arm was getting tighter and tighter around my neck. I tried to scream but nothing came out because of the pressure around my throat. I thought, I'm going to die. Right now. This is it. And who will find me?

Then blackness, then nothing.


When I came to I was lying on the ground, my pants were down around my ankles, the guy was gone. I tried to sit up but it hurt and my neck was so painful I could hardly move my head. There were little bloody cuts around my thighs. Maybe from his hands, his nails digging into me.

Getting up was hard because I was so trembly and my legs were tangled in my pants. When I did manage to stand and get my clothes back on they were all wet. I think I must have peed in them. They felt cold and clammy.

I couldn't go to the cops. They'd have to take me into custody because being down in the tunnels is criminal trespassing, plus legally I was a runaway. I wasn't going to spend another three days eating bologna sandwiches in Central Booking.

I was scared and hurt and I needed April. Only how was I going to go running around the station looking for her if I peed my pants?

And I couldn't stay in there, because what if he came back?

I hid in the darkest corner, wrapped myself in an old army blanket so even my head was covered. Ashamed to go out, afraid to stay there. I was shaking all over and crying and crying. I think I fell asleep that way.


Later, when I found April, she got me clean clothes from St. Agnes Church. She took me into the ladies' room and helped me wash and change, held me while I cried, even combed my hair for me. She said, "That fucking bastard, just show me who he is because I'm going to chop his balls off."

And for weeks, whenever we saw a man hanging around the waiting room who wasn't one of the regulars, she would ask me, "Tina, hey, is that the guy? Is he the one?" But it never was. I never saw him again.

I tried to forget him. I tried to forget it ever happened.

I HAVE A RUN-IN WITH Jacinta, who was my Big Sister when I first came to Samaritan. Nothing major, she just asks me to do some little thing and I give her an attitude and wind up on the Chair for it. They sentence me to a day at the dishpan. Plus, Nancy tells me I have to write a composition about my image and how it keeps tripping me up.

I'm going through all these changes. Crying a lot. Also I'm angry half the time at the people here, because it's hard for me accept their concern. Why can't they leave me alone? At the same time I know I'm just fighting the program, holding on to things that maybe I have to give up. April's identity, for one thing. I have to learn to be myself. But who is that?

I feel burned out and exhausted and I'm falling asleep in meetings and classes. I need a break, so I play sick and spend a day in bed, sleep until after noon. They send me a dinner plate from the kitchen, fried chicken. But I'm not hungry. I get some stationery and sit up in bed writing to my mom. Tell her how proud I am of her with her new job, tell her I want to come home for a visit soon. And that I miss her. I don't even realize I'm crying again until I see a tear fall onto the letter.

I want some crayons and a coloring book.


One of my roommates, Angela, reminds me of April. Sometimes I can't believe how much. Especially with wet hair. One night she comes out of the shower wearing a robe and her hair is wet and shiny dark and stuck to her face. I almost stop breathing for a minute because she looks so much like April.

I figured to get to Samaritan Village you would have to have gone through some horrible things. I don't know everybody's story, but I had figured it would be about the same as mine. You know, they were living on the streets and doing drugs and they hit bottom and wanted to get themselves cleaned up. But that isn't so. My situation was a lot worse than most of theirs.

It took a while for me to realize that, because I didn't let myself get too friendly with most of the others. It isn't until I see how bugged out they are when we watch my tape of *48 Hours* that I realize how different my experience was.

I had talked about *48 Hours* to a few of the girls in YDA, and Nancy heard about it. She asks if I can get a copy to show them. She says it would help me see how far I've come because I get discouraged a lot, and it would also be good for the others to see how much bigger my obstacles were because if I can get it together, they can too. So I write and ask Jamie to send me a video copy of the program.

We show the *48 Hours* tape on a Friday night in October, just for whoever is around and wants to see it. Girls and guys, maybe fifteen in all.

The first part shows the tunnels, and Harold Dow is talking to some of the older men who live down there. Then, when it gets to my part, everyone claps and whistles and goes, "Hey, man, lookit Tina!" until Nancy makes them be quiet.

It's so strange to be watching that program again. There's me, cigarette hanging from my mouth, looking tough or trying to, talking to Harold Dow and waiting for Harley to show up with the crack so we can spend the night getting high. That was definitely me. But look. This is me, too, stretched out on the floor of the YDA living room at Samaritan Village in upstate New York, wearing a clean sweater and new jeans Harriet sent me, watching TV with my hand stuck in a bag of potato chips. How many me's are there? For a minute I get a weird dizzy feeling wondering which is the true one.

When the show is over the others are saying things like, "Wow, you really lived down in those tunnels? That's wild." It surprises me, how impressed they are. One guy wants to know did we really have TV down there. To him, that's the most amazing part. And everybody is asking me, "How did you manage to live through that?"

I tell them, "Every day was just another day. It wasn't anything special."

And it wasn't all bad. Sometimes, I couldn't help remembering the fun parts. Being on the streets, doing what you wanted, not having anybody tell you that you can't do something because you're too young. All the crazy stuff we did.

86

WE WERE BROKE. APRIL SAID, "Wait there, I'm going to get us some money."

She walked into the men's room, and I stood close enough to the door to hear her make this loud announcement, "Okay, one of you gentlemen in here is gonna give me five bucks. Who's it gonna be?" She didn't sound threatening, just kind of cute and ballsy and, sure enough, about three minutes later she comes bouncing out, big grin on her face and a five-dollar bill in her hand. Tipped her baseball cap at me and said, "You want to split a pepperoni pizza?"

April usually had some kind of gimmick for panhandling, like sitting outside the station with a sign that said PLEASE CONTRIBUTE TO HELP THE HOMELESS! Crack slang for getting high is "Scotty beam me up," which is from *Star Trek*, and one time she had a sign that said, HELP ME FIND SCOTTY. I couldn't believe what she was doing, but no one understood what it meant. Another thing she would say was that she was working her way through Vassar. Anyway, a lot of people got a kick out of April and gave her money just for the hell of it.

For a long time I didn't have the courage to try panhandling. Finally I did, and it just came to me like that. As a matter of fact, some of my best times were probably panhandling in Grand Central, because everyone thought I was so young and cute, and I could get almost as much money as April could. That was one of the few things I could do as well.

This is how I started: One day I was sitting around doing nothing, and one of the guys suggested I try panhandling. I really needed money, so I said, "What the hell, I'll give it a shot." Went and stood by the ladies' room, but all I could do was watch the women going in and out, couldn't make myself say anything. I felt like a jerk.

Then this one lady came out, she was kind of plump and comfortable looking and she reminded me of a teacher I had in fourth grade. She stared at me. Maybe I reminded her of someone, too. I said real fast, " 'Scuse me, could you spare some change?"

She looked kind of surprised. Like she wasn't quite sure how to react. Then she said, "Well, how much do you need?" That really blew me away. She's asking how much to give me, like I was some neighborhood kid she's known my whole life.

I said, "A dollar?" With the question mark.

So she opened her big purse, sifted around and came out with a dollar bill. I said, "Thank you," as politely as I could, stuck the dollar in my pocket. I wondered what would have happened if I'd asked for twenty.

After that it got easy. It was all about eye contact. Because if they made eye contact, I felt they were really seeing me and wondering, "Well, what are you doing here? What's the matter with you?" They would want to help me.

Plus, I had a lot of advantages. Not only was I young and cute compared to most of the other panhandlers, I was also white. Commuters, at least the white ones, always saw white panhandlers easier than they saw the black ones. Another advantage, I was real small, so I wasn't intimidating. Also, it was around the holidays when I started, just before Thanksgiving, so people were feeling generous anyway. I remember one day I made almost fifty dollars in one hour. But usually it was much, much less.

After I'd been panhandling for a couple months I didn't worry about the eye contact thing anymore. I just asked anybody walking by. I'd turn from one side: " 'Scuse me, can you spare some change?" to the other side: " 'Scuse me, can you spare some change?" Zip, zip, zap, zap, thanks-a-lot, ma'am, thanks-a-lot, mister, shove the money in my pocket. Catch them coming both ways. I had the timing down real good.

I even had some regulars. People who came through the station every day at the same time, catching the same train home to Scarsdale or White Plains or whatever hole they crawled into when the sun went down. They'd look for me in my place, which was usually by the ladies' room, and they always had some change. Once in a while a dollar, mostly a couple of quarters or whatever they had handy. I told people, "I don't accept pennies." That was one of my lines and they usually thought it was funny. Of course I took pennies. Pennies, nickels, dimes, subway tokens, whatever. If it fit in my pocket, I took it.

One of my regulars was Jerry, the guy who owned the deli in Grand Central right off the main concourse. He was a big chunky white guy with a goatee and glasses, and I knew him through April. He used to give her free food sometimes, or slip her a dollar. One day I was panhandling near Jerry's deli, right by the steps to the lower level, which is where I liked to hang out. When business was slow I'd see him standing there by the door flipping a quarter up in the air with his thumb. He always caught it, I never saw one drop. One day he was doing it and I went over and said, "Got a quarter?" He flipped it at me and I caught it. After that, whenever I saw him by his store flipping quarters, I'd go and hit on him.

And then there was Hug Me. Jabba took credit for him. Jabba told me that one day, before I came on the scene, he saw this old guy buying a paper at the newsstand so he said, "Hey, April, Maria, you see that guy there? Well, I happen to know if you walk up and hug him, he'll give you some money."

April, she was game for anything, she went right over, threw her arms around him, gave him a big hug, and came back with a five-dollar bill. So then Maria did it, and the guy gave her five dollars too. They said, "Hey, Jabba, who is that guy and how did you know he'd pay for a hug?" Jabba started laughing. Turned out Jabba never saw the guy before in his life. He had no idea he would really pay April and Maria for a hug.

This guy came through the station all the time, so after that whenever April and Maria saw him they'd run up and give him a bear hug, and he'd give them money. Usually five, but sometimes as much as ten or twenty dollars. They called him Hug Me. One day April pointed him out to me and said, "Go hug that guy and he'll give you some money." I thought she was kidding so she took me over and introduced me. He was short and very pink with just a fringe of gray hair around his head, dressed really nice, but you got the feeling he was frail.

After that, whenever I'd see him I'd say, "Hi, Hug Me, how you doing today?" I'd give him a big hug and he'd pull out a five, once in a while a ten or twenty, and give it to me. And that was as far as it went. All he wanted was a hug.

Toward the end, when April was in really bad shape and didn't care about anything anymore, she pickpocketed him. He figured out who took his money and after that he wouldn't let April near him anymore. And after I turned Beverly on to him, and her friend Micki, he told me in private he didn't like the black girls to hug him. We started seeing him less and less. Then somebody told me he was sick. He had a heart attack, I think.

We never understood why he paid for hugs, but I didn't question it. You know the saying, Don't look a gift horse in the mouth.

My other regulars I never got as friendly with. And they never gave me as much as Hug Me. But I'd try to be nice, thank them, ask, "How are you today?" and they'd always say, "Fine, how are you?" A few would try to ask me personal questions, like what was I doing here, but I just gave them smart answers like "Having fun."

And I was having fun. I was doing something I was good at, and making honest money. The people could give it to me or not, it was up to them. I wasn't robbing, I was giving people a choice.

And I really did need money, because I had started messing with crack by then. Vials at that time were around ten dollars, unless you went uptown. You could get them a lot cheaper uptown.

THE THANKSGIVING DANCE AT SAMARITAN is my first dance and I'm really nervous. But I'm not as uncomfortable around the other people now, and I do have a couple friends. After showing *48 Hours* on movie night, things changed a little. It wasn't like I turned into a celebrity or anything, but I did get respect. I'm not sure what impressed them most, that I was on TV or that I lived such a crazy, dangerous life. But people started asking me questions about it and that pulled me out of my shell a little.

After I finished my work Contract I had to write a proposal about why I thought I was ready to leave Orientation again. In order to move up, you also have to get the people in the peer group you're leaving, and the people in the peer group you're going to be in, to agree that you're ready to make the move. And they did, so now I'm back in Lower Peer and feeling a lot better about myself.

For the Thanksgiving dance nearly everyone is dressing up, but you can wear whatever you want as long as it's clean and neat. I know I'm going to feel even more uncomfortable if I'm dressed up, so I wear jeans and a nice dark blue sweater.

The dance is in the Adult House, in the cafeteria. They moved all the tables and decorated the place for Thanksgiving. There are lots of refreshments and the music is loud disco rock. They never play slow music because there always has to be space between you and your partner.

The first half I spend stuck to the wall. A couple guys come over and ask me to dance but I tell them I don't know how. Anyway, I'm enjoying just watching it all.

One of my roommates brings me a cup of coffee. "You gotta try this," she says. I tell her I don't like coffee but she says it isn't regular coffee, it's called *Café Bustelo* and Upper Peer made it. She tells me they strained it with a special kind of filter to make it stronger, and the counselors are trying to get it banned because you can get a little high off it.

It's very, very strong but I drink it anyway. And while I'm drinking, this guy Roy comes over.

"You want to dance?" he asks.

I tell him, "I don't know how."

"Come on, everybody can dance. Even you."

"No," I tell him, "I never did it before."

"Well, then, I'm gonna teach you," he says.

We get on the dance floor and he shows me this back and forth, back and forth kind of step. He makes me copy him a couple times, then he says, "See? That's all you do," and he starts to dance. So I do too.

And it's working. It looks like I'm really dancing. The music is so loud the floor is buzzing, I can even feel the music inside me, and I make the back-and-forth step fit the beat and all of a sudden I'm dancing. Maybe the *Bustelo* kicked in.


Roy is one of my best friends at Samaritan. He's a nice guy, handsome but a little short, and he's kind of self-conscious about his size. He doesn't really talk to people much but he likes me. Like in boyfriend/girlfriend. But I don't feel the same for him.

Roy is an honest kind of person, that's what drew me to him. There's something very safe about him. And he would never, ever try to push himself on you. He helps me study for my GED exam, and we play handball and also take walks together. The trees and mountains are all different colors now, bright oranges and reds and yellows, like something an artist painted.


They tell me, "Tina, you got an emergency call," and I run to the phone making the sign of the cross all the way. I guess they thought it was an emergency call because it was long distance, from Florida, but it turns out to be my brother Frankie calling to say hello.

I think the last time I spoke to Frankie was when he was living with Vince in Queens, before I ran away. He sounds different now, he has sort of a Southern accent. He tells me Florida is great and he likes his landscaping job. "You should come down," he says, "because I have an extra bed and plenty of room. Why don't you come for Christmas?" I tell him I have to finish the program at Samaritan first and he says I should definitely come down to Florida afterwards and we could live together.

It's so hard to believe he just turned nineteen. I still picture the kid brother who was always tagging along after me on his bike. Frankie was a quiet kid, but he was pretty happy until we had the fire and had to move to the hotel. Not the Prince George where my mom went the second time, but the first one. We spent a year in the Martinique Hotel and then the city moved us to the Bronx, to the apartment on Fordham Road.

It was in the Martinique that Frankie started withdrawing. I remember later, on Fordham Road, he'd spend hours shut up in his closet just reading science books, math books, all kinds of books. He was totally into school and that's how he escaped. From us being so poor. And from Robert, who he couldn't stand. Finally when he was fourteen he moved in with Jessica's father, Vince. My mom didn't try to stop him.

I tell Frankie, "I'm going to try to write every week." And before we hang up I tell him I love him.

"I love you too, Tina," he says. He sounds lonely.


My roommate, Angela, left the program right before the Thanksgiving dance. I'm not ever going to see her again. When she left I cried all night. It was almost the same kind of pain as when I heard that April was dead.


On Thanksgiving we have turkey. That's the big thing, the dinner. You eat and eat and then you kind of lay back and relax. Watch TV.

It's better than the last few Thanksgivings. There was a time I knew what day and what time every church in midtown Manhattan served meals, so on Thanksgiving we went from church to church and had three or four dinners. The Salvation Army always had the best holiday dinners because they gave you the most. Turkey, mashed potatoes or yams, peas or another vegetable, and pie. And even though it was processed turkey, it *was* turkey. They did their best.

The last year I was in Grand Central I didn't bother to go for turkey. I don't think I even noticed it was Thanksgiving. Anyway, I was hardly ever hungry anymore.

I STARTED SMOKING CRACK FOR a couple of reasons. April was doing it, and I wanted to be like April. This was the end of 1985 and it seemed everyone was discovering crack, so it was the thing to do if you wanted to belong. Also, I guess I started because I didn't feel good about myself and I'd already learned that drugs can make you feel better about everything.

It was somewhere around Thanksgiving when I started, and it was Lorenzo who turned me on. Just like he turned April on a couple months before. Somebody told me, "Hey, Lorenzo's been looking for you and April." They said he was downstairs, so I went down to the lower level and he was all the way in back by the elevator with a couple of guys I didn't know.

Lorenzo gave them the nod to leave, and he asked where April was. I told him we were over at the bus terminal and she hadn't come back yet and he said, "Oh, 'cause I just went uptown and I have some rock for her." Then he kind of looked at me and said, "Well, you know, if she's not around nothing's stopping *you*. I'm not gonna blab."

He handed me his stem and lighter and stood in front of me, so if somebody happened to walk by they wouldn't see. What the hell, you know? I lit up.

And wow. It was magic. The first hit was magic. I had a sudden burst of energy and felt a rush like I never had before. My mind was floating away in a cloud.

But it didn't satisfy me, it made me want more. I took a couple hits, pulled hard as I could, but it didn't happen again. Only that first one sent me flying. All I was feeling now was hyped up.

"Hey, hey, hey," Lorenzo said, and he took his stem back. "You trying to smoke up my supply?"

I'm thinking, give me more, I want to catch that rush again, I gotta get back up there in the cloud. But Lorenzo took a couple of hits, then stuck the stem back in the seam of his fly. "You're practically slobbering for more," he said. "I think you'd roll over and die for another suck off my stem."

"Fuck off," I told him.

I guess when April got back they gave her the same message about Lorenzo, because twenty minutes later she came downstairs too. I was still with him, we were just standing around bullshitting. But she knew. Somehow she knew the minute she saw me.

She said, "You smoked it, didn't you?"

I was smoking a regular cigarette then, and first I thought that's what she was talking about. I just said, "What?"

She looked at Lorenzo, then back at me, and said again, "You smoked it." This time I knew what she meant.

"No," I said. "No, I didn't."

I could tell she wanted to belt me. "Don't fuckin' lie to me."

"Okay," I told her, "so I did smoke."

"Didn't I tell you not to touch that shit?"

"Look, April, you're not my goddamn mother."

"You're a stupid asshole," she told me, and she told Lorenzo, "And you're an even bigger one for giving it to her."

She turned and walked away and didn't come back. Maybe she holed up in a hotel with someone and some crack, because I didn't see her again for three days. I went looking for her too. In Bryant Park and in the little park on Second Avenue, also around Forty-second Street, on the steps of St. Agnes Church, outside the Pan Am Building, and all the places we hung out. But I couldn't find her.

I bought my crack stem on Forty-second Street. You can buy just the stem if you want. It comes without the pipe bowl. The pipe bowl is for free basing, which we didn't do.

You need a screen too. A little filter screen. You can buy it already inside the stem or you can buy it separately, because a lot of people like to make their own filters. I got mine separately. You fold the screen into a ball and put it inside the stem. If you fold it so it filters right, the resin from the crack, when it's melting, gets hard and white instead of dripping all the way down and turning into an oily film. Then you can flip the stem around, push the screen back a little, and smoke the other end. It's a lot more powerful because it's melted down and concentrated. Now you're smoking pure res, the best.

IN THE BEGINNING OF DECEMBER I go before the Middle Peer committee and tell them why I feel I meet the criteria to move up. I tell them I worked real hard to study for my GED, and also helped others with English and reading. I just took the GED exam and now I'm waiting to see if I passed, but I'm pretty sure I did.

I also tell the committee how responsible I am in my job in the dining room. I'm not carrying food trays anymore, I'm one of the supervisors. And it helps if you can show that you're working on patching things up with your family, so I tell how I'm in touch with my mom and my brother again.

Then, right before Christmas, they announce at one of the meetings that I made Middle Peer. Well, it took long enough. But finally I'm moving up in the program. You have more privileges in Middle Peer, too. You get more WAM money, you can go on home visits alone, and they let you use the game, room which has a pool table and arcade games. Also in Middle Peer you have more responsibilities, like being a Big Sister or Brother to someone new. But as it turns out, I didn't stay in Middle Peer long enough for that.

The same week I got to Middle Peer I found out I passed the GED exam. Passing is 225 and I got 269. First thing I do is call Harriet and George and write to my mom and Jamie. I tell them all, "Guess what, I finally got my high school diploma!" Almost twenty-one years old, but better late than never.

My Caseload group goes on a holiday trip to the city. We see an Off Broadway show in the afternoon, a one-woman play. All I remember about it is, it was boring. But then we go to see the giant Christmas tree at Rockefeller Center. It's so crowded there's hardly room to stand, but we stay a while because the tree is so beautiful and so are all the people skating on the rink down below. It looks like a storybook picture.

While we're waiting for the green light so we can cross the street to St. Patrick's Cathedral, I spot this guy, also waiting to cross, who looks familiar. Kind of youngish, dressed nice, carrying a briefcase. I'm trying to remember who he is, and then it hits me. He used to be one of my regulars. Every night he went through Grand Central, and whenever he saw me panhandling he'd give me some change. He'd say something like, "Hey, kid, how's life?" and dig in his pants pocket, give me whatever loose change he came up with.

I don't know if I want to say, "Hi, 'member me?" or hide real quick behind the other girls. Before I can figure out which it is, the light changes and we all cross Fifth Avenue together.


When my mom and I write it's mostly "Hi, how are you" stuff. Nothing deep or serious. That's the way it's always been between us.

When she writes that she's going to come up for a visit the day after Christmas I get nervous. It would be very awkward after the first "Hello, how are you?" What am I going to talk about? What am I going to do with all that time? I could show her around, but she wouldn't be too interested in the place. It would be hard to get a reaction out of her about anything. She'd just sit there the whole day unless I started the conversation or kept us moving. It would be up to me to make it work out right.


My last Christmas at home Mom said, "You're getting older now and Christmas is really for little kids."

In other words, don't expect anything under the fake tree this year.

So that year, Christmas was for Jessica and Robby. I said, "I understand, Ma," but really I didn't.

I pretended to be happy for the kids when they opened their gifts. I pretended Santa Claus left the toys for them, that it wasn't Mom and the welfare check she had to stretch between food and their gifts. And I decided then and there I wouldn't be a burden anymore, one more mouth to feed, one more kid to clothe. That's when I knew I would leave whenever the right time came. Frankie got out a year before. I was sixteen now and I should be able to support myself. Anyway, I couldn't stand Robert and the fighting and the way we had to live. All it was, was a place for me to leave.

I wanted something I could call my own, and a few months later I met April.


Christmas, they try to make it good for us at Samaritan. A couple days before, there's a big dance. They don't serve *Bustelo* anymore because Upper Peer got carried away with it. They get the most WAM money and some of them were spending it all on *Bustelo* and drinking a couple pots every night. So the counselors had to ban it forever.

A few days before Christmas we take turns picking a name from a box and everyone is given ten dollars to get a gift for that person. The girl who picked my name gives me pink bubble bath, and I also get Christmas cards from my mom and the kids and from Frankie, George and Harriet, and Jamie. I tape them up over my bed.

On Christmas Eve it snows. A blizzard. We all go sleigh riding on these big plastic sleds and that's one of the most fun things I've ever done in my life-time. One hill at Samaritan is about as long as one city block, and that's how far you can slide. It's like flying.

FLYING. I SPENT MOST OF my first Christmas at Grand Central high on crack. That year I could have had all the gifts I wanted, because on Christmas morning at Grand Central dozens of volunteers pop up out of nowhere with presents for the homeless wrapped in holiday paper and ribbons.

All the presents were practical. Because you wouldn't be handing out necklaces to homeless women or fancy ties to old homeless men. But they were nice gifts anyway: scarves, gloves, hats, warm socks, long underwear, pullover sweaters. Only I didn't bother to get anything and neither did April. I didn't really need a hat or a scarf or gloves, and if I did, I knew where to go. You go to the church, St. Agnes Church, or you could always try, if you talked a good talk, to get someone to buy you stuff. One guy who worked in a newsstand in Grand Central bought me two jackets. One I lost and the second I sold. I had a kid face. I could always get stuff.

And the holidays, like I said before, were the best time to get money. Me and April spent half of Christmas Day panhandling on Lexington Avenue so we could buy crack. I needed to get high. I didn't want to hear the Christmas carols being piped in over the sound system, didn't want to think about the people going through the station with suitcases and little kids and bags of presents. Those were the kinds of things that could make you think about your own family, and thinking about your family was the one thing you didn't want to do on Christmas Day at Grand Central.

So we got enough money and went uptown to Harlem, spent the rest of the holiday on a mission, running around getting high. And the day went by just like any other.

When we got back to Grand Central that night the cops had cleared out the waiting room. There were reporters and a couple of TV news crews, and George McDonald was there too, but they weren't letting anyone else in. Officer Korsoff was guarding one of the entrances. He was a nice cop, and he was also one of my first arresting officers, because it was him and two others who arrested me last summer in the boiler room. April asked him what the hell was going on, and he told us Mama had died.

Mama was one of April's favorite old people. Korsoff asked April if she knew Mama's real name or where she came from, because they were trying to find if there were any relatives and no one knew much about her because she could hardly speak English. April said she didn't. She asked, "What did she die from?"

Korsoff said they just found her dead on the bench in the afternoon. She might have been dead for hours, because everyone thought she was just sleeping until one of the cops banged on her bench with his nightstick, trying to make her move. Korsoff said, "You girls better clear out now. The waiting room's closed until morning."

"But I want to see her," April said. "I want to say good-bye."

"There's nothing to say good-bye to, they took her away already."

We got a can of beer and snuck down to the abandoned train. It was a cold night and there was no place else to go. A bunch of people were down there, Chewie and Jabba and Francisco and Maria. Hershey was there, too, with Lester and Sam—the other singers in his trio—and they were all sitting around a couple of candles talking about Mama.

April went down to the dark end of the car and pulled a blanket around herself, and I followed. She was shook up, I guess, but to tell the honest truth it didn't affect me too much. I cared that some old lady died, but I didn't really know Mama, and I was so focused in on April and our own tight little group that nothing else seemed very important.

We could hear Hershey telling everyone how last night, on Christmas Eve, Mama was coughing and breaking out in sweats, and right before the station closed Hershey told the cops they should call an ambulance. They just told him to mind his own business and vacate the premises because it was one-thirty now.

"She died 'cause she was sick and they wouldn't get her medical help," Hershey was telling everyone. "Looked to me like she had pneumonia."

Francisco said, "Shit, they should've sent her to the hospital, not out to sleep in twenty-degree cold. Old lady like that. Sick or not."

"Makes *me* feel sick," Hershey said. "Makes me feel scared. Because, wow, the way she died, all alone, no family, that could happen to me. I could die like that, any one of us could. You get my drift?"

He started singing then, it was "Amazing Grace," real low at first like it was coming from deep down inside and he was only singing it for himself. But then Lester joined in, then Sam, and everybody stopped talking and sat there just listening to the singing.

Me and April were passing the beer back and forth, but I was beat from all the running around that day so I fell asleep before the beer was finished. And that was Christmas 1985.

MY MOM DIDN'T MAKE IT up to Samaritan after all. Something came up with Uncle Tony, who was supposed to drive her. Anyway, they would probably have had to cancel because of all the snow. The roads were still bad from the blizzard.

Once in a while, if I'm sleepy after lunch, I sneak upstairs for a quick nap. I figure I'll probably just fall asleep in Seminar and get in trouble. But on this day Liz, another Middle Peer girl, walks in just as I'm stretching out on my bed. She says, "I'm going to write you up for this."

I am totally pissed. Now Liz is going to report me, and on top of that I'll still have to sit through Seminar. I'm not even going to get a nap out of it. I follow her out the door and say, under my breath, "Bitch."

She hears me, and she goes and tells that I called her out of her name, that I didn't use her right name. If it was just skipping Seminar they'd probably have put me on Contract for a day or two, but calling someone out of their name is a really bad thing at Samaritan. It means you aren't giving the person the right respect.

I wind up on the Chair again, and finally they call me in just before dinner and tell me I'm getting shot back down to Lower Peer. I was in Middle Peer exactly one week.

Right after I get demoted, one of the counselors finds out Roy has a crush on me. Getting too close to one person is called "tipping out" and there's a rule against it because you could be thinking up schemes about stuff, like sexually acting out or drugs. So they put me and Roy on a speaking ban and we're not allowed to talk to each other for two weeks.

It seems like every time I'm starting to get someplace, I slide back down again. The night they demote me to Lower Peer I go outside for a few minutes, even though it's icy cold. My special rock is covered with snow but I sit down anyway and light a cigarette. The windows of YDA are all lit up. It's about nine-thirty and most of the people are watching TV or cleaning up the house and getting ready for bed. I don't want to go back in. I don't fit. For whatever reason, I just don't fit there. And I'm sick of trying and sick of all the stupid rules.

Suppose I do finally manage to do okay in the program and graduate? Then what? There isn't anyone waiting for me, there isn't any*thing* waiting for me. So what am I going to do after I graduate? What really scares me is, I can't picture me doing anything at all. I can't picture me moving around in the real world in a normal way. And I can't think of one single thing I want to do, anyway.

I feel like I'm just existing. Going nowhere.


"You've been at Samaritan almost eight months," Nancy tells me, "and you still have trouble talking in Caseload."

I say, "Why should I? Where's it going to get me?"

"Well, for one thing, the more you work on your issues here the better chance you have of being promoted."

"So, I get promoted back to Middle Peer and a week later I'm going to wind up in Lower Peer again. It's like a seesaw."

"Maybe," Nancy tells me, "it's time to get off the seesaw. Maybe you need to get your butt out of the playground altogether."

"Oh, clever," I say.

"That's what they pay me for." It's hard to get mad at Nancy.

"Well, if Tina's not going to talk," one of the other girls says, "I got a letter from my boyfriend, and he wants to break up with me because I'm away so long and this is really bugging me."

"Let's give Tina a shot first," Nancy says, "and then we'll get to you. So, Tina, have *you* gotten any mail lately?"

"My mother."

"Does she write often?"

"We write back and forth, yeah. She was going to come up over Christmas but she couldn't."

"That must have been a disappointment," Nancy says. It wasn't, but I just nod my head.

"Hey, Tina," this girl, Kelly, says, "how'd your mother feel about you living in Grand Central Station?"

"Nothing she could do about it."

"Because if I ever tried something like that, my mom would have my dad after me with a shotgun."

"Maybe Tina's mother didn't care," another girl says.

"She cared," I say. "She just had her hands full. Other things on her mind."

"Tina," Nancy asks, "did your mom ever try to get you to come home?"

"Sure she did. Lots of times. I said she cared, didn't I? Once she even came to Grand Central looking for me."

ONE DAY AROUND CHRISTMAS WE were in Bryant Park hanging out, me and Corey and April and her friend Smokey, who was a dealer from Bryant Park. He and April got to be friends and then he started hanging around Grand Central, him and his friend, a Jamaican named Goofus.

Smokey was in his forties, black, short, missing some teeth. Always kind of scraggly looking, like his clothes were way too big for him. But he was a decent guy and he always made sure April had money to get high and to eat. Once he even took some of her clothes to a Laundromat and washed them. And she would look after him, give him money to get high if he needed it, share her food if he was hungry. Sometimes I got totally left out. April could go off with Smokey on a mission and be gone two days. It made me feel jealous. It made me feel alone.

Smokey had a lot of what he called "games" and he taught April one. She'd stand around the station looking cute until some horny commuter came on to her, then she'd bring him down to the lower level. The commuter would hardly have his zipper down before Smokey yoked him from behind and April emptied his pockets. April and Smokey got some cash, the commuter got what he deserved for hitting on a teenager while his wife was probably home in Yonkers cooking him dinner, and no one got hurt.

So on this day April and Smokey had some extra money and they were sharing it with me and Corey. We were lying around the benches in Bryant

Park smoking, drinking beer and vodka. Except Corey, he was just drinking. He'd smoke crack once in a while, but he was one of the few people who never did get into it.

I was just about to light up when April said, "Look, Tina, your mom," and sure enough, there was my mom coming up one of the paths. She had Jessica by the hand, Robby in a stroller, and Robert right behind her.

I said, "Holy shit."

"Who the hell's that?" Smokey asked.

"It's her mom," April said.

I told April, "I gotta get out of here."

My mom hollered, "Wait, Tina!" but I took off and Robert took off after me. I ran across the park to the Forty-first Street side, ran across the street, almost got hit by a Checker Cab, and kept running down Sixth Avenue. I didn't stop until Thirty-fourth Street. I found out later the only reason I got away was because Corey caught Robert and held on to him. By the time Robert tore loose, I was clear across the park.

I'll always wonder what would have happened if I'd gone home with my mom that day. My life might have been so different. But it was probably too late already, because now it wasn't only April keeping me there, it was crack.

April never stopped bugging me for smoking it, but what could she say? She was smoking it too. She knew there was no way I was going to say, "Oh, you want me to stop? Sure, I'll stop."

Probably the first time I smoked, it was too late. For most people, crack is an instant addiction. You want more and more until either you run out of money or your body gives out and you fall asleep for two days.

Trouble is, you only get that earthshaking rush on your first hit and it's only about a five-minute high. You're crazy for more, but each hit gives less and less. You won't get that magic again until you come all the way down, until it's a brand-new crack day and you're starting on your stem all over again. The rest of the time you're just chasing a dream.


They said they were professional football players. They said they played for one of the big teams, but they never said which one. They were trying to cop some crack on Ninth Avenue and they were pissed because they gave this guy fifty dollars and he disappeared.

April and me, we were on a binge, and these football players stopped us and asked did we know where to get some crack. One was black and two were white and they were all cute. At least I could tell April thought so.

We took them to Eighth Avenue near the strip place called Sex Kittens, because April had a dealer friend who worked that block, and they bought a couple bundles. A bundle is about ten vials in a plastic bag. And they asked us if we wanted to come back to their place and party with them. "Share the goodies," the black one said. April asked where their place was, and they told us New Jersey, but it wasn't far and they had a car.

"Well, I don't know," April said.

"Hey, come on," the black one said. "We won't bite."

"April," I whispered, "no."

One of the guys, who had curly black hair and looked a little like John Travolta, I guess he heard me. He told April, "Aw, come on, you don't have to chicken out just because your friend is scared. Leave her here."

And April would have. The John Travolta guy was the cutest one. So I went, too. I couldn't let her go alone.


She almost got killed. She did get beat up, and it probably would've been worse if I wasn't there. When they realized we weren't going to put out in exchange for the crack they gave us, they started getting nasty. April didn't help. She told them, "Not much you can do now, is there? You already let us smoke three vials."

"Dirty little whore," one of them said.

"Even if I was, I wouldn't do business with you fuckin' scumbags," April told them.

The John Travolta guy hit her in the face so hard her nose started bleeding. The funny thing is, I know she would have gone to bed with him in a second. She just wasn't going to take on his friends too. And me, I was freaking out. Here we were, alone in this house somewhere out in Jersey, with these three big angry guys who wanted us to put out. I was still having nightmares about what had happened to me in the tunnels, I was still waking up screaming once or twice a month. Now it's going to happen *again?*

Everything went in kind of a blur after April got hit. She started punching and yelling, and the black guy was holding her down while the John Travolta guy tried to get her jeans off. April was twisting and kicking, and I was trying to make the black guy let go of her, only it was like trying to move a tree, and the blood from April's nose was smudging all over the gray carpet. Next thing, the other white guy was there with a baseball bat. He raised it up and said, "I'll take care of this little piece of shit," and that's when I thought April was going to die. I thought he was going to bash her head in. And me next.

But it didn't go like that. What happened, I think, was that the guy with the bat scared the other guys, too. They must've realized it was getting out of hand. Because the John Travolta guy stopped trying to undress April, and the black guy let go of her, and they both started trying to calm down the guy with the bat.

And that's when we ran.

Through the kitchen, out the back door, down the driveway. April was so mad, she was crying and swearing and the blood and tears were smearing together all over her face. She looked gruesome, like a Halloween mask.

She stopped when we got in front of the house, and I saw she had her screwdriver out. She usually carried one in her pocket, we both did. "Wait," she said, "I'm going back to shred their fucking tires." But I grabbed her, pulled her, made her keep going. I was so scared I felt almost calm. It was weird. Or maybe it's because we were both still high. "Let go of me," she hollered. "Get your frigging hands off me, I'm gonna mess up their car and then I'm gonna kill those motherfuckers."

"Not with a screwdriver you won't," I told her.

Then she was just crying, and I kept her walking as fast as I could, and finally when we were far enough away we stopped in a little field. There were patches of snow all over, and I took handfuls and wiped off April's face. "Tina," she said, "don't leave me, don't leave me, don't leave me." It was hard to understand her, she was crying so hard.

"I'm not going anywhere," I told her, "so just hold still." The blood wasn't all from her nose. Once I got her cleaned up, I saw her lip was split and she had a big cut above her eyebrow too.

Then we started walking. It felt like we walked for a week but probably it was only an hour. Maybe less. But we were freezing because we had run out of the house without our jackets.

At a Texaco station we met some skeezy guy who gave us a ride to the PATH train in Jersey City. We looked so bad he didn't even try to come on to us.

MY TWENTY-FIRST BIRTHDAY IS ON January 6 and Jamie and her husband, Ron, and their two teenage kids come up to Samaritan to take me out. We go to a little restaurant in town for dinner. I have to have a buddy because I'm not in Middle Peer anymore, so one of my roommates, Carla, comes.

After we order, Jamie holds up her water glass. "This is a toast to Tina," she says, "in honor of her hard work and accomplishments. I know she gets discouraged sometimes and it looks like an endless road ahead. But I was with Tina on her last birthday, too, and I just want to say, you've come a long way, baby, and we're all very proud."

The year before, on my twentieth birthday, I was living in a cardboard box on a ledge outside Grand Central Station. I remember when I woke up on my birthday I raised the flap and saw snow coming down, covering the ledge and the streets below. But the box—I called it the Clubhouse—was covered with a tarp, I was bundled up in a hundred layers of clothes, and there were a bunch of blankets in there too. So I was warm and dry.

And I remember when Hug Me came through the station he gave me five dollars, but when I told him it was my birthday, he threw in an extra twenty. So while I was panhandling that day I told everyone it was my birthday. I don't know if they believed me, but I took in a lot more paper money than usual.

Also, Jamie came up to Grand Central to give me a gift: a navy sweatshirt.

I took her up to the Clubhouse so she could see where I was living now. I was proud, because it was better than the tunnels even if it was just a big old box.

Then me and this guy Shiv, who'd found the box we made into the Clubhouse, pooled our money and bought a couple bundles of crack. We climbed back up the ledge to the Clubhouse and spent the rest of the day in there getting high. So that was how I spent my twentieth birthday.

At the end of dinner, on my twenty-first birthday, the waitress comes over to the table with a cake that Jamie and Ron brought up from the city. It has white icing with pink and green flowers, it says *Happy Birthday Tina*, and it has twenty-two candles, all lit. When Jamie, Ron, their kids, and Carla start singing "Happy Birthday," the waitress joins in and so do the people at the next table. By the time the song is over, everyone in the restaurant is singing "Happy Birthday" to me.

I can't blow the candles out. I'm crying like a baby.


I don't know why I had to make things even worse at Samaritan, but I did.

One of my friends in YDA is a pretty black girl, Cerisse. She's really smart, she wants to be a doctor, but she keeps messing up on account of her drug problem. It wasn't me that made the first move. But she starts coming on to me and sending me notes, and I don't say no.

We sneak into the schoolhouse one night through a window that I left unlocked that afternoon. While we're climbing out we hear someone else around the other side. I'm scared stiff. I'm sure we're going to be caught. The only thing is, if it's someone else they're not going to tell on us, because what is their explanation for being in the locked-up schoolhouse at nine o'clock at night?

We do get caught, but only because Cerisse winds up telling. Drops her guilt. They make her leave the program, her parents come up and get her. Me, I not only get sent back to Orientation, they put me on a three-week work Contract.

The weird thing is, you know what I feel when the counselors tell me I'm getting demoted again? Glad. I feel glad. It takes me a while to figure out that I'm frightened of being let loose again. I'm not in any hurry to get out of this program.


I have another dream about Grand Central. We're all sitting in the waiting room talking and joking, and April comes up to me and says, "Don't believe what you hear about me and Roy. He's just hanging around me until they lift the speaking ban between you two."

But it doesn't make any sense, even in the dream, because it's Rio she's talking about, from Grand Central, not Roy who is my friend at Samaritan.

APRIL AND I MET RIO together. This was in January, right after my seventeenth birthday. April had turned seventeen last summer. For my birthday I stole myself a little box of Godiva chocolates from the candy store in the waiting room. Happy birthday to Tina from Tina. Thank you very much.

One afternoon right before my birthday we were sitting on the stairs by Jerry's deli. Not doing anything special but probably going to go on a crack mission soon. And this guy comes over, a good-looking Hispanic with a head full of curly black hair. I'd seen him before selling newspapers over by the train gates.

He said, "What's up, girls? You don't look so happy." He said "girls" but he was looking at April.

"Who wants to know?" April said.

"Oh, 'scuse me, I'll introduce myself." He was real polite. "My name's Rio. I've seen you around here, right?"

"I'm April and this is my very good friend, Tina." April was acting real polite now too. I thought, uh-oh. Because April was always getting tied up with some guy. They never lasted long, but I always knew I wasn't going to be seeing much of her while she was hooked up. They'd be off on a mission or maybe just crashing for a day or two down in the tunnels. Once in a while I got included but usually I was left on my own. I could tell I was going to be having some more time to myself soon.

"So what's up?" Rio said.

"You already asked that," I told him.

April said, "Tina, shut up."

"You girls hungry?"

"No," I said.

"Yes," April said.

"Because if you were hungry, I got a little money on me at the moment and I could buy you a sandwich. They got real good sandwiches in this deli." He meant Jerry's.

"See, we just had a big meal," April said. *Liar.* "But I probably could go for a little bite of something."

Rio wound up getting us two turkey sandwiches and a couple of pickles on the side. Then he said he had to go sell newspapers with his cousin, and he told us to come say hello when we had time. After he left, April polished off her sandwich, half of mine, and both pickles.

Afterwards, when we went to see Rio over by the train gates, he gave April a white rose. And before you could say "I told you so," April was with Rio every minute he wasn't selling papers. But since he mostly worked from three in the afternoon until eleven, April and I were still hanging out a lot together.

Rio was ten years older than April and he'd been in jail a couple of years on a robbery charge. The other thing he did now, besides selling newspapers, was the credit-card scam. There were guys who did nothing but stand around pretending to talk on the pay phones by the main concourse, and when they saw someone next to them dialing a credit-card number they would write it down quick, then sell the use of it. Lots of Pakistanis and Middle Easterners, also some Mexicans, came around whenever they needed to call home. For ten dollars, the credit-card guys would dial up their number and let them talk as long as they wanted. It was a safe and easy way to make money, and Rio sometimes did it too.

Rio used to do a lot of drugs, but at the time he met April he was clean. He told April he wanted to stay that way, he told April he didn't want her doing drugs, either. A little reefer, that was okay, but nothing more. This is how much April loved him: She stopped smoking crack.

Every night when Rio was done work they'd go to their spot. It was an old employees' bathroom up on the third floor. Rio broke into it. But he didn't want April bringing anyone else there because he was scared the cops would see.

And Rio didn't want April to hang out with me anymore, either, on account of I was still smoking crack. But you couldn't stop April from doing anything she really wanted to do, so we were still running around together whenever she wasn't with Rio or I wasn't on a mission. The rest of the time, I was on my own.

It was around this time that I met the Foot Guy. I was sitting by Jerry's deli in my usual spot and I saw this man walk by, stop, give me the once-over. He was short, Puerto Rican I think, and he was wearing one of those blue uniform-type outfits like janitors or building superintendents wear.

"Hey," I said when I saw him eyeing me, "you got a quarter?"

He came over to me then. "You want to make five dollars?"

I told him to fuck off, but he got all apologetic. "No, no, that's not what I mean, I'm so sorry. Please don't be insulted. All I want is to see your feet. Just show me your feet, I'll give you five dollars. I swear I won't touch you, nothing."

I figured, why not, I sure could use five dollars.

We went down to the lower level and I took off my sneakers and socks. My feet were pretty dirty but he didn't seem to mind. He just stared at them a couple minutes, then said, "Oh, you have such pretty feet!" Then he thanked me, gave me a fiver, and left.

Well, hell. Whatever floats your boat, you know?

I was still sleeping in the same spot under the platform of Track 100, where me and April had been since around Thanksgiving. These spots, how you got into them was through the gratings under the platform's overhang. The gratings were about three feet wide, and some were loose. You jumped down onto the tracks, pried off the grating, crawled inside and pulled the grating back in place after you.

April's friend Smokey, and his friend Goofus, were also sleeping in this spot. Goofus got hit on the head with an iron when he was a kid and his brain stopped growing or something. Smokey was like a big brother to him. Made sure he didn't get himself in trouble, made sure no one was picking on him.

Also in the spot were a couple others I didn't know too well, and Beverly. That's around the time I first met her. She wasn't so skinny back then, just a friendly little black lady with a crack habit. She was some relation to Smokey, so she would come by with her friend Micki to see him, get something to smoke, and pretty soon she was hanging out in Grand Central full-time, too.

We'd all get high together. But even getting high wasn't the same anymore. I missed April, missed being her closest friend. And I was jealous. She didn't usually stick with a guy more than a couple weeks, and I hadn't expected her to last this long with Rio.

The Foot Guy came around again about a week later and this time he invited me out to lunch. I wasn't hungry because it was Wednesday, and on Wednesdays the soup kitchen at St. Joseph's Church usually had spaghetti and meatballs. So I'd had a really good lunch an hour ago, but I liked the idea of going to a restaurant. I told the Foot Guy sure. Besides, I could always stuff in an extra meal.

We went to a little diner on Second Avenue. He was very polite, held my elbow when we crossed the street, opened the door for me at the diner, asked me if this place was okay. I said it was fine.

We sat at a table in back. He told me his name was Manuel and he was head of maintenance at one of the buildings next to Grand Central. He asked my name, and I told him, but when he tried to ask where I came from, I said, "That's my business, okay?"

"Well, I just want to ask you one favor, Tina," he said. "Order anything you want, but it would make me so happy if you could please take off your shoes and socks for me."

The whole time I was eating my hamburger and french fries with extra pickles he had my feet in his lap, playing with them. He didn't order anything, didn't eat, just played with my bare feet under the table. The waitress never saw.

I had trouble not laughing because at times it tickled.

I think Rio had April brainwashed. She stopped talking to everyone. It was like he had her thinking she was better than the rest of us because we were doing crack and she wasn't. Plus she wasn't sleeping in the tunnels anymore, and she was eating well and he was buying her clothes and taking care of her. I wanted to get right in her face and shout, "Hey, April, remember me? We're blood sisters and you said we'll always be part of each other!"

I saw her going down to the lower level one day and followed her. When I got there she was waiting for me. Somehow, she knew I was on her tail. She was wearing designer jeans and a red sweater, not the usual giveaway stuff from the churches. Also her sneakers were new. And she was clean. She was always clean now from living in that bathroom.

She didn't look mad, and for a minute I thought maybe now we'd get to talk. Down here, where Rio wouldn't know. I said, "Hey. So what's up?"

She said, "You're following me. Why?"

"I'm your friend. I don't understand why we can't talk."

"Because," she said, "you're smoking crack. As long as you're smoking crack I don't want to talk to you. So get out of my face."

"Fine," I said, "that's fine." But what I was thinking was: Well, what am I supposed to do now? I had a feeling of being lost, deep down lost.

I went and found Smokey. He had a couple of vials. We went to Central Park and smoked it all. He told me, "Don't take it so personal 'cause nowadays April don't talk to me neither."

Next time I saw April, I was standing around near the ticket windows shooting the breeze with this lady cop and Officer Borden. Borden was one of the other two cops, besides Korsoff, who arrested me in the boiler room, but I didn't blame them because they were just doing their job.

When I saw April coming I thought maybe she wanted to talk to the lady cop, because they were friends, but she took me aside and said, "Come on, you want to see where me and Rio live?"

I told her, "Sure, why not?"

So April snuck me up there and Rio never knew it. He was selling newspapers. I have no idea why she did that, but you usually had no idea why April did anything.

To get to their place we took one of the little elevators, then had to walk up a flight of stairs. April stuck a card in the door, sprang the lock, and switched on the light. "You should've seen how dirty this place was when we first came," she told me. "I bet nobody was in here for years. I stole some Comet and Lysol and Mr. Clean off one of the porter's carts and worked my ass off cleaning."

There were a couple of toilets and sinks, a long mirror, and a big mattress in the middle of the bathroom covered with a blue quilt. April told me Rio found the mattress and quilt behind some swanky hotel. The quilt looked almost new.

Rio had strung a rope across the end of the room and one of his shirts was hanging on it, also some socks and April's black underwear. April said every day she washed out their clothes and hung them to dry on the line, so now they always had clean stuff to wear.

On one of the sinks was a mayonnaise jar full of purple flowers. Rio also bought April some stuffed kittens and teddy bears and a little white seal, and she had them lined up on the bed. They all had names. April loved stuffed animals. Once she and one of her robbing partners, Jackie, broke into a car just because she wanted the teddy bear that was on the backseat.

We sat on the mattress together, smoked reefer, drank blackberry brandy. It was almost like old times. She told me how great Rio was, how he took her to the movies twice already this week and they went to a restaurant and she had lasagna, and he brought home flowers every night. It's a good thing April was doing enough talking for both of us because I had a lump in my throat and I wouldn't have sounded too normal.

——— • ———

I met Jackie through April. He was one of the new people who popped up. That's how it was around Grand Central, people came and people went. Maria and Bonnie were gone. Maria moved to Puerto Rico to live with an aunt, and R.J. said he thought Bonnie was staying someplace with her baby. Lorenzo was gone. Someone said he got murdered, or maybe he went back to El Salvador. Also, Francisco wasn't around. I heard he got arrested trying to break into a limousine in a garage in Lincoln Center.

And sometimes a person would just disappear. You never saw them again and you never found out where they went.

Jackie was a skinny little white kid, not yet seventeen, and he and April had known each other for a few years, from when they were in a group home together. I didn't know where Jackie slept, but it was someplace cleaner than the tunnels because he never looked dirty and he always had neat clothes. He also had a big crush on April, even though he probably knew nobody else stood a chance with Rio around.

Jackie was a crackhead, his specialty was breaking into cars, and April had gotten to be his main robbing partner. It didn't seem to bother her that Jackie smoked crack, but I guess that was because she was making money with him.

When Jackie got high he would hide his stem and forget where he hid it, so he was always looking for someone who'd share theirs. That's how we got to be friends. It was rush hour and I was sitting halfway up the double staircase on the main concourse, drinking a Dr Pepper and watching the people coming down the giant escalators from the Pan Am Building. They didn't look real, the way they stood so still and straight and let themselves be moved down into the station by the escalator. From where I was sitting they looked like store dummies; you expected them to tumble over when their step hit bottom. It was so weird to see them suddenly snap alive again, start rushing for trains, like someone turned their switch back on.

Jackie came up the stairs and sat down next to me. He had a pointy little face that made him look mouse-ish. "You got a stem on you?" he asked. "Because I need to borrow one."

We went down to the lower level to one of the platforms that wasn't in use. I took a hit and passed him my stem.

"Hush," he said. "You hear that?"

"Hear what?" It was just the normal station noises. Footsteps, luggage carts, voices all mixed together.

"No, listen."

I listened.

"They know I'm here. They're coming."

"I don't hear anything on this platform. Just the people out there."

He said, "They're coming!" one more time and took off running, down toward the end of the platform where it was dark and shadowy. I took another hit and waited a couple minutes in case he came back. I could see now how he was always losing stems.

I went back to the double staircase and sat there until rush hour was over, watching the store dummies go down the escalators.



In the spot I was sharing with Smokey and Goofus, under the platform of Track 100, there were people coming and going. Most spots, strangers weren't welcome, but here, as long as you were known by someone, you could stay. A lot of people had been sleeping on ramps and in stairwells, but now it was getting cold and everyone wanted to go deeper into the tunnels where it was warmer.

There were three mattresses, and three or four people on each one. People who couldn't find mattress space slept on the floor on flattened cardboard boxes or big ad posters ripped from bus stops and subways. You could make a bed, too—you could lay an old door across two milk crates. It was a little wobbly, but when you're up off the ground the rats won't run over you while you're sleeping.

Also, there was an old black-and-white TV. It only had one channel, but nobody minded because it showed reruns of *The Honeymooners* late at night and everyone loved that show.

I stayed maybe a month. I stayed there until Rio got sent to jail and April invited me to share the employees' bathroom with her. She didn't have to ask twice.



Rio got in a big fight while he was drinking in a bar up the street from Grand Central. He was supposed to be meeting April later, but he never showed. She didn't find out for two days what happened. Someone who was with Rio in Central Booking told her that he got arrested for assault and sentenced to thirty days on Rikers Island.

That's how I wound up living in the employees' bathroom with April—me and Smokey, at first. Then Smokey invited Beverly and Beverly brought Micki, and Goofus came and brought one of the guys from the spot. Even though Rio had told April nobody else could sleep there, April said no way was she staying alone.

One promise she did keep to Rio, she didn't smoke crack while he was gone even though everyone around her was doing it. "You want to know why I'm not smoking?" she whispered one night. We were lying on the mattress, under the quilt. There were two or three other people in there, too, but I think they were sleeping. "Because I could, now. He'd never know."

"So why aren't you?"

"You gotta promise not to tell." So I promised. "You gotta swear." So I swore. "I'm pregnant," she said, "and I'm gonna have this baby, too."

I asked her, "Does Rio know?" and she said no. I told her she was nuts. How could she take care of a baby? Anyhow, Rio wasn't going to want her to have it.

She said maybe he wouldn't, but once he saw the baby he'd change. "He'll have a change of heart," is the way she said it. "First time he looks at our baby, he'll have a change of heart. And then we'll live together like a real family."

I said, "Where? In this bathroom?"

She told me Rio had a plan that now that he wasn't doing drugs anymore he could save up money from selling newspapers and the phone scam, because him and his cousin wanted to open up a flower shop upstate, where everything was cheaper.

She had some of her stuffed animals under the covers with her, and all the while we were having this talk she was hugging a teddy bear that was dressed in shorts with little suspenders. April had a cold, and her nose was red and runny. She kept wiping it on her sleeve. She didn't look like somebody who was old enough to be having a kid. She looked like she was a little kid.

About a week later April went to visit Rio on Rikers. Smokey bought her a blue dress and she got some high-heeled shoes from one of the churches. She even put on makeup, like eye stuff and blush, and pinned up her hair. She looked great. But when she came back that night her makeup was smeared and her hair was all over the place and she looked like she'd been crying. She told me she and Rio had a big fight and Rio said no way was he going to let her have this baby. He wasn't even sure it was his.

I DON'T KNOW IF THE counselors at Samaritan Village think being sent back to Orientation and getting put on Contract again is helping me, but if they do, they're wrong. I have no privileges, have to sit through all those dumb Orientation classes again every day, can't go anywhere without a buddy. Practically everyone I started out with in the program is in Middle or Upper Peer now, and I'm really embarrassed to be back in Orientation with the new people.

And every free minute, I'm washing or dusting or scrubbing or sweeping or vacuuming or polishing or shoveling snow, never a minute to myself except when I'm sleeping. Sometimes the anger boils up and I want to hit someone or kick a wall or smash a dish. I want to take off and run and run, anywhere, it doesn't matter, just until I outrun the anger. Until I leave it somewhere behind.

Only I'm not allowed outside alone.


I'm doing the dinner dishes one night, me and this jerky guy Serge who is also on Contract. I go over and get the box of detergent from him, pour a little in my sink, set the box down, and while I'm running hot water Serge stomps over, snatches the box, and takes it back to his sink. He starts digging out big handfuls of powder and I tell him, "Well, you might as well take the rest because now there's hardly any left for me."

He says, real nasty, "That's your problem, isn't it?"

Now I'm pissed. I go over and grab the box so hard some of the powder flies out and splashes him. He says something like, "Now look what you did," but I just ignore him and keep washing dishes.

Our sinks are at opposite ends of the kitchen and we're facing away from each other so I don't see him leave. After I mop up I'm starting back to YDA when an Upper Peer meets me at the door and tells me Melissa, the counselor, wants to see me.

The minute I step outside, I know why. There's an ambulance in the driveway and an EMS guy is helping Serge, who is in a wheelchair, into the ambulance. From where I'm standing, it looks like Serge's face is bright red.

I go to Melissa's office. "Report to the Chair first thing in the morning," she tells me.

"That little bastard, how could he make such a big deal over some soap powder?"

"It got in his eyes, Tina," Melissa says, "and he had a severe allergic reaction. We'll talk in the morning."

I'm in deep shit and I'm terrified. I feel like I'm either going to explode from anger or break down and cry forever. I lie awake in bed all night while the other girls sleep, trying to keep from screaming and banging my head against the wall.

Vodka. It used to help so much. God, I want a drink of vodka. On the streets, if I was hurting, I could get high or drink. If only I was back there now. Just for an hour, give me one lousy hour. Or maybe in Bellevue, in the psychiatric ward, where they gave me medication to get calm and I could lie back and just be a couch potato.

What if Samaritan discharges me? Three people from the Adult House got terminated this week. If they kick me out, I'll never have enough guts to get myself back into another program. I don't want to think about where I'll wind up then.


Next morning I sit on the Chair for two hours before they call me into the office. There are three of them, Melissa and Nancy and another counselor, Hank. I feel like I'm facing the death squad.

"Do you know why you're here?" Hank asks.

"Do I know why I'm here? Listen, he probably just rubbed it into his eyes on purpose because he doesn't like me and he wanted to get me in trouble. Anyway, what the hell kind of soap do you have in this place that turns your skin all red?"

"Tina," Nancy says, "take a deep breath and calm down. Then we'd like to hear your version of what happened."

So I tell them, calm as possible, that I didn't mean for the damn stuff to fly up and hit the little fucker, I just wanted the soap back. I tell them I'm sure Serge played it up so he could get me in trouble.

"We're thinking of discharging you," Melissa says.

"But he probably made it sound like I did it intentionally and that wasn't how it happened. I swear. I know I shouldn't have gotten mad at him but that's *all* I did. I didn't throw the damn powder in his face, I don't care what that asshole says."

I sit on the Chair another twenty minutes while they discuss what to do with me. Twenty minutes can feel like eternity when your life is hanging by a thread.

I decide if they kick me out I'm going on a suicide mission. That's a mission for crack where you just keep going and going and going. You don't stop, you don't care what the fuck happens, you just keep going until you die.


Well, they don't kick me out. Not this time. But it takes them a while to figure what my punishment is going to be. They can't demote me any lower because I'm already back to Orientation, they can't put me on Contract because I'm already on Contract. So they decide my punishment is to wear a big cardboard sign around my neck that says RESPONDING TO ANGER IS NOT THE ANSWER—RELATING IS.

Every single day for two weeks I have to face everyone in the place with that big stupid sign hanging around my neck. I can only take it off to eat and sleep.

I never came so close to walking off the property and hitching a ride back to New York. I want more than anything in the world to drug myself into oblivion.

WHEN APRIL HEARD COREY AND me had angel dust she said she wanted to get high too. Rio was still in jail. I said I thought he didn't want her doing drugs and she told me, "Well, he never said anything about dust."

We smoked it uptown, then came back to Grand Central. It was just me and April by then. April didn't feel good, her stomach was messed up, so we went to Jerry's deli and stole a quart of milk. Angel dust has embalming fluid in it and sometimes it makes you nauseous, so you have to drink milk to coat your stomach.

We sat down in the waiting room, and while April started swigging milk, these two guys on the next bench were eyeing us. They started saying dumb things like, "Oooh, that milk looks so good, could we have some, too?" and they were talking to each other about how cute April was. They both had Spanish accents.

"I think it's time to move to another bench," April said to me, real loud so they could hear.

"Oh, don't leave," one of them said, "because we want to go out with you."

She told them, "Well, we don't want to go out with you, so shut your face."

Then it all happened so fast. They said, "Oh, you don't like to do it with boys, you like girls," and April told them to get the fuck out and they called April something so bad I don't even want to say it. She yelled back, "I'll kill you both, you dirty motherfuckers!"

Next thing I knew, the milk went flying. April had good aim. The carton hit one of the guys and covered them both with milk, but it also sprayed two other benches and a couple of commuters.

The cops were there in a second. They said, "Okay, let's go." I tried to tell them the guys started it, but they didn't give us a chance to explain.

In the back of the Metro North precinct, in the station's balcony, is a cell, and that's where they put April and me. I knew one of the cops who arrested us; it was Officer Borden. April knew both of them. They had both arrested her a few times before.

April right away lay down on the floor. She still wasn't feeling good. "I might puke," she said.

I told her maybe it wasn't the dust, maybe it was from being pregnant. "No," she said. "Because I'm not pregnant anymore."

"What do you mean, you're not pregnant anymore?"

"What the hell do you think I mean?"

"You had an abortion." I looked down at her. She was flat on the floor with her jacket under her head and her hands on her stomach, staring up at the top of the cell bars. I could see tears start in her eyes.

"I was going to name him after my brother," she said. "I was going to name him Travis." The tears were overflowing, sliding down the sides of her cheeks, wetting her ears and running into her hair. I wanted to cry, too.

"I have brandy. A bottle of blackberry brandy in my jacket. Maybe that'll help your stomach."

"You know," she said, "it's not right to get rid of your kid."

They let me out after about an hour, let me sit in the office with them after they finished typing up all the information, like my name and my mom's address and stuff. April was passed out on the floor of the cell, probably from the brandy on top of all that dust. The cops knew I had the bottle. They didn't care. In fact, I even offered them some. They said, "No thanks, we don't want to catch anything," so I polished it off myself, right in front of them.

It was late at night and Borden and this other cop, Mansky, were the only cops around. They were joking with me, telling me how lucky I was because I was seventeen and could still got away with a lot of shit. "Once you're eighteen," Borden said, "you'll go to Rikers and the women there will eat you alive."

Mansky said, "Yeah, you and April are going to be somebody's dessert."

I told them, "Not if we don't get caught."

"Well, you didn't have much luck today, did you? In fact, we've gotta ship April over to Central Booking for this, because she's got an outstanding warrant on her."

By then I was feeling no pain. I was dozing off at Mansky's desk when Sergeant Johnson came in. He was a short guy, deep voice, black hair in a crew cut, he looked like a Marine. I didn't know him too well, but he knew April. When he saw her sleeping in the cell he said, "Oh, I see our star boarder is back."

I heard the other cops telling him about the Spanish guys and the milk and all, and then I think I dozed off because the next thing I knew the sergeant was shaking me and telling me it was time to take a shower. I said, "But when are you going to let us go?"

"Soon," he said. "We got a certain amount of procedure before we can release you. First the shower."

I didn't think taking a shower was part of procedure, but hey, what did I know? Anyway, I was too out of it to question anything.

Sergeant Johnson took me up to their locker room on the floor above, where the shower was, and Borden and Mansky came, too. The hot water felt good. I couldn't remember the last time I took a real shower. And I was high enough not to care that I was totally naked and three cops were watching.

When I turned off the water I was freezing, goose bumps all over. The sergeant said, "Tell you what. We won't take April in on the warrant, and you'll do me a little favor." He was sitting on a chair with a towel, covering his lap. He told me, "If you want the towel, come and get it." I don't remember if he still had his pants on underneath or not, but I went and got the towel. I knew what I was supposed to do.

Borden and Mansky were still in the doorway, watching. I closed my eyes really tight and tried to pretend I wasn't there.

Afterwards the sergeant left, Borden gave me my clothes, I got dressed, and they took me back downstairs to the cell. April was still out cold on the floor.

When they let us out a couple hours later we found Corey. He still had some dust and we all got high again.

I never told April what happened with the sergeant. She thought some things were okay for her to do, but not for me, so I think she would've been really pissed. But it didn't bother me much, what I did. I was too high to care at the time and, anyway, I did it for April. I only did it for April.

About three days before Rio got out of jail, the cops padlocked the employees' bathroom because there were so many people coming and going. I moved back under the platform of Track 100 with Smokey, Beverly, and

Goofus, and Rio and April moved to a hotel in the Bronx. Rio still came to sell newspapers, but for a while I hardly saw April because she stayed at the hotel, sleeping half the day and watching soap operas on TV.

Corey told me he heard Rio was messing with heroin again. Not shooting it, but sniffing it. He said the word was, so was April.

JUST WHEN IT SEEMS LIKE it can't get any worse and I'm ready to tell the world, and especially Samaritan Village, to go fuck off, everything starts going right again. First the sign comes off my neck, then a week later I submit a proposal to get back into Lower Peer and next day at House Meeting they announce I made it. A week after that, Nancy tells me I should go for Middle Peer again and, guess what, I made that too. It's like the powers that be figured my limit's been tested and they better start sending some good things my way or someone's going to have to scrape me off the wall.

Also, I have a new friend. Matt and I were both in Lower Peer in the fall. He got in trouble a few times too, and we spent a lot of time together on Contract, washing dishes. Now he's in Upper Peer, but he's the person I hang around with most. He actually came to Samaritan after me, but I've been knocked back to Orientation so many times that he's way ahead. He's a year younger, he has red hair, freckles, and a baby face. He still gets pimples.

We spend a lot of time together playing handball and taking walks, but not enough so they can say we're tipping out, like with Roy. There's a snowstorm in the beginning of March and we build a snowman out back, decorate it with stones and twigs. When the sun comes out we sit and watch it melt.

In March I put in for an Itinerary. Itinerary is when you write down what you want to do and what date you want to do it, maybe a visit home or to a friend or just a trip to the city. And they announce at House Meeting whether or not you get your request.

So I put in for a home visit. I finally got up the nerve to want to go home.

And they grant it. I can go into the city in the morning, on the van, and come back at night.

While I was at Harriet's last year my mom moved out of the welfare hotel. The city found her an apartment in the projects near Coney Island.

The first thing I notice when I walk in is one of those glass bead curtains hanging in the living room doorway. I know that's Robert's touch. The second thing I notice are the pictures on the wall. Me at my fifth-grade graduation, Jessica and Robby when they were babies, and the big painting of Jessica that Vince, her father, had one of his friends do when Jessica was two. He painted it from a Polaroid. I remember it was a big thing because the thumb came out looking like a penis and my mom didn't like it. So Vince brought it back to his friend, but his friend never really fixed it right. Every time I saw it, I noticed the way that thumb was sticking out.

I haven't seen any of those pictures in years, not since we lived in the house in Astoria. I thought they were probably ruined during the fire. I wonder where they've been all this time.

The apartment has two bedrooms, a living room, and a kitchen. It's small, but there's a whole lot more space than there was at the Prince George. The furniture, I haven't seen any of it before. Some looks a little beat up and secondhand, but the rest of it—the beds and the living room couch and chairs and the TV—looks pretty new. My mom tells me that her brother, my uncle Tony, helped buy most of it.

Even at the Prince George, some of my stuff was there. I'd go over, stay a few days, get some clean clothes. But this is the first home my family lived in where I've never been. Where there is nothing of mine around. Nothing, except my fifth-grade graduation picture, that says I'm part of this place too. Or of this family.

The kids are a little shy at first. It's been almost a year since they saw me. I don't try to hug them because I know how uncomfortable that can be for a little kid. They kind of hang around watching while I introduce Tanika, the Samaritan buddy who came with me, to my mom. Then Jessica says, "We have hamsters and their names are Mork and Mindy," so we go into the kids' room to see them. There's a wire cage on the bureau and in it are two furry, taffy-colored hamsters.

Jessica takes Mork and Mindy out and we all sit on the floor and play with them. I'm watching the kids more than the hamsters. Jessica doesn't have a baby face anymore. You can already see how she's going to look when she's a teenager. Robby got taller, but he looks too scrawny for a six-year-old. He holds up Jessica's hamster and laughs when she tries to get it back, and I can see his teeth are rotten. I ask my mom later if Robby goes to a dentist and she says no. She says it's okay if his teeth are bad, because they're just baby teeth and they're all going to fall out anyway. She says when he gets his second teeth she'll take him to the dentist.

When the kids get bored with the hamsters we play darts, and then Tanika goes into the living room to watch TV. Robert's home now and he's in there watching basketball or hockey or something. I help my mom with supper. She tells me Frankie is going to try and call from Florida, because she wrote him that I was going to be there today. When I ask how he is, she tells me, "He's in jail." I kind of giggle, because I think she's joking. She gives me a mad look and tells me to set the table.

"He's really in jail?"

"That's what I said."

Frankie in jail? No way, not Frankie. "But what did he *do?*"

"If he calls," my mom says, "you can ask him."


For supper my mom has to borrow chairs from a neighbor because there's her and Robert and the kids and me and Tanika, and Uncle Tony comes, too, as a surprise for me. Uncle Tony is an interior decorator, and I really love him. I was in touch with him for a while when I was in Grand Central, but finally he got fed up with me, so I stopped calling him.

I give him a big hug when he walks in, and he tells me how great I look and how proud he is that I'm getting my life together. He wants to know all about Samaritan Village, and how I'm doing there. All the kind of stuff my mom doesn't think to ask, or maybe she just doesn't want to hear about it.

We lived with Uncle Tony for a while when I was twelve. After the fire. It was the best place I ever lived. If I didn't feel so guilty I would have been totally happy there. I never told anyone, I couldn't tell anyone, not even Uncle Tony, that it was mostly because of me that we got to be homeless.


We moved to the two-family house on Astoria Boulevard in Queens when I was five. The house had reddish cardboard shingles and a little yard. Back then, it was just me and Frankie and our mom and dad. This was way before Jessica and Robby were born, and a year or two before my dad left us.

We were like a regular family for a while. Even though my dad was drinking a lot and he was definitely what you'd call abusive, I have some good memories, too. He worked nights as a security guard and he was off in the daytime. Sometimes he used to pick me up at kindergarten and carry me all the way home on his shoulders. I felt like a queen. I have a picture of my dad. He was so handsome, it was easy to see why my mom fell in love with him.

Then he left and Vince moved in. A couple years later Jessica was born. Frankie and I resented Vince because he tried to take our father's place. He wasn't old enough to be our father anyway, he was only nineteen or twenty when he came to live with us. But even though things weren't great we were still a family, with a mom and kids and a sort-of-dad—and after Jessica was born Vince really was a dad—and we even had a dog. Vince brought her home one Christmas. She was part shepherd, part Doberman, and we named her Cleo. I really loved her. She knew it. She wound up being mostly my dog.

Our backyard was connected to the neighbors' yard. We had cleaned up our side, but they had lots of wood and garbage on their side and that's where the fire started. It was at night and Jessica was asleep in her crib and Frankie and me had just had our baths. We could see the fire from our back window, blazing up in the yard next door.

My mom said, "Tina, run down the block and pull the fire alarm. Hurry!"

I ran down the stairs, got to the door, then realized I was in my pajamas with no shoes on. And I stopped right there. I was just too embarrassed to be running down the street like that to pull the alarm. So I never went.

Someone else must have called the fire department because they did come. Only by the time the firemen got there, the neighbors' half of the building was on fire. And our roofs were connected, so they had to spray down our roof too. The fire never got to our side, but we had bad water damage and all our furniture was ruined. The building was condemned and we lost everything. We left with just some clothes that we'd saved.

I never told my mom I didn't run and pull the alarm. I never told anyone. I was too ashamed.

We moved in with Vince's parents for a few months. They lived in Astoria too. Then my mom and Vince broke up and we didn't have anyplace to go so my uncle Tony told us to come stay with him, in Manhattan. His apartment only had one bedroom, and he was gay and his boyfriend was living with him, so Mom and me and Frankie and the baby had to sleep in the living room. But I didn't mind. It was the most beautiful place I ever saw, wall-to-wall carpeting and expensive furniture and Egyptian decorations.

We didn't take Cleo when we moved. Nobody had room for us with a dog. So she stayed behind in our yard on Astoria Boulevard. It wasn't far from Vince's parents, and even after we moved to Manhattan I rode my bike back to Queens, across the Fifty-ninth Street Bridge, every day after school to visit and feed her. I collected soda cans to get change to buy dog food. Before I left each time I hugged her good-bye and told her as soon as we had our own place again we'd come get her.

Then my aunt in Brooklyn said she could keep Cleo for a while, but that summer they condemned her building too, and my aunt moved in with friends. She just left Cleo there. Frankie and I went to Brooklyn once to look for her, and she was still there, living in the abandoned building with some other dogs. She was skinny and her coat was matted and either she was mad at me for staying away or she didn't recognize me anymore, because she growled and showed her teeth when we got close. We never went back. I tried very hard to forget Cleo. I didn't know what else to do.

After Uncle Tony had to move from his apartment we wound up in the Martinique Hotel, which was one of the rottenest, most dangerous welfare hotels in the city. We stayed there a year.

When the fire happened I was twelve, and that's when everything changed forever. That was the end of being a kid in a more or less stable home and the beginning of moving around from relatives to welfare hotels to city projects. And I've always felt guilty about it. I always felt it was my fault we had to leave home. If I'd gone and pulled that alarm, maybe the firemen would have come sooner.

Ma, if you're reading this now, I'm so sorry.


Frankie, when he calls, says he was arrested for breaking into someone's house. It's hard to picture the little brother who used to sit in his closet reading books all day breaking into someone's house. Even harder to picture him in jail.

I try to give him some advice. I tell him I was in jail too, a few times, which he didn't know because we were out of touch during my Grand Central years. "Keep to yourself, Frankie," I tell him. "Try to mind your own business. That's the best way to stay out of trouble."

"Yeah, but I'm afraid I'm gonna be here a few years if I don't get parole."

"Well, don't ever forget we're with you, even if we're far away." Now I'm feeling like I'm going to cry, so I have to hand the phone back to my mom.

I do get tears in my eyes when it's time to leave. So I say to myself, Okay, let me just say good-bye real quick, hurry up and get out and take a couple deep breaths, then I'll be all right.

And that's what I do. It's a fast, "Okay, good-bye, see you soon," and I'm out the door with Tanika.

How I started robbing cars was, Jackie came by one night and asked if I wanted to stand lookout. I said okay. It was a slow night for panhandling. We walked to a quiet street that wasn't too well lit and Jackie told me to stand on the corner and whistle if I saw anybody coming.

It took five minutes for Jackie to do two cars and I didn't have to whistle. He got two radios and a tan trench coat. The second car was a red Honda parked near me, and I saw how he jammed a screwdriver in the groove along the window, pushed the screwdriver all the way back, and bingo, the window shattered. Then he stuck his hand in and opened the door. The whole thing took a minute.

We moved to another block and Jackie did three more cars. He got another radio, a radar buster, a thermos, a couple dollars in change, and half a carton of Marlboro cigarettes. I went with him over to Tenth Avenue to this taxi company, Metro Cabs, and a guy there gave Jackie five bucks apiece for the three radios and the radar buster. Jackie threw in the thermos for free.

We split the twenty dollars and the spare change, so we each came out with about eleven dollars for half an hour's work. We split the carton of cigarettes too. Jackie kept the trench coat. He threw the jacket he was wearing into a Dumpster and wore the coat back to Grand Central. "See," he said, "it's important to keep changing clothes so people can't identify you."

Sometimes I went panhandling with Dwayne, the guy who got his face scarred up on a radiator when he was nodding out on heroin. He didn't do heroin anymore, only crack. At that time, he did more crack than practically anybody else.

Dwayne never slept in Grand Central because he got a monthly SSI check for his disability, so usually he managed to go to a fleabag hotel at night. He made his extra money panhandling in the subways. Dwayne could be so weird he scared me. And not just because his face was all scarred and he sometimes had seizures. He was a white guy, and his skin was so pale he looked like a picture I saw once of a corpse getting an autopsy. His eyes were always kind of wild, even when he wasn't high. You had the feeling he might explode at any minute.

I came back from panhandling with Dwayne one rush hour and went into the ladies' room to sneak a hit in one of the stalls. When I came out, April was standing at a mirror putting on lipstick and eyeliner.

That was the first time I'd seen her in a couple weeks. She'd been looking wasted from all the crack, but now she'd put on weight plus she was wearing neat clothes, jeans and a cute blouse, and her hair was shiny. She didn't look like someone who lived in Grand Central anymore.

She saw me in the mirror, coming out of the stall, the same time I saw her. She said, "You were in there sneaking a blast."

I told her, "Don't say hello."

"You know that shit's going to kill you."

"Oh," I said, "and you're not sniffing dope?"

She didn't deny it or even ask how I knew. She walked out of the ladies' room and I followed her. She said, "I'm really glad I'm not living here anymore. Did I tell you me and Rio are staying in the Bronx? We bought a hot plate for our room and every night I cook him rice and beans. I'm just hanging around now until he's finished work. He likes me to come with him." She looked at her watch. It was a new red Swatch.

I told her, "April, you're no different from me. In fact, you're worse because you're sniffing dope and you have a habit now."

"Well, dope is better. All you have to do with dope is spend ten dollars and you're straight for the day. With crack you're always on a mission. You don't eat, don't sleep, you're either smoking it or looking for a way to get it."

"Listen," I asked her, "where're you going?" Because she was heading for one of the Forty-second Street doors.

"No place with you," she said.

She went out the door and I kept following her. I guess I thought maybe if she turned around and saw me, really saw *me,* Tina, her friend, her blood sister, she'd remember how important we were to each other. But all she said was, "Would you stop following me like some dumb-ass puppy? I told you I'm not hanging around with you, because you're still smoking that shit."

April was right, in a way, about heroin. But I heard the worst kind of withdrawal in the whole world was heroin withdrawal. Getting over crack was easy, a couple days and you were fine, but getting clean from heroin was a trip to hell.

So I don't know, heroin, crack, they both had their good and bad points.


The Foot Guy saw me sitting by Jerry's deli. He said, "Tina! Where have you been?" like I was his long-lost daughter, because he hadn't seen me in a couple weeks.

He had taken me out to lunch three or four times. I always ordered a hamburger, french fries, and pickles and took my sneakers off, and he always played with my feet the whole time I ate. Afterwards, he'd slip me five dollars. One time, on the way back to Grand Central, he took me into a store and bought me two pairs of white tube socks. He said, "You should only wear pretty new socks on those pretty little feet."

I thought he was going to ask me to lunch again, but this time he said he wanted me to come to his office with him. I said, "What office? You said you were a maintenance man."

He said, "I am, and it's a maintenance office. Come with me, I'll give you ten dollars this time."

The building he worked in was one of those big office buildings connected to Grand Central. He made me follow a few steps behind so no one could tell I was with him. Inside the office there was a desk and lots of cleaning equipment like mops and buckets. He pointed to a sink by the door and told me to wash my feet good, so I scrubbed and scrubbed until my arms ached, until my feet were cleaner than they'd been in a year.

We went into the closet so if someone came in they wouldn't see us. He put a chair in there for me but he stayed standing, and he picked up my right leg and started sucking on my toes. I thought he was just going to play with my feet like he always did. I never expected this. I never even heard of this. It was so weird I almost busted out laughing.

First he sucked all the toes on my right foot, then he did my left foot. There was a dreamy look on his face and he made little slurpy noises. I bit down on the inside of my cheeks, tried to think of other things, anything, to make myself sit there quiet until he finished.

Just when I thought I couldn't keep the giggles inside any longer, he stopped. It wasn't like sex, he didn't come or anything, he just stopped. "Oh," he said, "you have the most wonderful little feet."

I said, "Thank you."

"Here is the ten dollars I promised you. I must see you again soon, Tina."

"Well, sure," I said. "Anytime."


The Foot Guy came back a couple days later, found me sitting in my spot by Jerry's deli. "I have a present for you," he said, and he gave me a bag with a pack of three pairs of white socks. He said, "You must take good care of your feet for me."

I followed him to his building again, to the maintenance office, and we went through the same routine. I washed my feet good, we went in the closet, he sucked my toes, he gave me ten dollars.

I thought, Oh, this is so cool. I can get ten bucks for nothing. For *feet*.

After that, I saw him at least once a week. A couple times we went to lunch and he played with my feet under the table while I ate, but mostly we'd go to his office and he'd suck my toes. After the first two or three times I didn't have any trouble keeping a straight face. I guess I got used to having my toes sucked on. Actually, I got to like it.

How it ended was, after a couple months I just didn't see him around anymore.


Smokey was worried about April. Because whenever she was around the station all she did was sleep. Ten dollars, she'd get high, then nod off. In the waiting room. On the lower level ramp. In the tunnels. Anywhere. Rio was nodding off all the time too. Sometimes they didn't even bother to go back to their hotel when he was done selling newspapers, they'd just fall asleep in the station.

Smokey tried to talk to April, get her to stop sniffing dope or at least cut back. She wouldn't listen so he asked me to try. But she just said, "Well, you know what? Crack is much worse than heroin. Because I'm not running around all day like you are, I can get rest and sleep."

"Yeah, but that's all you can do," I told her.

"Fuck off, crackhead," she said, and walked away.


I was panhandling one morning when Rio came by. Asked me, "Where's April?"

I said, "How should I know where April is?"

He looked around a minute or two, like maybe she was right nearby but hiding, then he asked was I making any money today. I told him a couple dollars. He looked around again and said, "Goddamn bitch." I know he meant April, not me. They hadn't been getting along lately. "Well, look," he said, "if you want to knock off, you can come uptown with me. I'm gonna buy a little dope, come right back downtown because I gotta sell newspapers at three."

I said sure. Sure I'll come.

We got on the uptown train. Rio bought a token but I just jumped the turnstile. I had money, but it was the principle of the thing. I never paid to get on a train unless, of course, there was a cop standing there.

It was strange to be going somewhere with Rio because even though we weren't enemies anymore, we weren't really friends. But if I couldn't be with April, I could at least be with the person she loved. It made me feel closer to her, and, in a crazy way, it also made me feel a little *like* her.

We rode up to Harlem and walked three blocks and there was a guy standing on the corner, a dealer, a black string-bean guy with a shaved head. He said, "Yo, Rio, what's up?" Rio bought a bag of dope and the guy said, "She's buying?" He had no front teeth. Rio said, "No, just along for the trip."

"Well, that's a shame," the guy said to me, "because this is not shit, I got premium-quality dope here. Can't find anything better around the city this week."

"Thanks, but no thanks," I told him, and me and Rio started walking back to the train. Rio put a straw in the bag, stuck the other end in his nostril and sniffed, then stuck the straw in the other nostril. He did it while we were walking, and it was the middle of the afternoon, but nobody cared. This was 113th Street, who's going to look at you?

I thought, Oh, what the hell. Why not. I told Rio, "Give it here."

By the time we got back to Grand Central, about twenty minutes later, I was sick. Puked all over the stairs coming up from the train. Rio said, "Don't worry, that's normal. After you get sick you'll feel the heroin working and it'll be great."

And he was right, because once I threw up the nauseous feeling stopped. And then I felt relaxed, I was floating, everything was happening in a dream. It's so different from crack because heroin is a such a down thing. You don't have to be always in motion, moving, running, like when you're high on crack. Heroin, it's like taking a vacation.

There's a ledge in the stairwell on the Lexington Avenue side of the station, where Rio and I came up from the train, and I climbed up on it and nodded out. I don't know how long I was out, but when I woke up I was still high. The effects of the heroin lasted nearly eight hours. I walked around, got a beer and a hot dog, nodded off again, did a little panhandling, got some chili when the Salvation Army truck came by at nine.

That first heroin high, I really liked it. That scared me.

IN CASELOAD, NANCY WANTS ME to talk about my home visit. Talking in Caseload still isn't easy. "So okay, it was a nice visit," she says. "But what was nice about it?"

I tell about my mom's apartment, and how I was glad to see them out of the welfare hotel. Nancy asks how long they were in the welfare hotel and I tell her, "About three years at the Prince George, but that was the second time. The first time, when I was twelve, we were at the Martinique Hotel a year."

"Must have been rough."

"Yeah. The Martinique, it was full of rats and roaches and people doing drugs. There were fights in the halls, somebody even got raped. We had to stay in the room most of the time. My mom got really, really depressed."

"How could you tell she was depressed?"

"I don't remember."

She says, "Why do I think you do?"

I ask, "Is that a real question?"

"Tina," Nancy says, "it's been rough for you here, but you're finally making progress. Whatever you're feeling now, try to push through it and get to the other side."

So I do it. I tell them how my mom is pretty strong, but it was hard on her not to have her own place, to have to keep moving around. Especially with three kids. So sure, she got depressed in the welfare hotel. Who wouldn't? And finally one night she just flipped out and started screaming, said she couldn't live like this anymore and she was going to jump out the window. She ran into the bathroom and locked the door. We were all really scared because the bathroom had a window and we were sixteen flights up. Robert was living with us by then, and when he couldn't make her come out of the bathroom he told us, "Talk to your mother, tell her you love her, tell her you need her."

So Frankie and I were banging on the bathroom door, crying and hollering, "Don't jump, Ma, we love you, we need you!" Even Jessica, who was only three or four, was hollering, "Don't jump!" Finally I think Robert broke the lock and got her out.

"Oh, Tina, you must have felt terrified," Nancy says.

"Sure, terrified. And guilty."

Nancy says, "Why guilty?" so then I tell how I didn't pull the alarm when we had the fire so it was my fault we were homeless. This is the first time I ever told anyone about that. I guess I'm crying, because one of the girls passes me a box of Kleenex.

"Tina," Nancy says, "suppose you *had* gone out and pulled the fire alarm. Would you still feel guilty?"

I grab a bunch of tissues, rub at my eyes. "Probably," I tell her, "because then I'd think maybe I should've run faster."


So I'm back in Middle Peer now, second time around. I have responsibilities again too, I'm in charge of the dining room setup. Things are going good.

One day I'm working in the dining room when one of the counselors brings this girl over to me, tells me she's new and I'm going to be her Big Sister. I'm a little surprised that they're trusting me and giving me this responsibility, since I've been in so much trouble.

After dinner I take Rosalie over to YDA and show her the room they assigned her. I get her a little commissary pack—it has stuff like shampoo, soap, toothpaste—and introduce her to some of the other YDA people. Rosalie is one of these outgoing girls, and it's weird because I'm kind of shy and I'm supposed to try and make her feel comfortable.

She tells me she was a crackhead. She's my age and has brown hair, shoulder length. I think she looks like April a little bit.


Sometimes, at Samaritan Village, they have things like fashion shows and Talent Night. Talent Night is where anybody can get up onstage and do an act, and the best one gets a prize. In April they announce there's going to be a Talent Night just for lip-synching to records.

Matt tells me, "You should enter it," and I tell him, No way, Jose, am I getting up in front of all those people and making a fool of myself. And Matt says, "You could do 'Hit Me with Your Best Shot,' because you know that really good." That's by Pat Benatar and it's one of my favorites.

I tell him I don't have anything to wear and my roommate Susie says I can wear her black shirt and pants. "I'll even do your makeup," she says. "I'll make you look like a rock star."

My other roommates are saying, "Yeah, Tina, you should enter it." Even my Little Sister, Rosalie, is saying, "Go on, I dare you." And Matt tells me, "Look, I'm gonna help you with the act. You'll see."

Then everything is happening and I never even actually say, "Okay, I'll do it." Next thing I know I'm walking out on the stage they rigged in the cafeteria. I'm all dressed in black with half a ton of makeup on, and there's a couple hundred people in the audience and I'm so scared I want to puke. But the music starts, so I just start lip-synching to it because I really do know those words by heart, and right away everyone is laughing.

At first I think they're laughing at me, but then I realize Matt and another guy are behind me pretending like they're two crazy boxers having a fight. I can't see much of what they're doing, but they must be funny because the laughter never stops. And the more the audience laughs, the more I ham it up. When the record is finished we all take bows, and everybody claps and cheers.

And guess what. I win first prize. Me. I can't believe it. The prize is a bottle of perfume, which I'm never going to use but I think I'll always keep.

I am wearing nail polish now, though. My nails are growing here, just like I am.


Rosalie's starting to say things like, "Oh, that's a nice shirt you're wearing, you look real good in blue." And she brushes her hair in front of me a lot, and sometimes asks if I'll brush the back for her.

I think they gave me the wrong Little Sister.

In April there's a big Easter party. At the party Rosalie starts telling me how much she likes me, and I'm thinking, Oh no, don't do this to me, please, I just got back to Middle Peer. I keep telling myself, Tina, you worked real hard to get where you are and you want to keep moving up in the program. So just walk away.

But I don't. Rosalie and I sneak out and go upstairs to my room, because I figure we have a little while before the next fire check, which is every hour. But I'm wrong. About five minutes after we get up there the monitor, Jasmine, opens my door. Rosalie is sitting in a chair and I'm leaning over her, but Jasmine just closes the door again. So I figure maybe she didn't see anything. Right away Rosalie and I go back down to the party.

Next morning they call me into the staff office. There's two counselors there, Nancy and Sherelle, and Nancy says, "I think you know what this is about, Tina." She looks really, really serious. Like somebody just died.

I tell them, "I don't have any idea."

"Okay," she says, "go take the Chair."

Two hours later they call me in again.

"Where were we?" Nancy says.

"Look," I tell them, "I didn't do anything."

"Come on, Tina," Sherelle says, "cut the crap. Jasmine saw it. You and Rosalie were breaking a cardinal rule."

"No, no, that's not what happened. She had something in her eye. I was getting something out of Rosalie's eye."

I'm not surprised they don't believe me. Who would? I probably wouldn't even believe me, with my track record.

They have a House Meeting and everyone in the place is there, because the rule is you're allowed to have your say in front of the family. I tell them the same thing I told Sherelle and Nancy, that Rosalie had something in her eye and I was bending over her trying to get it out. Then they send me out to the Chair, and call Rosalie in. I don't know what she says, but then she's sent out too, so everyone in the house can make the decision about what to do with us.

The whole time I'm waiting I think I know what's going to happen. But when they call me back and tell me that everyone has decided it would be in their best interest if I left, I'm devastated. Just hearing those words is like a gunshot. I think somewhere inside me I always thought no matter what I did, it wouldn't come to this.

They keep Rosalie, though. They keep her and kick me out because they feel she's more workable than me.

So what am I going to do now? I want to scream and holler and tell them I didn't mean it and they have to let me stay because I'm really sorry and anyway I have no place else to go. And if that doesn't work I'll throw a tantrum and tear the whole fucking place apart.

What *am* I going to do now? This is a problem. I spend the rest of the day in my room, packing and crying. Nothing else to do, because nobody's allowed to talk to me.

I wonder if they'll remember me in Grand Central. Or would I just be walking into a place that used to be home to find out that now I'm a stranger?

Will I fit in there again?

Do I want to fit in there again?

Maybe.

Maybe not.

I've been upstate almost a year. Once you've had a taste of something good you don't want to lose it.

They let me call Harriet that night. I don't want to call her. God, I don't want to call her. I just can't think of anything else in the world to do. "Hi, Harriet, I got kicked out."

"You got kicked out?"

"From Samaritan."

"Oh, Tina! What happened?"

I don't know what to say to her. What *didn't* happen, you know?

That night I sit outside on the big rock until bedtime, thinking about the future and trying to picture me in it. Harriet told me I could stay with them again until we get something worked out.

In a way, I wouldn't mind going back to Grand Central. It's the easiest thing.

And, actually, lots of people go away from Grand Central for a while, like to jail and even the nuthouse, and when they come back people still remember them. If I go back now, I'll still have friends. And when I think about lighting up and taking a blast, I get shivery inside.

But I'm going to miss the country. I'm going to miss the night sky. I imagine how the sky would feel, soft and warm and safe. I'd like to touch a star.

The night I found out April died, I was in jail. I looked out through the bars of my cell, I stared at the sky and the stars a long, long time. It made me feel closer to April. It made me feel so close that after a while I started talking to her. I told her, Listen, April, if you can hear me, could you please just send some kind of a sign so I know you're okay? And about two minutes later, I swear to God this is true, about two minutes later I saw a shooting star.

So tonight I'm sitting out back on the rock at Samaritan, and I'm looking up at the sky and I start talking to April again. I tell her, April, I really fucked up. I had a chance and I fucked it up and maybe I don't deserve another chance. Maybe Grand Central really is the right place for me.

And it happens again. I see another shooting star go streaking across the sky. I almost can't believe it because it's the kind of thing you always see in movies.

Then she's talking back to me. She's telling me I have to keep on trying, and if I just keep trying and don't give up, somehow I'm going to be all right in the end. Only she's not saying it in words, she's saying it in feelings. And if all this sounds crazy, so okay, I'm crazy.

I tell her, Thank you, April.

I tell her from now on I'm going to be living my life for both of us.

# PART THREE

WE BOTH MISSED APRIL. THAT was the main thing I had in common with Jackie. She had started brushing him off, too, which I guess was why he was asking me to be lookout when he robbed cars. We didn't talk about April much but it was something understood, that she had hurt us both. Jackie didn't have many friends. He was a loner and I liked that about him.

Usually I'd stand lookout, but once in a while Jackie gave me the screwdriver and I popped the window. His favorite cars were the ones that had NYP on their plates, which stands for New York Press. And there were always a bunch of them parked around the Daily News Building on Forty-second Street. You could find good stuff in the trunks of press cars: expensive cameras, camera equipment, tape recorders. He'd pawn the stuff and split the money with me and we'd go to one of his spots to get high and to sleep.

Where he mainly lived was a bathroom in the Roosevelt Hotel on Forty-seventh and Lexington. I don't think Jackie knew anybody at the Roosevelt, I think he'd just found a door he could pry open. And you could tell the bathroom hadn't been used in a long time because it was full of garbage—torn blankets and towels, a busted chair, a file cabinet, lamp shades, and stacks of yellowed magazines. Jackie put down a blanket and we had to squeeze together to sit or lie down because there wasn't much floor space.

We smoked a little. He didn't get paranoid there like he usually did. It was like this little bathroom was a cocoon for him, where he felt safe.

"I come from a respectable family," he told me the first time I stayed with him, "and I can't go home. My mom teaches high school math. She won't talk to me anymore."

"What do you expect, smoking crack all the time and busting into cars?"

"Yeah," he said. "They sent me away to a group home when I was twelve, one of those places for messed-up kids. Did April ever tell you that's where we met? But I don't even blame my family because I was a real pain in the ass. Still am. I been smoking crack now for two years. It really gets into your head. Sometimes I think I've gotta kill myself because people won't stop following me."

I told him, "You better stop smoking for a while."

He asked me if that happens to me, if people seem to be following me, and I told him no. "Well," he said, "maybe they haven't found you yet. But they will."

He woke me before dawn so we could get out without anyone seeing us. Before we left he pulled open one of the file cabinet drawers and I could see it was crammed with clothes. He changed into khakis and a striped shirt and we snuck out.

At least once a week now, if I had ten dollars, I'd go uptown with Rio when he went to buy dope and get my own bag. He went in the morning, usually early, while April was still at the hotel sleeping. We'd cop some dope, then split up. I'd go back to Grand Central and he'd go pick up his newspapers.

I still got nauseated about fifteen or twenty minutes after I sniffed, and sometimes I'd throw up, but then the sick feeling would pass and I'd just have a really great high. I could ride it for hours and maybe nod off a little, too. If I had the money, I'd also get some crack. Heroin is such a downer, and crack is an upper, so if you smoke a little crack with the heroin, it brings you up and levels you off. That's the opposite reason you drink when you're smoking crack. When you're smoking crack, you need a little brandy or vodka to help keep you down. You couldn't drink with heroin, though. Two downers, that would really knock your ass on the floor.

Corey was on my case about the heroin. He was pissing me off. "April got you on crack," he said, "and now you're sniffing heroin. You're going to wind up all fucked up, just like her."

I told him, "April didn't get me on crack, she tried to keep me from smoking it. And she didn't get me on heroin, either."

"But you're doing it because of April. Everything she does, you have to do. Or maybe you haven't figured that out yet."

"Corey, go blow it out your ass," I told him. Because he was right. I hadn't figured that out yet.


I heard injecting heroin was even better than sniffing. So when this guy Tyrone invited me to come with him to a shooting gallery, I figured why not? It can't hurt to just try it once.

I didn't know Tyrone well. He came around Grand Central sometimes, but he wasn't one of the regulars. I think he was a friend of Smokey's friend Goofus.

We took a train to East New York, to a neighborhood that looked like somebody bombed it. Sort of like where Chewie lived in the South Bronx. The shooting gallery was in a building that was only half standing. Out front a guy was slouched on a plastic milk crate, a black guy in holey jeans and a jacket that said HARVARD. He was nodding out but aware, because as soon as we got near the door he raised up his eyes—like only his eyes could still move, not his head—checked me and Tyrone out, then said, "Go on in."

We had to climb over boards and bricks to get inside. I couldn't see well because the windows were bricked up with cinder blocks and there were only a couple candles for light. Maybe eight or ten others were in there, but at first they just looked like shadows on crates. And it was quiet. Nobody talking. Just cooking up their stuff, tying off their arm and shooting, or nodding out, gone to another world altogether. The place smelled of pee and moldy plaster.

Tyrone gave the head guy money, bought the dope and a fresh needle. He told me you can buy fresh needles in wrappers or you can pay less and rent somebody else's. "But it's safer to use a fresh needle," Tyrone said, and I watched while he put the heroin in a spoon, poured on just enough water so it didn't spill over, lit a flame underneath, cooked it until it was a sticky syrup. Then he wrapped his arm tight with a piece of rubber so the vein bulged, sucked up the heroin in the syringe, and stuck the needle in his vein. Just before he injected the dope he pulled a little blood out into the syringe, then pulled the plunger out farther and jammed it all the way in, jammed all the dope into his vein.

By now my eyes were a little more used to the darkness and I could see some of the other people. Two, I think, were women, but it was hard to tell for sure because they were so wasted. Those people, they gave me the creeps. It was like being in a room full of zombies. I wondered if Tyrone was going to look like them someday.

He yanked out the needle and handed it to me. "No," I said. "Never mind."

Looking around that place, I think I realized this was one line I didn't want to cross. I sniffed a little dope and we took the train back to Grand Central. I went my way and Tyrone went his.

If I thought sniffing heroin would make me and April friends again, I was wrong. When she came to Grand Central she didn't hang out with anyone, just sat with Rio and his cousin while they sold newspapers. She'd say, "Hey, what's up?" when she saw me, and maybe we'd talk a little, but not about anything important. It was like she hardly knew me. I was seeing more of Rio than April.

I wasn't smoking much crack. Sometimes I'd use it to bring me up from the heroin, and sometimes I'd smoke a couple of vials on days I wasn't sniffing. But the drive wasn't there for crack, now that I had heroin.

I was more relaxed on heroin. It's like, dum de dum de dum de dum, I'm fine, I can just enjoy the day instead of all the time running around on a mission. It was definitely a more comfortable life. And it kept me from hurting too much about anything.

Lots of times when I went uptown with Rio to cop, his friend Hector would be with us. We'd go to some guy's apartment on 103rd Street and Second Avenue, because Hector used a needle and that was a place where he could shoot up.

At some point I noticed Rio wasn't just sniffing anymore, he was shooting it too. I remember him telling Hector, "You should buy your own needle," but then it turned out they didn't have enough money to buy the dope and an extra needle, so Rio said, "Okay, you could use mine and I'll make sure there's no blood in it."

After that, Rio never sniffed anymore, he always injected it. And when Hector was along they shared a needle. I asked Rio once if April was using a needle now, too. He said, "Fuck, no, she's not shooting. I told her a hundred times, if I ever catch her shooting up I'm going to smack the shit outta her. I love that girl better than my life."

Jerry, the guy who ran the deli, was pretty friendly with me by then. He'd come over to the lower-level stairs when I'd be hanging out and talk to me. Sometimes he'd sit down on the step and say stuff like, "Well, did you blow some big dick today?" I'd try to laugh it off or say things like, "What, are you jealous?" Sometimes I'd tell him to shut the fuck up. But I put up with it because, basically, Jerry was an okay guy.

He'd always flip me a quarter when I was panhandling, and if I came into the deli when he was in the right mood, he'd let me have a sandwich and a pickle, maybe a cup of soup and a little cake. He'd ask what was going on in my life, or what I did last night, or where I slept. Not nosy, but like he cared.

One day while I was panhandling at rush hour he told me, "Hey, kid, get a job."

I said, "Maybe you got one for me?"

He said yeah, he did. Said I could work in his store a couple hours a day. "I could use a little help in the stockroom, and you can run some deliveries. No salary but you get all the food you can eat, plus delivery tips."

It turned out that I liked working at the deli. It gave me something to do for a couple hours every day. I'd unpack cartons, stock the shelves, and make sure the old stuff was in front and the new stuff in back. Also I'd make deliveries to offices. Jerry had two guys for that, but sometimes there were enough orders so we'd all be running. Each time I made a delivery I'd get a tip, usually two or three dollars. I could make fifteen dollars in a couple hours just delivering sandwiches and coffee. And the guys behind the deli counter were instructed to let me have whatever I wanted to eat.

The only condition Jerry had was that I couldn't come to work when I was high. I thought that was fair enough.

It was a rainy night in March or April, and Corey told me to wait because he was going to get some money. He didn't say where he was getting the money so I didn't ask, but then we were going to the Roxy to see a kung fu movie. Corey loved kung fu movies. And I liked the Roxy because it was open twenty-four hours and it was enough of a fleabag so they'd let you sleep there most of the night, as long as you didn't do anything real outrageous like beat up another customer or pee on the floor.

So I was sitting on the stairs near the deli, just watching people pass, and here comes April and she sits down right next to me. "Hey," she said, "what's happening?" Like nothing ever changed between us. She took a pack of Marlboros from her jeans pocket. "You want a cigarette?"

"Sure."

"Well, you can't have one," she said, and pretended to put it back. That was an old joke between us. We both laughed, she lit two cigarettes, and for a couple minutes we sat and smoked. Looked around. Watched people. I was being so totally cool.

"I'm waiting for Rio to get done," she said.

"I'm waiting for Corey. We're going to a movie."

"Oh yeah? Too bad. Because we're going back to the Bronx, and Rio and Hector are going to cop and we're going to get high, so I thought you might want to come."

"Well," I said, "I might."

Sorry, Corey.

It wasn't an actual hotel where April lived with Rio, it was more like a motel with separate entrances outside. It was rundown, a skeezy kind of place with stains on the carpets.

They had two rooms, one where April and Rio lived and one right next to it where Hector was staying. I never did see where April lived because the guys told us to wait in Hector's room while they went out to get the dope.

April turned on the TV, opened a bag of potato chips, and we stretched out on the bed. "You know," she said, "Rio's shooting up now."

I told her yeah, I knew. I didn't tell her I was with him sometimes. I stuffed some potato chips in my mouth and passed the bag back to her.

"Shooting dope, it's changing him," she said. "Sometimes he doesn't come home at night anymore. I think he's going to leave me."

"Maybe you're better off without him."

"I've been losing people my whole life. If Rio leaves, I'll kill myself."

What I wanted to say was, Can't you see you'll always have me? What I did say was, "Don't talk crazy."

"If I had that baby," she said, "everything would have been different. We would've been a family together."

We watched a rerun of *M\*A\*S\*H* and ate all the potato chips. By the time the guys came back we were both asleep. I woke up when they came in, but Rio had to shake April, tell her, "Wake up, baby." When she finally opened her eyes she smiled, all sleepy and lovey, threw her arms around him, and said, "Where *were* you?" like every second he'd been away had hurt.

I guess I expected when April invited me to come that Rio and Hector would shoot up, and April and me would sniff dope, and we'd all get high together. But Rio took April by the hand and led her out of Hector's room. She was yawning, still half asleep, and she never even said good-bye. A minute later I could hear their door, right next to Hector's, slam shut.

Hector turned off the TV. The walls were thin and I could hear Rio talking in the next room. "So," Hector said, "you want to do it?" I never was alone with Hector before, and it felt uncomfortable to be in a hotel room with him.

"Sure," I said. I thought he was talking about heroin, but he started unbuttoning his shirt. I sat there on the bed and watched while he took off his shirt, took off the T-shirt underneath, started to unbuckle his belt. I asked him, "What're you doing?"

"What does it look like I'm doing? You want to fuck with your clothes on?"

"Hold it," I said. "Wait a minute. I'm not doing that."

He kept unbuckling his belt. Hector was short and kind of heavyset. Meaty. Leaning over like that made his breasts hang down, like a girl's. He said, "I got some good dope. We share everything or nothing."

I wondered, Did April know about this when she asked me to come? Did she expect me to do it with Hector? She couldn't have. She wouldn't.

Unless maybe Rio told her to.

Now Hector was stripped down to orange and green boxer shorts. His belly and legs were covered with dark furry hair. I got up from the bed, started looking underneath it for my sneakers, told him, "I just remembered an important appointment."

"Aw, Tina, come on," he said. "We'll party." On the other side of the wall, April laughed.

"Party without me," I told him. I shoved my feet into my sneakers, didn't even bother tying them, just walked the fuck out of there.

Hector hollered, "Bitch!"

I took the train back to the city, dozed off in one of the plazas on Second Avenue until Grand Central opened at dawn, then went and found Smokey and Goofus. I spent the whole day high on crack and I never touched heroin again.

HARRIET HAD TOLD ME TO take a taxi to her house when the van dropped me off in Queens. She said she'd be out, but George's son would be there and he'd pay for the taxi. I'd met him a couple times. He's about twenty-eight and he's from George's first marriage.

The son tells me to turn on the TV and get something to eat. But I'm so nervous all I can do is sit there and wait for George and Harriet to come home. I don't know what's going to happen.

But nothing much does. George comes down and says hi, and Harriet talks to me for a few minutes and tells me I can stay until they find someplace else. I guess she talked to someone at Samaritan, because she already knows why I got kicked out. They don't have much time now because someone is upstairs waiting for them, business stuff, but at least they don't seem angry.

Abigail is glad to see me when she comes home from school. She's gotten taller and her face has lost its chubbiness. She's about twelve but probably could pass for sixteen. We have dinner together and spend the whole evening watching TV.

Late that night I go out to the stoop to smoke. The streets are so quiet, it's almost like in the country. A whole year has passed since the last time I sat out here. It feels like I lived a lifetime in that year, but in another way it feels like I never left. Like Samaritan Village was only something I dreamed.

Harriet says, "I thought you were happy at Samaritan, Tina. Why didn't you try harder?"

"Things kept happening. Lots of other people were doing the same stuff, you know? I was just getting caught all the time."

"So have you thought about what you want to do now?"

Have *I* thought about it? I thought *she* was going to. I have no idea what I want to do. Like, what are my choices, anyway? I can't see any.

I'm coming out of a place where people told me what to do every single minute of every single day, where they totally structured my life and helped me set goals. And then wham, bam, I'm out of there. Just like that. Without being prepared or deprogrammed or anything. And I'm in shock.


Harriet makes phone calls to Wendy Kaplan, at Samaritan in Queens, trying to get me a second chance. Only in my case, it would be more like a twentieth chance. They say no, finally, and I don't blame them. I sure as hell wouldn't take me back.

I pick up Abigail at school every day. It gives me something to do. Otherwise, I don't go out much. Suppose someone from Grand Central sees me? Suppose they say, "Hey, Tina, come on," and suppose I go? I get goose bumps thinking about it, and it isn't all from fear.

George says he'll pay me to clean out the backyard, but I never get around to it. Harriet calls Daytop Village, another rehab program, and arranges for me to go see them.

My mom, when I call and tell her I'm at Harriet's, asks, "Are you okay?" I tell her I'm fine. She asks why I'm not at Samaritan and I tell her they kicked me out because I broke one of the cardinal rules. She doesn't ask for details.


Daytop turns me down. I don't fit their qualifications because I was in Samaritan so long that I don't have a real drug problem now. I'm glad they didn't take me. Someone told me if you get on Contract there, they shave your head. For sure I'd come back bald.

Harriet tells me to go to some NA meetings. That's Narcotics Anonymous. She says, "We'll find one that's nearby. You've got to be doing something, Tina."

What Harriet is doing, with George, is putting a new organization together. It's called Ready, Willing & Able and it will give homeless people jobs building homes for homeless families. George is getting contracts with the city to rebuild or renovate abandoned buildings. Harriet says if we can't find me another rehab facility, or even just a job, we should maybe think about me joining this program.

Harriet explains to me that people will live at Ready, Willing & Able, in Brooklyn, while they get trained in construction. They'll be paid six or seven dollars an hour to work on the crews. Part of their salary will get saved for them, and by the time they finish the program nine months later, they'll have a thousand dollars. Then Ready, Willing & Able will match it with another thousand and help the person find a place to live and a job. Harriet says they'll be opening in a few weeks.

The NA meeting is on First Avenue, around Ninetieth Street. At the start, everyone takes turns saying, "Hi, I'm so-and-so and I'm a drug addict." Then people get up in front and tell their stories about how they got involved with drugs, also about how they hit bottom, because that's when your recovery really starts. So this goes on for a couple hours, with coffee and refreshments thrown in. It ends with the Serenity Prayer, and they tell everyone to keep coming back.

I'm the youngest person there. Everyone else, I think, is over thirty. Each time I go I sit way in the back. Drink two or three cups of coffee and eat the refreshments, but I never say a word. By the fourth time, they know my face. At the end of the meeting two of the women come up to me and say, "Honey, next time you've got to push yourself to get up and talk. Remember, you're among friends."

I tell them okay and I never go back.

The only thing I got from those meetings was, I learned to like coffee. I used to drink it once in a while, but I never really got to like it until the NA meetings.

I don't tell Harriet I'm not going anymore. I don't have the guts. So on NA nights I leave the house after dinner and walk over to First Avenue. In the beginning I just sit around outside the building for two hours. But two hours is a long time to kill, so I start taking walks.

When I was twelve, after the fire made us homeless and we were living in Manhattan with Uncle Tony on East Thirty-eighth Street, there was a nearby park where my mom used to take us. It was one of my happiest times because I loved living at Uncle Tony's, and my mom, for once, wasn't all wrapped up in a boyfriend. She had just broken up with Jessica's father, Vince, and she hadn't met Robert yet. For the first time, I had her to myself. We would have conversations, I helped with the younger kids, she even asked my opinion about things. My mom and I were closer than we've ever been.

On NA nights I start walking downtown. I buy a Coke and sit in the park where my mom used to take us. It's dark, but I sit in the sandbox where I showed Jessica how to build castles, or I climb up the monkey bars where Frankie and I had contests to see who could hang by one leg the longest. I stay in the park until eight-thirty or nine, then walk back uptown to Harriet's and tell her, when she asks, that the NA meeting went fine.

I write letters to my brother and to Matt. I feel lonely and I miss being at Samaritan. Especially I miss Matt, and my roommates Susie and Dana. I feel like I don't belong anywhere.

I had an awful dream last night. I dreamed I relapsed and didn't even care.

"So what did you do today, Tina?" George always asks at dinner.

And always I say something lame like, "Well, I picked Abigail up at school." Or, "I went to the grocery store for Harriet."

"Any job prospects?"

Like, sure, George. I got an offer to be a receptionist at Donald Trump's office, and Mayor Koch wants to know if I'll work for him as his personal assistant. But I'm considering taking the brain surgeon gig at Mt. Sinai because the pay is terrific.

What the fuck, George. I'm supposed to go do this on my own, using some of my many connections?

There is friction between us.

It's frightening that Grand Central is so close now. And when I walk downtown to the playground by Uncle Tony's, I'm passing just five or six blocks from it.

So walking downtown is like walking a tightrope. Gotta keep my eyes straight ahead. Concentrate on each step I take, concentrate on looking where I'm going. Because if I look off to the left or the right I'm going to lose my balance and fall.

WHEN RIO BROKE UP WITH her, April right away started smoking crack again. All she wanted to do was walk around the city all day, smoking and talking about Rio. How Rio told her they had to break up because he was no good, and if they stayed together he'd only screw her up too. How she begged him not to leave her, how she told him she'd rather be screwed up than live without him.

It seemed like April couldn't stay in one place more than five minutes. She was really bugged out. So I was sticking close.

We were up on one of the overpasses above the FDR Drive, smoking, watching a barge going down the East River. It looked like it was going to rain and the wind came up, whipping our hair and making our jackets puff out. April had just finished a bottle of blackberry brandy and she threw it over the rail into the water. It made a little splash but it didn't sink. I told her, "Let's go. It's too windy to light up here."

"I murdered my baby for him," she said.

"That wasn't murder. It was an abortion."

"Same thing. And I lost them both."

"Come on," I said. I was halfway down the steps before I realized April wasn't behind me.

When I saw her hanging off the railing, over the water, I was back up in a second. I don't think my feet even touched the steps. I grabbed her jacket and pulled her back, I yelled something like, "What the fuck are you doing!"

and she yelled something but the wind took it away. And then I was standing there holding her empty jacket in my hand and she was back at the railing, climbing over again. This time I grabbed one of her legs. She started kicking me in the face and chest, trying to shake me loose, saying she wanted her brother, but I held on hard as I could and pulled until she toppled backwards off the railing. We both fell in a heap, April on top.

I grabbed her around the waist to keep her there, but she didn't try to get up again. Just lay there crying, crying so hard she couldn't catch her breath. I held on to her until she stopped.


And then she went upstate with this couple, Tom and Katy, who worked with the homeless. Tom actually had been homeless once, and they'd gotten friendly with April. They saw she was getting more and more messed up, and they were going on a camping trip with their two kids, so they talked April into coming. She told me she wasn't going unless I got invited too.

The way I found out she went was, I just didn't see her around for a couple days and finally Dwayne or Beverly or someone told me she'd gone camping. I didn't see her for three weeks.

So I was on my own again.


It was around this time I met Shiv. I was hanging out by the liquor store in one of the west corridors, panhandling. Sometimes when I got enough money I'd ask someone to go in and buy me a pint of blackberry brandy. They weren't going to sell it to me, of course. I was seventeen and didn't even look that old.

I started noticing this tall, slim black guy, looked to be in his thirties, passing by two or three times a week. Whenever he saw me sitting by the liquor store he'd start singing this song: "There she was, just a-walkin' down the street, singing doo-wop diddy diddy dum diddy dum." Sometimes he'd throw in a little dance step. Mostly, I pretended I didn't see.

Then he started saying things like "Hey there" or "How ya' doing?" when he'd pass, and one day he sat down next to me and took a T-shirt out of his knapsack. "Go put this on," he said, " 'cause I'm tired of seeing you in dirty clothes."

"So who asked you to look?"

"Cut the smart talk, little white girl. How old are you, anyway?" I told him nineteen, but he said, "Aw shit, you're not a day over fourteen."

"I happen to be seventeen. Like it's any of your goddamn business."

Shiv was grinning at me. He had a tiny beard and big teeth, very straight and very white, and the kind of smile that didn't just happen to his mouth, it went all the way up to his eyes.

I took the shirt into the ladies' room and changed. When I got back he was still sitting on the step, watching people go by, tapping his foot and whistling the "There she was" song. He told me, "Give the dirty shirt here. I'll throw it in with my wash next time."

I gave him the shirt—it wasn't even mine, it was an old green thermal I found in the tunnels—and he stuffed it in his knapsack and left before I could even ask him to buy me some brandy.

A day or two later he was back. He took the thermal shirt from his knapsack all clean and folded neat, like my mom used to fold my clothes when I was a kid. He said, "When's the last time you took a shower?"

I told him, "Don't remember."

"That's what I figured. You're too cute to stink." He told me to come with him, and I went. I guess I was beginning to trust him, or maybe it was just that I liked his smile.

He had a locker on the lower level, full of clean clothes. He found a pair of jeans that looked small enough to fit me, and some socks, and even a bottle of Prell shampoo. He put it all in his knapsack and took me to the YWCA on Fifty-third Street, where, for about two dollars, you get to use the facilities for the day. So he paid, I took a shower, washed my hair, put on the clean clothes, and met him outside half an hour later.

A few days later he came around Grand Central looking for me again. He had washed and folded my dirty clothes. I didn't need them because the stuff I had on wasn't dirty yet, so he put them down in his locker.

After that, it got to be a routine. Every couple weeks he would take me to the Y so I could shower and put on the clean stuff he'd dug out of his locker. He even started keeping a toothbrush and toothpaste for me. If I hadn't eaten that day, he'd buy me a hamburger or pizza. It was kind of the way Smokey was with April. Always taking care of her, making sure she had food and clean clothes. Now I had someone too.

Shiv said he lived with his sister out on Long Island. I wasn't sure why he came around Grand Central because in those days, when we first got to be friends, he didn't smoke crack. Angel dust and reefer, but nothing more. He had a couple friends who hung around the station, mostly this older guy who was called Blackie. And me, of course.

I made it real clear from the start that sex wasn't going to be part of the friendship, but that didn't seem to bother him. It was almost like he thought of me as a little kid that he needed to take care of.


After April went away camping, I stayed in a spot with Chewie for a couple weeks. It was a little platform way high above the tracks, maybe twenty feet, and you had to climb a ladder to get there. Chewie called it the birdcage. The floor was just metal grating, and he had put cardboard and blankets down so it would be comfortable to sleep on. Sometimes Corey stayed with us, and once in a while Beverly, but there wasn't room for more than four, at the most.

There were a bunch of those birdcages way above the tracks. If you weren't scared of heights or of climbing the ladder, they had advantages. Rats didn't go up that high and neither did the cops. Only it wasn't a good place to stay if you were a sleepwalker.

I didn't pick the man, he picked me. He'd always stare when he passed, eyebrows up like he was asking a question, and I'd always shake my head no. On this night I shook my head, yeah.

He had those saggy cheeks a lot of older guys have, and a suit and brief-case—the uniform. I told him I wanted ten dollars up front and watched while he took the wallet from his pants pocket and pulled out a ten. There was a wad in there. And that's when I knew for sure I was going to go through with this thing.

He followed me down to the lower level, to the boiler room, and I jimmied the door open. He asked me, "Is this place safe?" I told him sure, and he followed me down the stairs. I had the upper hand but I was as scared as he was. I could feel my heart going bu-bump, bu-bump, bu-bump inside my chest. I couldn't believe he couldn't hear it.

I climbed the ladder to one of the catwalks, it was about four feet high, and he followed one step behind. Up on the catwalk was the first time we were actually close enough for me to notice he'd been drinking. I don't think he was drunk, but he'd had enough liquor to smell of it.

I knew what I wanted to do, I just wasn't exactly sure I could make it work. I told him, "Take off your pants," and he did—first his shoes, then his pants—and hung the pants over the railing. Now he was standing there in his shirt, jacket, tie, high black socks, and a pair of navy briefs about the size of a bikini. He was trying to smile and be cool, but he looked nervous, like maybe he was having second thoughts. He wasn't the only one.

"Underwear too," I told him, trying to sound tough and growly. And while he was bent over I grabbed the pants, jumped the railing, and started running.

I heard him holler, "Hey, hey, hey, where are you going?" and then, "Stop!" and what's crazy is, I actually did stop for a second. I saw him climbing down the stairs, he had his shoes back on and his bare legs looked white and chicken-scrawny. He was trying to run down after me, but he had to keep hold of the railing for balance. When he saw I'd stopped he yelled, "Come back with my trousers, you little whore!" and I took off again, running toward the stairs, holding his pants tight against me. All the while I was thinking, What the hell am I doing?

—— • ——

I don't know why I went back to Grand Central the same night. I spent the money on crack and I guess I was too high to be thinking straight. Officer Korsoff grabbed me as soon as I walked into the waiting room, and I admitted the charge because the guy was going to ID me, anyway. He was there in the precinct too, but I never saw him. I guess he was in one of the back rooms. He must have still been in his bikini underpants.

The funny thing is, the guy told the cops some bullshit story. He said there were two men with me, and they forced him down to the boiler room at knifepoint, made him take off his pants and I ran out with them. I told the cops, Korsoff and DelGardo, that there was nobody with me, the guy paid me ten dollars for a blow job and I took him downstairs all by myself. They questioned me a little, but I could tell they believed my version. Because the other one didn't make sense and, anyway, Korsoff told me the guy kept changing his description of the two men.

They asked what I did with the pants and I told them I didn't remember. Korsoff said, "Come on, Tina, the guy needs his pants. We can't send him back to Greenwich without his pants."

DelGardo said, "Yeah, what's his wife going to say?"

I told them, "Maybe he oughta think about that the next time he propositions some teenaged kid."

Finally Korsoff said, "Look, Tina, if you cooperate and tell us, it'll be easier for you." That made sense and, anyway, I liked Korsoff. He was always a pretty fair cop. So I told them I dumped the pants in a garbage can across the street, under the Park Avenue underpass. I had thrown the wallet somewhere on Second Avenue after I spent the money, but I had no idea exactly where. Anyway, nobody ever asked me about the wallet.

They sent somebody out to get the pants but they couldn't find them, so Korsoff came and opened my cell and said I had to show them. "Do we have to put handcuffs on you?" he asked.

"No," I told them. "You know me, and anyway where am I gonna run to?"

DelGardo came with me, we went to the garbage cans that were under the Park Avenue ramp. I found the right can and pulled the pants out. They were a little wrinkled, but not too dirty considering where they'd been.

DelGardo came back to my cell a couple minutes after we got back. "Tina, the guy wants to know where his belt is."

"I don't know where the hell his belt is. I guess someone took it."

DelGardo went back down the hall and I could hear him telling someone, "Poor bastard, I bet he's in no hurry to get home tonight."

I don't totally understand what made me take that guy downstairs and rob him. I know I was sick of the way some of the middle-aged commuters looked at me like I was merchandise, of the way they'd either make a "Wanna come with me?" gesture or just tell me what they wanted in a really disgusting way. If I was in a good mood, I'd ignore them. If I wasn't in a good mood, I'd tell them to go fuck themselves and save their money.

And then there was this: April was gone again, on that camping trip, and I was on my own. When she was with Rio I went around feeling lost, but now I was thinking maybe, instead, I should be more like her. Learn to be tough and take care of myself, learn how to survive, learn how to get more money and not just by panhandling. As long as I didn't hurt anybody.

Plus, I think at this point I felt like I had nothing left to lose.


I spent three days in Central Booking. Just like the first time, I was in a cell by myself because I was under eighteen.

On the third day I got released. The lawyer explained that they can only hold you seventy-two hours without an indictment and they didn't have an indictment against me. In other words, the guy I robbed never showed up. So they set a new court date and told me to come back in six weeks, in July.

But the guy didn't show in July, either. So they dismissed the case.


It was also in July that I had the miscarriage in Jerry's stockroom and wound up in the psycho ward in Bellevue Hospital. I didn't even know I was pregnant. I had no idea what the hell was happening. I was wearing farmer-type overalls that day, I felt like I had to pee, and next thing there was blood all over the overalls. Jerry's sister-in-law, who was working the cash register, called an ambulance and they took me to Bellevue. Jerry met me there, and while I was still in the emergency room my mom and my aunt came. My mom didn't say much but she looked real upset. Then my aunt took her out of the room and she didn't come back.

But a while later, Jerry did. He said, "Listen, Tina, your mom had a talk with the doctor and they want you to spend a little time upstairs in the psychiatric ward."

I said, "The psychiatric ward? Hell, no, I'm not crazy."

"No," Jerry said, "but it's just for observation. They think you have problems and they want to get you straightened out."

"I don't want to get straightened out. They can't make me stay."

"Yeah," said Jerry, "they can."

I told Jerry, "I want to talk to my mom. Where's my mom?" and that's when he told me she left. He told me she no longer knew what to do with me so she was going to make me a ward of the court. I said, "So why didn't she come in here and tell me herself?"

"Well, she had to get home in a hurry."

"Fine. Good riddance to her."

Before Jerry left he gave me a couple dollars for cigarette money and said, "Hey, kid, you don't have to tell me if you don't want to, but who was the father?"

I said, "What father?" because somehow, even though I knew I'd just had a miscarriage, it didn't seem connected with things like a baby or a father of the baby.

"Oh, excuse me," Jerry said, "I think we got the goddamn Virgin Mary here."

I thought about it after he left, while I was lying there in the emergency room waiting for them to take me upstairs. I guess the father had to be either Corey or, possibly, Chewie. I pictured them both in my mind. They didn't go with the word *father* at all.

It turned out I didn't mind being in the nuthouse because it was almost a vacation. But I minded what my mom did. I'd never let her know, but wow, that really hurt.

I was in Bellevue over a month. It wasn't so bad, I played cards and watched TV all day. I wasn't in a ward with any violent people, everyone was pretty sedated and they slept a lot. They were always dozing off in front of the television or in the middle of a Monopoly game. Plus this guy Stan, who helped the Salvation Army give out soup and sandwiches at Grand Central every night, sent me a little money every week for the candy cart. Regular meals, money, candy, cigarettes, TV, what more could I want? I gained ten pounds in the psycho ward. I was kind of disappointed when they finally decided I wasn't crazy. I didn't want to leave.

April never came to see me even though I was allowed to have visitors. But Corey did, and Smokey. I asked them both how come April didn't come and Smokey said she was real messed up. He said, "April's selling her soul to the crack devil."

Jerry visited me a couple of times. Told me this was a new start. I was clean now, no drugs in my system, I was young, I didn't belong in Grand Central, I didn't belong with crackheads, I could start a new life, I had to think of my future, I had to go to school and get an education.

I told him, "Bullshit, Jerry, I don't have to do anything. My mom gave me up so I'm my own boss now. I'm totally free."

Jerry said that wasn't true because now the court was my guardian, but as far as I was concerned it was true. My mom gave up her responsibility to me so, the way I figured, I didn't have any responsibility to her now, either. And that's what made me free.

————— • —————

In the beginning of September, Bellevue released me into the custody of the Bureau of Child Welfare, and the social worker told me I had to get put in a group home.

The group home they sent me to was on Staten Island. It was over-crowded, no supervision, little kids jumping on the beds and smearing snot all over the walls. You know how easy it was for me to leave that place? I just opened a door the next morning and walked out. Kept walking until I got to a gas station with a pay phone and made a collect call to Stan, who happened to live on Staten Island. He picked me up at the gas station and drove me back to the city.

Nobody from the group home ever came after me, that I know of. I was seventeen so I guess they thought, why bother? I wonder if they even noticed I was gone.

I got back to Grand Central, and wow, it was like coming home. Everyone was happy to see me, even April made a big deal about it. It was, "Hey, guess what, Tina's back!" and everyone laying free crack on me. Party time.

Smoking, wow, after being clean a month, it was just as powerful as the rush I got with my very first hit. It was like dying and going to heaven.

Jerry never offered me my job back at the deli and I never asked him. The first time I saw him, when I went in with Dwayne to buy cigarettes, I think he knew right away I was bingeing. All he said was, "Hi, kid," and rang up the cigarettes, but he was looking at me like he was really disappointed. Like he gave me a job and he tried to help me and be a friend, and I let him down. I had to look away. That's the first time I ever felt ashamed.

I stayed high a week.

IF YOU HOLD YOUR BREATH for the longest you can, if you inhale real deep and hold it until you feel like bursting, then let it out slowly, slowly, slowly so you get light-headed and your heart starts to beat really fast, that's a little bit like the rush of getting high.

At Harriet's, I think about that feeling every day. It's a part of me, crack is, something I've done that will always be a part of me whether I like it or not.

Harriet says, "George is not happy with you." I'm helping her fold laundry at the kitchen counter.

"What do you mean, George isn't happy with me?"

"He feels you're not doing anything."

I don't say anything, just keep folding towels, but now I'm pissed. I'd be happy to do something, but I don't know where to start. I thought that's what they were going to help me with.

When he comes home that night, he says, "Tina, let's talk." We sit upstairs in the living room, Harriet is there too, and George says, "What are your plans?"

"I don't have any plans."

He says, "You know you can't stay here forever, don't you?"

"Of course I know that." Deep down, though, I wish I could. They give you the feeling that if only you could be a part of them you would finally be in a place that was safe. "Anyway," I tell him, "it's just been two weeks. It's not like I've been here a year or something."

I can tell George is getting mad. He's trying not to show it, but I can see it in his eyes. "Listen, kiddo, we got you into Samaritan and you screwed that up. You want to wind up on the streets again smoking crack and swigging vodka, I can't stop you. If that's not what you want, you'd better get your ass in gear."

Now I'm getting mad too. "Oh, right, George, you expect me to find a place to live, but I have no money. You expect me to find a job, but I have no experience. You expect me to stay clean, but I see you guys drink. Who the fuck do you think you are, God?"

Silence. Terrible icy silence. George sits looking at me for a minute or two. I think his teeth are clenched. I'm waiting for him to fly out of his chair and smack me, but all that happens is that he gets up, goes into his bedroom, and shuts the door.

"Tina," Harriet says, "you'd better go downstairs."

I spend the entire evening in Abigail's room, lying on my bed. I can hear them in the kitchen having dinner, and then I can hear Abigail watching TV. When she comes to bed I pretend to be asleep.

I feel so worthless and stupid. I fucked everything up at Samaritan Village and they kicked me out, and now I fucked everything up at George and Harriet's. After Abigail puts out her light I cry myself to sleep.

In the morning I stay in bed until I'm sure Abigail and George have left. When I come out, Harriet is sitting at the counter with a cup of cappuccino. "Have some breakfast," she says.

"No, thanks."

"You've got to eat something. Make some toast at least. Or we have English muffins."

I slice a muffin and stick it in the toaster, butter it, put it on a plate, and sit down at the table. Harriet's still drinking her coffee at the counter, watching me. I can't eat the muffin.

"I can't eat."

"What got into you last night?"

"George is always on my case—do this, do that, get off your ass, you're screwing up. I guess I finally bugged out. And I'm sorry what I said about drinking, but I'm not used to seeing people drink anymore, you know? At Samaritan they're always telling you drinking is as bad as drugging."

"That's no excuse for the way you spoke to George."

"I know."

"And you're going to come across people every day who are drinking. It's called social drinking. So what are you going to do, tell them they can't drink in front of you?"

I just sit there. Pick the crumbs off my muffin. My eyes feel puffy from all the crying.

"You said you'd give Ready, Willing & Able a try if we couldn't place you in another rehab facility."

"Yeah. Sure."

There is one problem with Ready, Willing & Able, though. You have to be in a shelter for a couple of weeks before you can go there, but the shelter I have to go to won't have room for me for two weeks. I don't feel comfortable staying with George and Harriet now, not after acting like such an ass. Things wouldn't be the same anymore. So I do what I always do—run. Only this time I know I don't want to run back to Grand Central.

I call Jamie. She has a talk with Harriet to find out what's going on, then she tells me I can come stay with her family until there's room in the shelter. So I pack my stuff and move downtown. Sleep on the top of her son's bunk bed, take their dog for walks, watch a lot of TV. It's a weird two weeks, because all I'm doing is waiting.


The shelter is on 123rd Street, smack-dab in the middle of Harlem. I don't really understand why I have to go there except that it's one of the requirements for getting into Ready, Willing & Able. They can only take people who are in the shelter system because that's part of the deal they made with the city.

The idea of a shelter always turned me off because I've heard how skeezy most of them are. To say nothing of dangerous. But this one isn't so bad, maybe because it's church-run. In most shelters you sleep dorm style, but here you have your own room that you share with another person. My roommate is a big heavyset girl, Spanish, and she has a TV. She tells me, "You could watch my TV with me, but if I'm not in here you keep your hands off it, you hear?" I tell her no problem. Last thing I want here is a problem. Keep my head down, mind my business.

Whatever free time I have, I stay indoors. I'm not up to testing myself against Harlem streets.

There are two others at the shelter who are also going to Ready, Willing & Able—Sailor and Ralph. Sailor is a nice, quiet guy, black like most of them, with big round glasses. He's called Sailor because he was in the navy. Both him and Ralph have families somewhere. Ralph doesn't talk about it, but Sailor carries pictures of his two little boys and whips out his wallet to show anybody who'll stand still long enough. He wants to go home but his wife won't let him until he's been clean for a year.

Even though we're living in the shelter and the Ready, Willing & Able facility isn't set up yet, they've started the work crews already. So every morning a van comes and picks us up and takes us to a construction site. They start us on rubbish removal, but the supervisor says we'll get training as we go along. It's not that I want to learn construction as a career, the main thing is that when you complete the program you'll have two thousand dollars and they'll help you find a job.

And it bails me out of the void. At least now I know where I'm going next.

MORE AND MORE, APRIL WAS on a mission. More and more, she didn't have time to do anything but chase after crack, smoke it, crash for a couple days, then get up and start all over again. Sometimes no one saw her for a week. When she was around, if she wasn't sleeping, she was with Smokey or Corey or, once in a while, Jackie. She didn't seem to have many other friends anymore.

Smokey was her smoking partner and they robbed people together, usually with April bringing a commuter down to one of the platforms where Smokey was waiting. Jackie and April were still friends because she was his main partner for hitting on cars.

All the profits went for crack. Everything in her life was about crack now. And it wasn't just April. Ever since I got back from Bellevue it seemed it wasn't about having fun and hanging out or being a big family anymore, it was all about crack. Everything had changed. Or maybe it had been like that for a while but I had to go away a month before I noticed.

Shiv was glad to see me. He said he figured either I went back home, or I got picked up and put into some detention place. I told him no, I was in the hospital.

He said, "Well, you want to get high?"

"You mean, crack?"

"Don't mean reefer."

I asked when he started smoking crack and he said, "Recently." Said he got tired watching everyone else have a good time.

So even Shiv had changed. Now it seemed like everyone was smoking except the old people lying around the waiting room. For them, it was only about drinking. That was all they knew or cared about.


Shiv robbed bums. The crazy ones, who got SSI checks. On the first of the month when they got their money, he'd go around and cut off their pockets while they were sleeping. You could get as much as two or three hundred dollars a bum, but only at the beginning of the month. The rest of the time, all they had in their pockets was whatever they managed to panhandle that day.

When he got a lot of money he'd take me to a hotel up on 145th Street for a few days, buy us crack and vodka or beer, maybe brandy for me. We'd get high, eat, watch TV, sleep, get high all over again.

Robbing bums was an easy way to get a lot of money but, personally, I thought it stunk. It was like taking money from your own, because we were all in the same boat. I told Shiv, "Why don't you leave them alone? Go after guys who really have money, not some poor nutcase with an SSI check." But Shiv didn't see it that way. Or maybe he did, but he was too scared to pick on somebody who could fight back.


I went over to Bryant Park one day looking for April, because someone said they saw her there with Smokey. Maybe if I found her she might be in a friendly mood and we'd hang out together. Once in a while that still happened.

I walked all around the park and I didn't see April or Smokey. But I did see this guy selling reefer who I remembered seeing sometimes with Smokey. Big black guy, with curly hair in clumpy dreadlocks. I asked him if he'd seen April or Smokey today and he said as a matter of fact, he did, but they went uptown to cop.

I started to walk away, but he told me to wait a minute and he rolled a woolly. Took a smoke, passed it to me, and after we were done I said thanks and left. He called after me, "Hey, I didn't get the name."

"It's Tina," I yelled back.

I went to Jerry's for a Coke and a pack of cigarettes. Jerry was standing in the doorway flipping quarters. He said, "Hey, kid, how's it going?" He was still friendly, but it was just the kind of friendly he was to everybody. I sat on the lower-level steps feeling sorry for myself and sick of my shitty life. Finished the soda, crumpled the can, checked in my pocket to see if I had enough money to get someone to buy me brandy. And while I'm digging through my pockets I hear, "Want a little company, Tina?"

It's the guy from the park. The guy with the dreadlocks. "No," I said. "Just a pint of brandy."

"Well, can I treat you?"

Can he treat me? Hell, yeah, he can treat me. You don't have to belong to a special club for that.

I get up, toss the soda can in a trash basket, and follow him to the liquor store. "By the way," he says, "the name's Harley."


This is how Shiv and I found the Clubhouse: One night about two A.M. we were walking around looking for a place to sleep. The station was closed, so we couldn't go there, and it was too late for Shiv to go to Long Island, which is where he lived most of the time. We were heading over to this park on First Avenue and we passed a bunch of empty boxes stacked in front of an apartment building.

"Let's take some cardboard to sleep on," Shiv said. I started to rip up a box but Shiv told me wait a minute. "We gotta take this one," he said. It was an enormous box, the kind refrigerators come in. "Help me carry it."

I said, "Carry it where?" He said back to Grand Central. "For what? Grand Central's closed."

He told me hush up, he said, "Don't I always know what I'm doing?" So we lugged the damn thing six or seven blocks, him carrying the front end and me following with the back.

We carried the box up the ramp to the elevated street that circles Grand Central, which put us alongside the second floor of the station. There's an entrance up there, it's mainly for the cops because it's right next to their precinct in the station's balcony. Near that entrance is a big toolshed, six or seven feet high, and behind the toolshed is a ledge about four feet off the ground. And that's where we put the box. Shiv climbed up there and I shoved it up to him. He laid the box down on its side, and you could hardly see it because of the toolshed.

"Brilliant, huh?" he said. "Now we got our own private little house."


It *was* brilliant, too. I don't know how Shiv even knew about this spot. I didn't. The toolshed hid the box and helped protect it from wind and rain, and also since we were outside the station we couldn't get arrested for criminal trespass. It was just squatting, which didn't carry any charges.

The second night, it rained, and Shiv got a plastic tarp to put over the box to keep it dry. When it started getting chilly, because it was late September already, he snuck into a moving van, stole one of those big quilted blankets that movers use, put that underneath the plastic tarp. It wrapped the whole box up and insulated it. Later, in October, Shiv brought some wooden planks to lay on the roof to make the box stronger and warmer. We had blankets and also we started keeping clothes in there, and the shampoo and toothpaste and stuff for when Shiv took me to the Y.

Shiv said, "You tell even one person about this place, we're going to have everyone and his brother tromping around. Then the cops are gonna kick us out on our butts."

Some of the cops knew about the Clubhouse because they'd see us coming in and out of that entrance every day. It was never discussed, but we knew they knew, and we knew they didn't mind because it wasn't trespassing. But if a bunch of people started coming in and out, the cops weren't going to be so nice about it anymore.

I did tell April. And later, after Shiv got arrested, I found her sleeping up there once in a while. Shiv said don't tell anyone, but April wasn't "anyone."

I'm the one who started calling it the Clubhouse. My house in Astoria, the house where we had the fire, had a little yard behind it. Me and my brother Frankie and a couple other kids built a little clubhouse from some lumber we found at a construction site. We worked real hard on it, and it was a neat clubhouse. We had secret meetings and used it for a fort, and when we got our dog, Cleo, she slept in there.

But this Clubhouse was even better. The one in Astoria fell apart after about a year, but the Clubhouse at Grand Central Station stayed in one piece longer than I did.


April was sitting on a bench in the waiting room all by herself, which seemed strange to me. Then I realized why. In all the time I'd known her, April always had people around. But now, more and more, when you saw her—if you saw her—she was alone. I'm not sure how much of that was April's choice, because she was so into crack now that friends didn't matter anymore, and how much was because people just weren't attracted to her like they used to be.

"Hey," she said, "look at this." She was sitting Indian style, legs crossed, and she took my hand and stuck it down the back of her jeans. There was plenty of room because the jeans were too big. "Feel that? Feel that lump down there?" She moved my hand around a little, and then I did. You couldn't miss it. It was a hard lump, a knob, sticking up under the skin.

"Yeah. I feel it."

"So what do you think it is?"

I sat down next to her. I never saw April look scared before. "I don't know."

"Well, but is it normal? Because I happened to notice it the other day and I was wondering if it was normal, you know?"

"Probably," I said.

"But do you have one?"

"No. I never noticed it, anyway. Maybe some people have them and some people don't. If you're worried, you could go over to the clinic at Bellevue."

"Aaaah, fuck the clinic. Spend the day waiting in line, I got better things to do with my time."

April had a can of beer in a paper bag and I sat there while she finished it. I wish I knew then that the lump April was so worried about was only her tailbone. I could've saved us both some worry. She had lost so much weight it was sticking way out.

We didn't talk anymore, about the lump or anything else. But I know what we were both thinking about—AIDS. Because there were all these stories coming out about how you could get AIDS not just from being gay or shooting drugs, but also from having lots of sexual partners.

It hit me then that it was possible April really did have AIDS. And this was the first time death was an issue with someone I was close to. The first time I realized it could happen to any one of us. Including me. There was also a lot of talk that you could get AIDS from a toilet seat, or from someone sneezing, or even from someone touching you, and the thing that worried me most was remembering how April and me had cut our fingers and put them together to be blood sisters. That was a scary thought. But I kept it to myself.

April finished her beer, bummed a couple Newports off me, said, "See ya," and she was gone.


Hershey and his gospel trio were rehearsing in the waiting room. He wanted them to work on this one song, "He's Got the Whole World in His Hands," before rush hour. He said last time they sang it they sounded like they were at a funeral. "This is a happy song, boys," he told Lester and Sam, "and you got to sing it happy."

I was sitting on the bench being their audience when Mac, one of the guys who sold credit-card numbers, came looking for me. "I got a customer wants a girl," he told me. "You interested?"

"I don't do that shit. Go ask Beverly or Micki."

"Well," he said, "who says you actually have to *do* something?"

Then I caught the drift. Why not? I did it before, in the boiler room. I said, "Okay, what the hell," and Mac said, "You have to cut me in."

Hershey was starting the song over for the third time. I told Hershey, "Later," and he said to Lester and Sam, "Now look, you're singing so bad you chased Tina away."

Mac brought the guy to me over by the ticket windows and left us. I told the guy, "Ten bucks for a blow job and you've gotta pay up front." Watched while he took out his wallet, pulled out two fives, shoved the wallet back in his pocket. He had a lot more bills in there.

The guy was an Arab type, like most of the ones who bought credit-card numbers. Small, with dark hair, very polite. He had an accent and his name, which I didn't know at the time but saw later on one of the police reports, was Hassan Abdul. I took him to the Clubhouse, had to help him up to the ledge. He should have been nervous coming up there with me, but he wasn't. I was the only one who was nervous.

I closed the front flap so only a little daylight leaked in. You couldn't stand in there because the box was on its side. I told Abdul to take off his pants, but it wasn't easy because he was half kneeling and trying to peel them off one leg at a time, without losing his balance.

And suddenly everything was light, because someone had opened the flap. I couldn't see the person's face at first, just the lower half, but from the skinny jeans and black lace-up sneakers I knew it was Shiv. He leaned over, reached in, got my arm, and pulled me out. I didn't know what the hell was going on, all I knew was he was really mad. I never saw him so mad before.

He crawled into the box and I heard Abdul say, "Don't hurt me!" and then sounds of fighting. I knew Shiv was beating the guy up. He was going at it so hard the Clubhouse was bouncing around like a scene in a cartoon. This wasn't supposed to happen. The guy wasn't supposed to get hurt.

Shiv came busting out waving the guy's wallet. "Come on," he said. On Park Avenue he stopped a cab. I asked, when we were inside, heading uptown, "Why did you hurt that guy?" because I never saw Shiv get violent before. But he didn't answer. He was going through the wallet, counting bills.

I never found out how Shiv knew I was in the Clubhouse or why he beat Abdul up, but what I think is maybe he knew Abdul already and there was bad blood between them. And maybe he saw me with Abdul and followed us to the Clubhouse, or maybe Mac went and told him. But there must have been a couple hundred dollars in the wallet. We checked into the hotel on 145th Street for four days and Shiv bought us new jeans, Reebok sneakers for me, and enough crack to stay high the whole time.


Shiv got picked up for assaulting Abdul the day after we came back to Grand Central. He had Abdul's wallet and credit cards in his pocket, so probably he didn't even try to deny it. I wasn't there at the time. I didn't even know he got picked up until a few days later, when they came for me.

So I spent another two days in Central Booking. Bologna sandwiches and cold tea again. At least I had an almost-full pack of cigarettes when I got picked up.

The judge told me to come back next month for a hearing, and let me go. But they didn't let Shiv go. He was sentenced to one to three years in an upstate prison. It was almost a year and a half before I saw him again.

FOR THE NEXT NINE MONTHS Ready, Willing & Able is my home. I have a place to live, the structure of a job, plus my independence. For the first time in my life I'm putting in a full day's work and getting regular paychecks. So I think it turned out okay that Samaritan didn't take me back and Harriet couldn't get me into Daytop Village. I think that Ready, Willing & Able was exactly the right thing for me at exactly the right time.

Ready, Willing & Able is on Gates Avenue in Brooklyn, in an old three-story building that used to be a school for blind people. On the top floor is the men's quarters. The main floor has a living room and a hall with double doors that leads to the women's quarters. The women's quarters are smaller than the men's, because there's more than twenty guys but only six women. I share a room with Matty, a big, tough black girl. She has two little babies who live in the Bronx with her mom.

The kitchen is down in the basement, and so are the offices. That's where George and Harriet usually are. My first day, I go in to say hi to Harriet and she gives me a big hug. Which is a relief, because I was worried that maybe she didn't like me anymore. She asks how I'm settling in and I tell her, fine. It's not really like going to a strange place because I came here with Sailor and Ralph, I already know George and Harriet, plus everyone else is also new because the place is just opening.

I ask, "Is George still mad at me?" and she says, "No, Tina, it's forgotten." And I guess it is, because George, whenever I see him, always gives me a hug. George was never really warm, but he is definitely always friendly.

Harriet asks me how the work is going. I tell her I actually like rubbish removal, because in those old apartments you can find some interesting stuff.

The rubbish removal crew cleans out the building before the demolition crew comes, dumps all the shit into heavy-duty garbage bags and hauls it outside. The buildings we work on are city owned, either abandoned or the people got kicked out because it was a drug house. Sometimes it's kind of sad. People leave behind rotting garbage, dirty pots and pans, torn and even bloody clothes, and busted furniture. Some of the refrigerators, the stink inside can make you puke. There are also love letters, moldy family photographs stuck together, broken dolls, used sanitary pads. In a lot of the apartments where the people probably had their electricity shut off, there are candles all over. You name it, it's there and it has to be cleaned up. They give us rubber gloves to handle the nasty stuff. Like in the places that were crack houses or shooting galleries, the floors are covered with syringes and bent spoons and crack vials.

But you can find good stuff too: TVs, VCRs, usable furniture. We're allowed to either keep the stuff or sell it and split the profit. The first week, Sailor found two hundred dollars stashed under a mattress and he split it with us. He sent most of his cut home to help support his kids. About a month later another guy on my crew found a hundred dollars in a bureau drawer. After that we keep expecting to find more money, but except for some old coins from someone's collection, we never do.

We get paid on Fridays. It's actually two hundred a week, but they take sixty-five dollars out of your salary for room and board and thirty a week to put in your savings account. That leaves me with one hundred and five dollars, and that's a lot to me. This is the first time I ever had that much money in my pocket that I earned honestly.

My first payday I sit on my bed with a pen and paper and work out a budget. I never did this before. Okay. Let's see, now, what are my basic needs? We have to buy our lunch on work days, so I have to put aside lunch money, also cigarette money, for one week. Figure five dollars a day covers a sandwich, soda, and cigarettes. Times five days, that's twenty-five dollars, and a few extra for cigarettes on the weekend.

I stick three tens in an envelope, put it in one of my bureau drawers. That leaves me seventy-five dollars a week. Enough to live on, get stuff like shampoo and deodorant and toothpaste and all those little things you're always running out of, even maybe new sneakers or jeans if I save up.

So each week seventy-five dollars goes into my pocket. Literally. To this day I always carry my money, loose, in my front pocket, because I know if people are going to rob you they're going to go for your wallet.

I notice, after about the second week, I'm getting the habit of walking around with my hands in my pockets so I can jingle all my change.

No drugs are allowed at Ready, Willing & Able, but they never said we couldn't drink. On Friday nights some of the guys go around to the corner liquor store, buy a bottle, and stand around drinking and bullshitting. So I start hanging out too. Buy a bottle of vodka and join the group. Those first drinks, boy, they don't go down easy. My throat is on fire.

I tell myself people here drink, half the world probably drinks, so, hell, it's okay for me to do it too. How else can I hang out with these guys? Maybe this is what Harriet meant when she talked about social drinking.

IN THE TUNNELS, WHEN YOU'RE smoking, the shadows move. Only they're not real shadows, they're the black spots you sometimes get in front of your eyes. Take a hit and stare at the black spots a minute and they seem to be moving shapes. So you have to keep watching the light where the entrance hole is, because now you think somebody came in.

Maybe it's real, maybe it's not. Doesn't matter. There isn't any difference between real and unreal when you're high. You push back as far as you can go into the darkness, slide the milk crate until it hits a pipe or concrete wall. You're all the way back in the cottony dark now where it's quiet and still. You should be safe. You can take another hit. But as soon as you do, you see in the corner of your eye that the shapes have started to move again.

April and I were sitting in her spot in the tunnels, smoking, watching the shadows move. Not talking much but sharing just the same. Together in the dark with our stems and the crack and the shadows.

April asked me, "Could I have your res?"

"Yeah," I told her. Nobody gives that away, but it meant more to make her happy than for me to have the best part. We had twenty or twenty-five vials, anyway. Sounds like a lot, but when you're slam-dunking you can go through it easy in a couple hours. Slam-dunking is when you jam one or two vials in the stem and smoke the whole thing up at once. Because once you get a tolerance you can't feel anything with a little sliver. You have to use more and more.

She scraped out the res with a piece of wire hanger and I watched the shapes that were gathering in the corner of my vision, got all caught up concentrating on them, how they were sliding from side to side. "Cool," I said, out loud, "that's very cool."

We stayed there long after our stems were empty. Finished a pint of vodka. Smoked a bunch of cigarettes. It must've been late at night by then because you couldn't hear any trains running. I figured now April would want to go on another mission, because she could never stop for long. I knew if she did go, I'd go, too. Even though all I wanted now was sleep.

"This life sucks," April said. "You know what I'm talking about?" She waved her arm around the spot. It was tiny and square, full of low-hanging pipes and other people's trash and burnt-down candles. Somebody left a pile of shit by the side of the tracks, right under the entrance. When you gotta go, you gotta go, but you're supposed to do it as far from the spots as possible. Maybe this guy just couldn't hold it, crack will do that to you. You could smell it in the spot, and if you weren't high, it was really disgusting. "What we need," April said, "is education."

"For what?"

"To better ourselves. You want to be forty years old smoking crack in a train tunnel? I think we should enroll in secretarial school. I saw some ads in the *Daily News* for secretarial schools."

"Those places cost money." I was having trouble staying awake. There were blankets in the corner, or maybe a pile of old clothes. Whatever, it looked soft. The hard plastic of the milk crate was starting to cut into my rear end.

April was getting excited. "We could get jobs and earn money and work our way through school. That's what lots of people do."

Tired as I was, every time April said, We need this, or We could do that, I got a little tingle of happiness. The "we" she was talking about was her and me. Tina and April, together again. "Well, what kind of job could we do?"

"I bet I'd be terrific in a pet shop," she said. "I really like animals."

"Me, too. I like animals, too."

"So tomorrow we go looking. I think there's a couple pet shops around Thirty-fourth Street and I know there's a big one on Fourteenth Street. Then, soon as we're employed, we register for secretarial school."

"Okay."

"*Okay.* Tomorrow we start a new life. Maybe eventually we could move to Florida."

We cuddled up back-to-back on the blankets. I tried to stay awake just to have a longer time to feel her next to me. Soon she was making little snores. She moved and her back pressed into mine. I could feel her backbone through her sweatshirt, she was that skinny.

I fell asleep thinking about a new life. I didn't care as much about that as I did about her saying we were going to start it together.


I woke up first. I could hear people walking around the platforms, trains pulling in and out, conductors hollering to get on board, so I figured it was daytime.

April was sleeping on her back, arms and legs stretched out. I'd wound up almost on the floor because she was taking up the whole pile of blankets. My back and arms ached, my head ached from all the shit we smoked. But I was ready to go job hunting. The more I thought about it, the better it sounded. April was right that life in Grand Central sucked. I didn't know how to get out of it on my own, but I could do it with April. And working in a pet shop could be a really fun kind of job, especially if it was the kind that sold puppies and kittens and not just tropical fish.

I didn't know about the secretarial school part, though. I couldn't see myself sitting behind a goddamn desk all day, taking orders from some fat old fart who thought he was the boss of me. But I wasn't going to worry about that yet. Probably, when April realized what it was like to be a secretary, she'd change her mind about it. April wasn't going to take orders from any fat old fart, either.

I tried to wake her up. I whispered, "April!" Nothing. I shook her arm. It was loose and limp. I said, real loud, "April!" and finally she opened one eye. "Come on, April. We gotta go job hunting."

"Jesus, who *is* that?" she said, squinting up at me, trying to focus.

"Me. Tina. Wake up."

"Go 'way, leave me alone." She put her hands over her eyes, to block me out.

"Come on, get up. You said we were going to get jobs in a pet store today."

"Will you let me sleep, for Chrissake?" She turned over and curled into a tight ball. So I curled up next to her, and we both went back to sleep.


Later, I went with her to the West Side to see the dealer on Eighth Avenue who sometimes gave her a discount. He was the same guy who sold us the crack for those football players last winter, an Hispanic guy named Ramon. He looked like a weight lifter, he was short and chunky with muscles you could even see under his coat.

He was very friendly to April. She only had about ten dollars but he gave her five vials of crack. Then he said, "It's cold out here. Come to my place and you can smoke there."

So we went up to his room in some busted-down building on Tenth Avenue, and Ramon, after we'd been there two or three hours, or maybe six or eight, said to us, "Okay, now you gotta pay me back what you smoked." April asked him what the hell he was talking about and he said we had smoked up his supply. He said, "I figure you owe me about a hundred dollars now."

"No way, you gave it to us."

"No, no, April, you're mistaken. I gave you ten dollars' worth. More than ten dollars' worth, because I'm a generous man and you're a good customer. But you two girls have been here half the night and you smoked up at least another hundred dollars. Now you have to make some money and pay me back. Fair is fair."

He had a couple drawers full of women's clothes, he told us to pick out something sexy and put it on and he'd be right back. When he left I said, "The bastard's a *pimp*."

"Don't worry about it," April said. She had already picked out a black dress with sequins.

"What do you mean, don't worry about it? I'm not gonna go out there and be a goddamn prostitute."

"You don't have to. Just change your clothes and play along. He'll watch us until somebody picks us up, so you'll have to get in the car. Get the money first, then get out and run. Just bring back half the cash to Ramon and he'll never get wise."

I started to say, You've done this before, haven't you? But I didn't.

Out on the street Ramon stuck to us like glue, like April said he would. He stood just a few feet away in a doorway, smoking and eating candy bars, but no one driving by could see him.

It was cold and the wind was blowing off the Hudson River. All April had on was the dress with sequins and a little black jacket, all I was wearing was silver shorts and a tank top with a denim jacket. And bright red boots that were about twenty sizes too big.

I wanted to run but I knew if I did, one of Ramon's friends would get me even if Ramon didn't.

"April," I said, "'member the plans you were making last night? The pet store and secretarial school?"

"What of it?"

"Well, do you still want to do it?" My teeth were starting to chatter. I could tell April was freezing too, she was jumping from one foot to another trying to keep warm. Which wasn't easy because she was wearing high heels.

"Nah," she said. "I talked to my father last week and he wants me to live with him in California. I told him I'll probably come."

Everything drained out of me. Like when you prick a balloon and it shrivels right up. A car stopped, blue with Jersey plates. April gave me a push and I went over. The guy rolled down his window, said, "Hey, sexy girl, you working?"

I didn't say anything, didn't look back at April or even to see if Ramon was watching, just opened the car door and got in. "Forty dollars for a blow job and I want it up front."

The guy told me not so fast because he didn't want a blow job, he wanted to do oral sex on me. Except he used different words which I don't want to say here. "And," he said, "I'm not paying any forty dollars."

"Thirty or I'm out the door." I wouldn't have gotten out, because we were still parked in front of Ramon's doorway, but he didn't know that. He said, "Okay. Deal," and started the car.

We drove to West Thirty-third Street, to a little alley. I could have gotten out and run. I had the money and he never would have caught me. But he wasn't a bad guy. He was in his twenties and cute, blond hair that hung over his forehead and a nice smile. He had a little teddy bear hanging from his car mirror, and he showed me how you could wind it up and it played music. He said his girlfriend gave it to him. "You have a girlfriend?" I asked him.

"Not exactly. We're engaged, so now she's my fiancée."

"So why . . . ?"

"Because there's certain things she won't do. And I don't mind paying for it."

If he'd wanted a blow job, probably I would have run. But oral sex, what the hell.

I wasn't even sure what to expect, exactly, because I never had anyone do that to me before. The main thing was, he was going to be doing the act, not me, so I felt like I was going to be in control.

I stayed. He did it. I pretended to love it. After, he said, "Wasn't that good?"

I said, "Yeah." But not as good as your thirty bucks.

I had him drop me off ten blocks from Ramon. Went straight to Grand Central. Found Beverly in the waiting room. She and Micki were doing their hair, rolling it into tight little bunches. All the hair stuff was spread on the bench, an Afro pick and jars of cream and oil and hair clips and tiny colored barrettes. Beverly started laughing when she saw me. "Goddamn, girl, did you go into business or is this Halloween?"

I told her, "Shut up and find me some real clothes, will you?"

She finished the braid she was working on, told Micki to watch the hair stuff, and took me down to her spot in the tunnels. When volunteers came around handing out clothes, they'd always give the extra to Beverly, because they knew she'd save it and give stuff out when people needed it.

Beverly dug me out a pair of jeans, a flannel shirt, and socks. The only sneakers that fit were a rundown pair of Keds, but I had to take them. My good Reeboks that Shiv bought me on 145th Street were in Ramon's room, and I sure as hell couldn't go back to get them. It was going to be a long time before I could go back to the West Side at all.

I told myself I didn't give a damn where April was or what she was doing. And for a little while, I think that was true. I was still being a shriveled-up balloon. Shriveled-up balloons have no feelings. They don't care about anything, not even people leaving for California.

In November I had to go back to court about the robbery in the Clubhouse. Shiv was at Rikers, he was being held there until his sentencing. I got charged with Robbery 1 and 2 because they thought I set the guy up, but they released me on my own recognizance and gave me a date in January to come back again to be sentenced.

So Shiv was in jail. Maybe Francisco was in jail, too. Chewie had disappeared. He might've gone home, he might've gone to jail, or maybe something bad happened to him. Nobody knew. I saw his cousin Jabba around a couple times, but he didn't know where Chewie was, either.

I'd see Corey sometimes. He always had a little money on him, and we'd go to Bryant Park and get some reefer. We went to the movies a lot, usually the Roxy on Forty-second Street because they always had kung fu movies.

Corey was hanging out with some guy he met, Alex, a light-skinned black like Corey, good-looking in a kind of girly way. He had three little gold earrings in his left ear that he said were twenty-four carat. Corey told me Alex could go into any public men's room and come out with twenty or thirty dollars. Once I saw Corey going into the men's room at Grand Central with him, and when they came out they had enough money to rent a cheap hotel room. I know, because they invited me to come. I wanted to ask Corey if he was doing the same thing Alex was, but Corey always put down guys who sold their bodies so I figured he wouldn't tell me.

At the hotel Corey had reefer and beer, plus some crack for me. Alex went out to get us pizza and Corey told me, "I know the only reason you're here is because I have crack for you."

I sat on the bed and put my arm around him. I told him, "That's not true." But maybe it was. Crack was getting to mean a lot more to me than Corey.

I said before that crack had changed Grand Central. One of the ways was that people weren't hanging around as much anymore. Used to be, you could walk into the waiting room and everybody would be there, goofing around, joking, glad to see you. Now they were all out smoking crack or getting the money to buy it. Since it was cheaper uptown, that's where everybody went, and half the time they didn't come back to Grand Central to sleep, they'd just crash wherever they happened to be. In a park, a doorway, the subway, a dealer's apartment. When Beverly and Harley and a few others started selling in Grand Central, some of the people went back to hanging out full-time. But that was later.

And even when people were around now, everything was about getting money. Robbing, panhandling, whatever. Smokey came up with a new "game": stealing the brass handrails from the staircases. He'd take them off late at night with a screwdriver or hammer. Also, there's lots of copper down on the tracks, because it's used to conduct electricity, and Smokey started stealing and selling that too. After a while other people caught on, and everyone was taking brass and copper from the station. Junkyards would pay maybe fifty cents a pound or whatever the going rate happened to be at the time. Smokey was always coming up with new resources.

One person who was still around pretty regular was Jackie. I hadn't hung out with him for a while, what with being in Bellevue and then getting friendly with Shiv, but we took up where we left off.

I went with him when he broke into cars, stood lookout, only now I was kind of nervous about it. He used to pick quiet streets and cars that were parked far from streetlights, but now he didn't care anymore. He didn't even try to be quiet. Sometimes he'd take a brick and just smash in the driver's window.

The guy with the dreadlocks, Harley, was getting in the habit of coming around to see me. He was a little like Shiv, always asking if I needed anything, sometimes bringing me warm clothes because it was getting to be winter. If he found out I didn't eat that day he'd take me to the coffee shop in Grand Central and order me a hamburger and fries, or maybe buy me pizza. A couple times he took me to the movies. Harley liked action pictures, the kind with fights and car chases. It was a nice change from kung fu.

Harley always had money on him, he always had crack, and he was very generous with both. It was easy to get used to hanging out with him.

One night, it was just starting to get dark, Harley and me were sitting in a little park on Sixth Avenue, smoking. Harley said to me, "Look there." It was April, walking that fast, jerky crack walk she started doing recently, arms flopping back and forth, and Smokey right behind her just barely keeping up. April was wired. She plopped down on a bench catty-corner from me and Harley, so I know she saw us, pulled her stem out of her jeans and started flicking her lighter under it. Before I could say, "Hey, April!" here comes George McDonald and a lady. The lady looked either pissed or upset, maybe both. Harley and I hid our stems quick.

April just ignored them. Torched up her stem and took another hit. The lady started talking to her, but she was talking low and from where I was sitting I couldn't hear. April looked up finally and said real loud, "Get out of my life, will you?"

I thought this lady was just somebody George had brought around, maybe a social worker, who knows? But then her voice rose and I heard her say, "But look at you, how dirty, how skinny. You look sick. I love you, why are you doing this to me?" That's when I realized it was her mom. The only time I saw her before was late at night when I went to her house with April. She was in a bathrobe then, with blond hair hanging loose, but now she was bundled up in a winter coat and she had on a hat or scarf. That's why I didn't recognize her at first.

"You never gave a shit about me," April said. "All you ever cared about was yourself. Well, guess what, all I care about is this." She held up her stem and took another hit.

The mom started to cry, and George said something to April I couldn't hear. Smokey, he was just sitting there next to April keeping his mouth shut, looking like he wished he was someplace else.

April told George, "You had no fucking business bringing her here. Anyway, I'm going to go live with my father because he wants me more than she ever did."

April's mom flipped out. "Where he wants you is anyplace that's away from him, that's where he's *always* wanted you!" She was yelling now, you could probably hear her in Brooklyn. April jumped up, grabbed the shoulder bag her mom was wearing, and started running across the park with it. Smokey took off after her.

I told Harley, "Wow, that's crazy even for April." We left the park right after they did, by a different exit. It was almost dark and I don't know if George had seen us, but in case he did we didn't want to get involved as witnesses if her mom pressed charges. Not with stems in our jeans and five or six vials of crack.

I looked back once, before we left the park. George was trying to sit April's mom down on the bench. She was making loud choking noises and at first I didn't realize they were sobs.

IN THE EARLY MORNINGS AT Ready, Willing & Able, when we're being driven to a work site, I notice the people on the streets. It's so easy to tell which ones are going to work and which ones have been up all night and are still out looking for money to get high. Even if they're clean, you can tell who's been in their clothes all night and who hasn't.

In June we start working on a site in Harlem. The first morning, on the way there, we go by a school on 119th Street. It's a big school, partly built up on columns, and the minute I see it I freeze. I'm thinking, Holy shit, because I used to go there, underneath that school, to smoke crack. Me and Smokey and Beverly, and later with Harley too. We'd go uptown to Harlem to buy, because it was cheaper, and sometimes we bought at a certain house on 116th Street. If we didn't want to wait until we got back to Grand Central we'd stop at this school to get high. There were always people smoking crack there, day and night. It's amazing there were never any cops around.

There are five or six people in that same spot now, getting high. I look real hard, trying to see if I know anybody. But we go by too fast to tell.

We pass that school twice a day for a week. Each time we're coming up on it I turn my head away. But at the last minute, I always sneak a look.

———— • ————

The Saturday morning after my first paycheck, I call my mom to tell her I just got paid and ask if I could come and stay overnight. My mom says "Sure, Tina, come on home." She says the kids will be excited.

And they're really excited when I tell them I'm going to sleep over. Because the last time I spent the night with them was a couple years ago when they were still in the Prince George Hotel, which Robby hardly remembers.

I stay outside with them all afternoon so they can ride their bikes around the projects, because they're not allowed out alone. When the Good Humor truck comes I buy them both Popsicles, which is a treat, because my mom doesn't always have enough money for extras like ice cream. It makes me feel good to be able to do things like that.

Robert isn't around at all. My mom says half the time now, he doesn't come home on weekends. She says, "It's fine with me. I wish he'd never come home."

Saturday night we all watch TV, and after the kids are in bed my mom and I sit around and talk. Just about little things, like always. She tells me Jessica will be switching schools in September because she was accepted into one of the gifted and talented programs. She asks if I like the work at Ready, Willing & Able. I tell her how I made out a weekly budget, and she says, "Oh, that's really good, Tina." We talk about the weather, how chilly it is for June, and by then we're both yawning so we say good night and go to bed.

On Sunday Uncle Tony comes for dinner, and we leave together so he can drive me to the train. Otherwise I'd have to take a bus to the train because it's too far to walk. The kids ask if I'll come back next weekend. My mom tells them, "Sure she will. Right, Tina?"

"Okay," I tell them. "I'll be back next Saturday."

Uncle Tony has this big Oldsmobile parked out front, it's about fifteen years old but he keeps it in great shape. He says, "You want to drive?"

"No way. I don't know how."

He drives around to the middle part of the projects where there's a short little road with hardly any traffic and tells me to get behind the wheel. I just sit there and look at him. "Go on," he says. "You can do it."

Uncle Tony has to keep showing me which is the brake and which is the gas pedal. I keep getting them mixed up, and when he tells me to pull over and stop I slam my foot down on the brake and the whole car jolts. I'm sure Uncle Tony's going to get whiplash. But all he says is, "Easy, Tina, easy." Uncle Tony is a Valium freak. He's always taking that stuff, so he's always real laid-back. Nothing bugs him out. He's a good type of person to teach someone to drive.

———— • ————

When I lived in Grand Central, I went to see Uncle Tony a couple of times. The last time, I remember, Corey came with me. Now Uncle Tony lives near Coney Island, but at that time he lived with his boyfriend in an apartment across from Brooklyn College. I went there to ask for money but he wouldn't give me any. He said, "You can shower, you can eat all you want, but I'm not giving you money." So I showered and he made dinner for me and Corey. He sat at the table with us while we were eating. He said, "You're making your mother crazy with worry."

I told him, "I can't help that."

"You should go home, Tina."

"I can't do that, either."

"You're smoking crack these days, I hear."

I knew Uncle Tony messed around with drugs himself. Nothing like crack, but he always had marijuana around the house, and tons of Valiums, which I remembered from when I was twelve. So in my opinion, Uncle Tony wasn't exactly lily white, either. "Right, I smoke crack," I told him, "but I'm not sharing any with *you*."

He didn't get mad, but I could tell he didn't especially care for my attitude. After that I didn't call or go over there again. Because the truth was, I thought Uncle Tony was a cool guy and I was ashamed I talked to him like that. Ashamed of myself, too, and the way I was living. I didn't see him again for a couple of years, until my home visit when I was in Samaritan Village.


Right next door to the Harlem apartment where we're doing rubbish removal, there's a bodega. At lunchtime I'm in there getting a sandwich and I hear meowing. Sounds like a bunch of kittens. The guy lets me go into the back room to see them. They're in a corner behind some garbage cans, in a torn cardboard box, and the poor little things are covered with plaster dust. Everything in the back room is covered with plaster dust, because the demolition crew has been knocking down half of the next-door building while we do the rubbish removal in another part.

I kneel down next to the box. There are seven kittens in there, all sleepy and squirmy. One is an orange tabby, and he looks just like the cat we had when I was little. He's lying on top of another kitten, sound asleep, and I reach in and pick him up. He fits in my hand and weighs almost nothing. His eyes open and he yawns, wide pink mouth, teeny white teeth. His paws are the size of my fingertips. I try to clean the dust off him with my shirtsleeve.

"You want him?" the guy says. "Because I gotta get rid of them." This guy, I can tell he doesn't give a damn about kittens. I can tell he's probably going to get rid of them the easiest possible way.

"Yeah," I say. "I want him."

I name him Lucky because that was the name of the orange tabby we had when I was little. Also, I think he's lucky I took him.

There's a new rule at Ready, Willing & Able because there were a couple fights on Friday nights, mostly from people drinking too much. So from now on, it's not just drugs that are forbidden, it's liquor too. You drink, you're out.

APRIL TOLD ME NOT TO smoke with the Jamaican guy. He was her friend, her newest smoking partner. One of the few she still had.

But he was looking for her and when he couldn't find her he said, "Okay, Tina, you can come with me. I have some smoke."

I followed him down to April's spot under the platform by Track 100, and while we were smoking I started hearing sounds. The grating being opened. Someone crawling in.

I told myself, "I'm just paranoid." Only this one time, I wasn't. It was April.

She said, "Didn't I tell you not to smoke with him, you little bitch?"

"Yeah, but we couldn't find you."

Then—*whack*—she hit me over the head with a bottle of Mr. Boston's Blackberry Brandy. It broke open all over me, and the brandy came pouring down my head. I could feel it dripping wet and warm onto my face, my ears, my neck. I climbed out of the spot, jumped up onto the platform. You're already paranoid just from smoking, but if someone really does come after you it's enough to give you a heart attack. I was shaking, my head hurt bad, and I was covered with brandy.

Way at the back of the platform was a big sink, for the workmen. I stuck my head under the faucet and washed myself. Tried to wash the brandy out of my jacket and flannel shirt too.

I had a headache for two days and a bump on my scalp for a week. And for a whole lot longer than that I walked around stinking like an alcoholic. Because the smell of Mr. Boston's Blackberry Brandy doesn't go away easy if you can't take a real shower.

Now I was really pissed at April, and tired of always trying to understand her. A few days later I saw her sitting in front of the ladies' room with a cup and a bent cardboard sign that said HELP ME GET TO SCOTTY. She was dirty and ragged, her hair was hanging tangled in her face, and she was rocking back and forth like she sometimes did when she was all cracked out.

I said, "What the hell are you doing?"

She said, "Asshole, what the hell do you think I'm doing?"

She didn't care. I could see it in her eyes. Just sitting there, dirty and rocking, with a sign and a cup. There was no dignity about her anymore.

That's when I stopped being mad. Seeing her like that, I realized she couldn't help what was happening. It wasn't up to her anymore.


I don't remember much about the holidays that year, Christmas and New Year's. I was high through most of it. I think I planned it that way. The first week in January was my eighteenth birthday and I do remember that, because that's when I turned legal. I wasn't a ward of the court, I wasn't a ward of my mom, and nobody could try to make me do anything anymore just because I was underage.

I thought it was going to be great. I thought it was going to be liberating. But when I finally turned eighteen I realized it didn't make any difference. I'd already been doing whatever I wanted for two years.


I was sleeping in the Clubhouse with Harley a couple weeks after my birthday and I heard someone saying, "Tina, you in there?" Then the flap was opened and I saw Officer Peterson, one of the station's cops, with a guy and a lady. The guy said, "Warrant squad, come on out."

They said they had to take me in on a bench warrant. They said I was supposed to have been in court last week to get sentenced for the crime with Shiv and that Abdul guy, but I never showed. Then I remembered how the judge, in November, gave me a January date to come back. But it totally slipped my mind. It wasn't like I kept a date book or anything.


The bus to Rikers was like a school bus, only it was blue and white with a couple of orange stripes and it said NEW YORK CITY CORRECTIONS across it. The windows had cage mesh in the glass. It was about half full, all women, mostly black. I sat low in my seat, kept my mouth shut, didn't look to the left or right. When no one was looking, I stuffed my stem down the back of the seat.

Rikers Island is in Elmhurst, Queens. The last part of the trip is over a bridge that goes to the island. La Guardia Airport is just across the water, and a big TWA plane came zooming down the runway, taking off right over us. It seemed so low I thought it was going to crash into our bus. But it passed over and I watched it sailing straight up into the sky. I wondered where it was going. Maybe Florida.


Before they take you into the Receiving Area, one of the Correction Officers tells you this is your chance to hand in your valuables. You don't have to, but they tell you if you don't, your stuff might get stolen while you're in jail. All I had was four dollars and some change, and a gold necklace that said "Tina." I don't think it was real gold, but I liked it and it was from Stan, the guy from Staten Island. I think it was a Christmas present, but I'm not sure because I was so high during the holidays.

I took off the necklace and gave it to the CO along with my money. She put it in a manila envelope, put my name and ID number on it, told me I'd get it back when I left. But I never saw it again. When they released me they gave me the envelope, and all that was in it was the four dollars and change. I asked where was my necklace and the CO said, "You never turned in any necklace."


I was on Rikers Island six days waiting for my case to get called in court. I spent the whole time in the Receiving Area, which was a big room with four large holding cells. They corralled us, me and the ten or fifteen other women who were on the bus, into the first cell. I felt like a cow getting herded into a pen. The cells were like the ones in Central Booking; each had one sink and one toilet and you had to do your business right in front of everybody.

Always before, in Central Booking, I was under eighteen so they kept me in a separate cell. But now that I was of age I was in with everybody else. They call you out one by one and do intake, get your vital information, and stand you up against the wall and take your picture. Then you go back and wait to get moved to the next cell.

By then it was late at night. There's one bench in every cell, but only the biggest, toughest women get that. So I lay down on the floor to sleep and folded up my coat for a pillow. One of the women, she had bruises all over her face and a bandaged hand, she told me, "I see you got half a pack of cigarettes, honey. If you don't want them stolen while you're sleeping, you better hold them close." She showed me how she was going to sleep, all curled up with her shoes and scarf held tight to her chest. She said, "Normally I'd tell you to hold on to your shoes, too, because they'll steal them right off your feet, but I don't think you got to worry about that pair." At least there was an advantage to having grungy secondhand sneakers.

She was snoring in a minute. A lot of the others were sleeping, too. I was just about to put my head down when I noticed something moving on my coat. First I thought my eyes were playing tricks on me, then I just wished they were. Because there were little bugs crawling and hopping all over my coat. Had to be fleas, because lice don't hop.

My coat was a navy pea coat I found the night before. Me and Harley were on our way back to the Clubhouse, it was freezing cold, and I saw this coat that someone had hung over the railing of a church. It looked warm, so I took it and left my windbreaker in its place. I had the pea coat on when the warrant squad woke me up that morning.

If fleas were on the coat, and I'd been wearing the coat since last night, they were probably on me too. God, all I'd need would be for some of the others to see me scratching. They'd love to find out the little white girl had bugs, they'd be taunting me and maybe even trying to pick a fight. I rolled the coat up and threw it across the cell so no one would know it was mine.

Now I was starting to itch, and I didn't know if it was really from the fleas or just the thought of them. But I didn't scratch. I lay there on the floor all night, holding my cigarettes tight, feeling real or imaginary fleas crawling on my back and my neck, then in my hair and on my arms and up my legs. I had to bite down on my lip sometimes, but I didn't scratch once.

In the morning they brought breakfast, the same as what you got in Central Booking: bologna sandwich and lukewarm tea. Then they called five names to go to the showers and one of them was mine. I whispered, "Thank you, God." They gave everybody the kind of soap that delouses you, so I washed until I was sure there wasn't a bug left alive on me. I was so relieved I didn't even mind having to shower with four others.

But the worst was coming. Before you get your clothes the COs tell you to line up against the wall. They go down the row wearing surgical gloves, checking everyone's mouth. Then they tell you to turn around, bend over, squat like you're getting ready to sprint, spread your cheeks, and cough. I must've looked horrified because one of the COs said, "We don't want to do this anymore than you do, so let's get it over with."

I tried to pretend I was somewhere else. Back in the Clubhouse, maybe, with Harley. Anywhere. Just not here. Not squatting naked and cold, with goose bumps, in front of those other women.

The COs, when they came to me, didn't make any mean remarks like, "Oh, what an ugly body," but even though they were just doing their job and probably didn't get any jollies from it, after it was over I still felt like something had been taken away from me.

I waited in the second cell another day and night, but at least now I was clean, and I made friends with an Hispanic girl by sharing my cigarettes. I felt a little safer and not as alone.

When you're in the third cell you get examined by a doctor. Then you see a psychiatrist and he asks you some questions, I guess to make sure you're not crazy. After that they sent me to the fourth cell and I spent two more days there, just waiting. Waiting for what, I didn't know. So I asked one of the COs, finally, and she said I was waiting for my court date. I said, "When is that?" and she said, "How the hell should I know?"

A day? A week? A year? How long was I going to be here? Sleeping on the floor, trying hard to use the toilet only at night when people were asleep, eating nothing but bologna sandwiches, almost out of cigarettes. The Hispanic girl was gone.

How long have I been here? That was another question. I was losing track of time because it's all the same. You sleep as much as possible to keep from thinking of crack, you eat a little, don't smoke too much because your cigarettes have to last. Move from cell to cell, watch the other women come and go. Four days, maybe five days I've been here, or it could have been six.

And then they called my name. Took me out, put me on the blue-and-white bus with orange stripes, drove me back to the city. It was time for me to go to court.

AT READY, WILLING & ABLE, jobs are broken down into steps. First on the site is the rubbish removal crew, then a demolition crew, then Sheetrocking, and the final crew is painting. The whole thing, from rubbish removal to painting, takes about five days. And there's usually five or six sites going at a time.

In demolition the supervisor gives us a list of everything that has to be done, which is usually knocking down walls and tearing down the ceilings. Sometimes they want us to remove the windows, break up the glass, and throw it in the garbage. Even if they don't ask us, we remove the windows anyway if they're aluminum, because we can get money for aluminum. Also from copper pipes. We put it all in a plastic bag, and, after work, if the supervisor who's driving the van that day is nice, he'll take us to one of the recycling places in Brooklyn where they pay by the pound for aluminum and copper.

In the older buildings, most of the ceilings are tin sheeting. It isn't all in one piece so you have to pull it down in strips with the hammer, and it's sharp. You can get sliced bad if you're not careful. Also, when you're peeling the ceiling off, years and years of dust are coming down on you. You've got a mask on and your hard hat, but you still wind up getting filthy.

The first week I'm on demolition, Charlie, the supervisor, starts making jokes about me. I'm hammering down walls and he says, "I'm glad I'm not the person you're thinking about." I stop for a minute, take a breath. The sweat is pouring down my face, my clothes are drenched, even my hair is soaked.

I put down my hammer, take a big swig of bottled water, and ask Charlie, "What do you mean?"

"Hey," he tells me, "it's a good way to get your frustrations out."

And that's when I realize I'm working harder than most of the other people, that I'm using the hammering and the bashing to get out a lot of stuff. And it feels good.

Before I know it I've got a reputation. The guys on my crew are telling each other, "Man, she's working harder than you." So I just keep going, going, going. Me and the Energizer Bunny. I want to show everyone what I can do.

Sometimes, even though I'm tired and hurting, I zone out. I'm not feeling the pain anymore, don't notice the sweat, don't hear anything around me. My body keeps banging down walls but I'm someplace else, someplace inside my head, thinking about my mom and about April and about all the other people and feelings that live in there.

When I go to my mom's on Saturdays I always take Lucky in his little carrier. Lucky runs all over the place, bouncing off the walls and climbing curtains. My mom doesn't think that's so cute, especially climbing the curtains, but Jessica and Robby think he's great.

Sometimes I take the kids to a movie. I'm trying hard to get to know them, to be a part of their life again.

Uncle Tony comes for Sunday dinner a couple times a month, and we usually leave together so he can take me to the train. I'm getting so good at driving that now he lets me drive the ten blocks to the station. We call his funky Oldsmobile the Batmobile.

One night I'm driving to the train and he says, "So where are you going to live after January?" Because January is when my nine months are up at Ready, Willing & Able.

I don't like to talk while I'm driving. I'm still new at it and talking blows my concentration. "I don't know," I tell him. That's something I haven't wanted to think about. At this stage of my life it's better to take one day at a time.

"You can move in with me, if you want. I've got two bedrooms and I'm just rattling around in there by myself."

"Well, sure, thanks," I say, "but only if you'll let me pay rent."

"How's fifty bucks a week?"

"That sounds fair." And then I have to stop talking, because I just missed plowing the Batmobile into a lady with a baby carriage.

Sheetrocking is hard to learn. You've got a certain amount of material to work with and you can't make mistakes and waste it. The measurements have to be exact, and it's all in inches so you're converting feet to inches. I've got to polish up my math.

If you're doing the ceiling, too, that goes up first. Then the walls. Then you do the taping. The tape is like paper, it's a thin strip in a roll, and you roll it along the seams and it attaches to the ceilings and walls. Then you compound it—"compound" is plaster—and sand it down. That's what you do in the corners so there isn't a hole.

I'm learning to work with screw guns and levelers and all kinds of tools I've never used before. It's a very satisfying feeling to see something come together piece by piece, seeing walls and ceilings go up where before there were just wooden beams and two-by-fours.

Painting is the last crew they put you on. It's not as easy as you'd think. You can't use a roller when you're painting near the ceiling, you have to do it with a paint brush that's tapered. It's something that not everybody can do, but I get really good at it. In fact, it's one of my specialties. It's called "cutting." I can paint along the top edge of the wall and never touch the ceiling.

Everything that's hard, I'm determined to master. I don't want to be just another employee of Ready, Willing & Able, I want to be the best at everything, because I have something to prove. I have to prove to Harriet I'm not a loser and I really do want help. And I think there's a few things I'm trying to prove to myself too.

For the first time I'm getting a sense of what it feels like to work hard. To push myself further than I ever thought I could.

My attorney met with me before we went to the judge and went over my case. He was young, and handsome in a nerdy way. He said, "Do you want to go home today?"

I said, "Yeah, of course I want to get out of here."

"Well," he said, "you can, if you take five years probation. Your other choice is to go back to Rikers and serve one year."

I said, "I'll take the probation. Of course." Not knowing that, in some ways, five years probation was going to be worse than one year in jail. At least with the jail time I'd have had it over with a lot sooner.


My first probation officer was a guy named Mr. Krohl. The first time I saw him he asked my name, address, date of birth, names of my parents, and went over the rules I had to follow for probation, then said, "Okay. Come back next month." So we made an appointment and I left. I figured, piece of cake.

One of the main probation rules was, I had to have a place to live. I wasn't a ward of the state anymore because I was over eighteen, and my mom said I could come live with them in the Prince George Hotel. Robert was still living with her, they were fighting as much as ever, and the room at the Prince George was even smaller than the one we had at the Martinique. Everyone was crammed into one boxy room with a tiny bathroom, two sets of bunk beds, and a black-and-white TV. My mom also had a small portable refrigerator and a hot plate for cooking. It was against the rules to cook in your room, but everybody did it. It was either that or eat all your meals at McDonald's.

Another rule of probation was that you had to have either a job or be in school, and Mr. Krohl told me he was going to get me enrolled in classes so I could get my general equivalency diploma.

I wasn't supposed to be doing drugs, of course, or going to Grand Central. But I figured, what the hell, it wouldn't hurt to stop by once in a while. I couldn't sit in that goddamn hotel room all the time. So I was going to Grand Central every couple days, hanging out with whoever happened to be around.

I saw April rushing through the waiting room one afternoon. "Hey," she said, "what's up?" She looked better than last time I saw her, when she was panhandling with the Scotty sign, because she wasn't as dirty and her hair was combed. But her hands, when she talked, were even jerkier than before. Flying all over the place like she had no control over them.

I told her about getting arrested and going to Rikers and she said something about, oh, that's no big deal, she was in and out of there all the time. She never really stopped moving while she stood there, it was like her motor was running full speed. I noticed for the first time that her mouth twitched when she talked.

I told her, "April, you're smoking too much." And knew, right away, I should've kept my mouth shut.

"It's okay, my father's coming soon. Gonna take me back to California." And she was gone. Damn. I chased her away.


Every time I came home past my curfew, Robert would be awake, watching TV. The bastard, he was waiting for me. He never said anything, but I know in the mornings he told my mom what time I came in, and my mom called Mr. Krohl. I know she also told Krohl I was probably hanging around Grand Central, because he called me into his office the third week and said he was transferring my case to the Intensive Supervision Program.

My new probation officer was a lady named Miss Reilly. Who told me, the first time I saw her, that ISP was for people who need more involvement than regular probation gives. She told me that in ISP you report at least three times a week, and she'd be making home visits at least twice a month. She asked if Krohl had gotten me signed up for general equivalency diploma classes yet and I told her I didn't know. She asked a few more questions, then she said, "Okay, you're free. Come back in two days. And by the way, I don't like to be called Miss Reilly. Maggy will do just fine."

Getting Maggy for a probation officer might have been one of the best things that happened to me, if it hadn't turned out she was going to be leaving soon. I have big abandonment issues.


At first I didn't like the idea of reporting to Maggy so often. Didn't know if I wanted a probation officer who was going to get "involved," like she put it. Whenever people tried to help me or get close, they always wound up making trouble. I needed to keep people out. But little by little, Maggy Reilly pushed her way in.

First thing she did was get me enrolled in school, taking classes for my GED. I didn't mind that much, going every day until two o'clock. It filled up the days.

After school, three or four times a week, Maggy had me come to her office and do my homework in the waiting room, then she'd go over it with me. She also made me start a diary. She kept it in her file cabinet, and whenever I didn't have a lot of homework I'd write in it, then bring it into her office and we'd go over what I wrote.

Maggy was slim and tiny with reddish-brown hair, but the first thing you noticed were her eyes. They were clear blue, almost the color of sky, and there was something warm about them that made me like her right away. Even though I didn't show it for a while. The other thing I liked was the way she never dressed in suits and office-type clothes, she always wore sweatpants, or maybe jeans with a sweatshirt. It made her comfortable to be with.

I wanted Maggy to be my friend. But, then again, I didn't.


I was trying to follow the rules, and now that I was going to school five days a week and reporting to Maggy three or four times a week, it was easier. I had structure again. What wasn't easy was being home with my mom and Robert. The good part was, he wasn't there much. He was hanging around Forty-second Street selling reefer, and he also had a girlfriend, which we found out in the summer after my mom followed him one day.

But even without Robert, it was hard to be there. My mom would go out and buy chicken wings for dinner, and she'd fry them up on the hot plate with the spicy Spanish seasoning Robert turned her on to. We ate out of plastic bowls, those three-pound plastic butter tubs you buy—my mom washed them out when the butter was gone. She'd put a couple chicken wings in each bowl, then suddenly pretend she wasn't hungry so there'd be more for Jessica and Robby and me.

I'd eat, but I'd feel so guilty that next day I'd make up some excuse to go out right before dinner. I'd walk around for about an hour, and when I came home my mom would say, "Tina, did you eat?" I'd tell her sure, Ma, I ate. What I wouldn't tell her was, it was a candy bar.

One weekend, after Robert didn't come home for four or five days, my mom went to Forty-second Street looking for him. It wasn't the first time she did that, and it wouldn't be the last. But this time someone told her he was in jail. My mom went to Rikers the next day to see him. He was waiting for his court date, she told me when she came home that night. I didn't ask what the charges were and she didn't tell me, but I'm sure it had to do with drugs.

Next day, after I came home from Maggy's, my mom told me to help her with spring cleaning. We scrubbed out the bathroom and made the kids sit on their bunks and watch TV while we swept and mopped. This sounds weird but I enjoyed it, me and my mom doing housework together. Then my mom packed all Robert's clothes in a box and shoved them under her bunk. My clothes, we hung on his hangers.

She wouldn't say so, but I knew she didn't want him back. None of us did. I hoped he'd stay out of our lives forever.


The main reason I was going to Grand Central when Krohl was my probation officer was because I hoped I'd see April. April was still the biggest thing in my life. Even though I hardly ever saw her anymore, even though when I did I never knew how she was going to treat me, I was still living life just waiting to see her.

I told Maggy about April, and how there were so many things about her I didn't understand, but I knew underneath all the drugs that were in her she was still my best friend. I told Maggy that even though April was going to California, I felt we would still be together someday. And there would be no drugs involved, or anything illegal, we would just be two normal people who were the best friends in the world.


One night I left home when my mom started dinner, because there was only a piece of liver and a can of corn and I knew it was going to be one of those times she'd say she wasn't hungry.

I walked uptown toward Grand Central, figured I'd sit in Bryant Park a while, buy myself a pretzel. But right outside the park I bumped into Corey. It was the first time I'd seen him in months. His face lit up, he yelled, "Hey, Tina, where the hell you been?"

I told him, on probation. I told him, "I'm studying for my GED. Might even go to college in the fall."

He said, "That's great, will you still be my friend when you're a hotshot college graduate?" I told him I'd always be his friend.

We sat in the park, smoked a little pot. He told me he was leaving New York soon, going home to Georgia. He just wanted to save up five hundred dollars first so he wouldn't be a burden on his family while he was looking for a job. I didn't ask how he was going to get the money, but I wondered if he was still friends with that guy Alex.

He told me he wasn't hanging around Grand Central much anymore because they were all turning into crackheads. "I'm not even hanging out with April," he said. "Little bitch stuck her hand in my pocket while we were sitting in the waiting room last week and ran away. She got at least ten dollars. How low do you have to be to steal from friends?"

"It's the crack," I told him. "It's not April."

Corey said, "What's the difference? There isn't any anymore."

He bought us hamburgers at McDonald's and a couple beers, then we went to the Roxy to see a kung fu movie. Next thing I knew, Corey was shaking me awake in my seat saying, "Tina, it's after two."

"Shit, I blew my curfew."

"I'm sorry," Corey told me. "I fell asleep too."

Corey said he'd come home with me and explain, but that would've only made it worse. My mom would figure out he was one of my Grand Central friends and she'd never believe we just fell asleep in a movie. It sounded like a stupid excuse even to me, right in there with "The dog ate my homework."

We stood out front of the movie arguing, Corey telling me I was only going to make things worse if I didn't go home now, me telling him to mind his own goddamn business. "Well, hell, Tina, it's your life," he said finally, and left. Crossed over Forty-second Street, heading toward Sixth Avenue.

So there I am, alone, standing in front of the Roxy at two A.M. Even if I wanted to go to Grand Central I couldn't, because it was closed. On top of everything, it was starting to rain.

I spent the night in the doorway of a dry cleaners on Thirty-eighth Street. Woke up at daylight, cold and damp and achy. All I could think was, "What am I going to tell Maggy?" Because I knew she'd find out. If I didn't tell her, my mom would.

It was still raining, so I sat in a coffee shop over a Danish and a Coke until eight-thirty, then went to a pay phone and called Maggy, collect. Said, "Maggy, I know you're going to get mad, but . . ." and told her I'd been out all night, told her what happened but left out the pot and the beer. I said, "I'm so sorry, Maggy, I know I did wrong. I should've gone home no matter how late it was, and I don't blame you if you think I'm lying about falling asleep in a movie. I don't even blame you if you don't want to be my probation officer anymore."

She said, "Get on the subway and come right down to my office."

I had to walk, though, because I didn't have enough to buy a token and no way was I going to risk jumping the turnstile. I was sure Maggy was going to yell at me, or transfer me to someone else, maybe even turn me in for violating, but what she actually did blew me away. She got up from her desk, hugged me tight, and said, "You're soaked."

I think that's when I realized Maggy wasn't just doing a job, she cared about me. And I was beginning to care about her. I talked a lot that day, about myself and some of the things I've done that I'm not too proud of. I spent most of the morning in her office. And it wasn't easy, talking. Good grief. There's things about myself I just don't want to face up to, and it's even harder to think about anyone else knowing. It's like, uh-oh, *intruder alert*.

Two weeks later, Maggy told me she was leaving. She was going to be a parole officer instead of a probation officer. At the end of July she was going to transfer my case to someone else.

So much for caring. Thank you very much, Maggy Reilly.

I think it was that same day, I came home to find Robert sleeping in the bunk bed. He looked even skeezier than usual, he needed a shave and his hair looked matted and greasy. His shirts were back on the hangers and someone, my mom I guess, had folded my clothes and stacked them at the foot of Robby's bed. The kids were sitting on the floor watching TV with the sound down low so it wouldn't wake Robert. My mom was there with them, and she pretended to be so interested in *Electric Company* she didn't see me come in.

Maggy was leaving in a month, and I had just started to trust her. Robert was back at home and so was all the fighting. Wherever I turned, it was shit.


Maggy had applied to Brooklyn College for me, and at the end of June they sent her a notice that I'd been accepted for fall. As long as, when I took my GED exam in July, I passed with a good score. The only classes that gave me trouble were math and social studies but I'd been working extra hard on them.

I think I was excited about going to college, but mainly because Maggy was. She treated it like such a big thing, so that's how I saw it. Because, really, I was only eighteen, and I had no concept of college. I hardly even knew anybody who'd gone, except for Maggy.

Maggy told me she could also fix it up for me to start seeing a therapist after she left. I told her no way, I told her, "I just want to be alone like I was before, okay? This caring stuff, it makes me too confused and tired and scared."

Maggy sat back in her chair and crossed her legs. She was wearing sweats, pants and a top, that almost matched the color of her eyes. "I know it isn't an easy time for you. Could you talk about how you're feeling?"

"No. I can't. Because I don't even know." Angry, maybe? Helpless too. This very important person was leaving and there wasn't a damn thing I could do about it.

I was grateful for having her as a probation officer. Maggy was strong and independent, she had an apartment and a job and she took care of herself, she didn't have to depend on a guy like my mom did. She was the first grown-up woman I ever really knew who I could look at and think, yeah, it would be okay to be like her.

On the other hand, I was furious at her for leaving. I guess deep down I felt if she really cared about me she would have found a way to stay.


In July Maggy went on vacation for a week. I figured maybe that was a good thing because I could practice doing without her. My intentions were good, anyway.

Near the end of the week I came in a few minutes past curfew. When I saw Robert looking at his watch to check the time I told him, "Mind your own damn business."

My mom was sleeping but he woke her up and started in on her anyway. "Are you going to let her talk to me like that? Aren't you going to do anything about it?"

"Tina," she said, "go to bed." I think she just wanted him to shut up so she could go back to sleep.

"I'm not tired," I told her.

"Hey," Robert said, "don't talk back to her."

"Get out of my face, will you? You're not my father, so don't tell me what to do."

Robert had been sitting on the floor by the TV. He jumped up and hollered, "I don't have to take any shit from you," at the same time my mom yelled, "Tina watch your mouth!" And I just walked out. I knew Robert wouldn't follow because all he had on was a long T-shirt over his jockey shorts, and a pair of scuzzy white socks.

I figured, Okay, I'll just wait out in the hall a while. Just until he calms down and she goes back to sleep. But before I could even light a cigarette, I heard him and my mom shouting at each other. Then Jessica was whining because they woke her up. I shoved my cigarettes back into my jacket and got the hell out of there.


When I went by Grand Central, Smokey told me April was over at St. Agnes Church, which is just a block from the station. She wasn't on the front steps where she usually sat so I went around to the back, and at first I thought she wasn't there, either. All I saw was a small pile of cardboard in the corner of the top step. But then the cardboard moved, and I saw there was somebody under it.

"It's a little house," April said, when I pushed one of the pieces off her. "I made a cozy little house where no one can see me. You wanna come in?" She moved over on the step to make room for me, I sat down next to her and she pulled the pieces back around us. It was dark under the boxes, but when my eyes got used to it I could see pretty good. April was wearing a navy sweatshirt and cutoff shorts, and she was so skinny her knees looked like doorknobs. "You can't have any of my smoke, though," she told me.

"That's okay."

"I'm laying low because everyone in that fucking station is an asshole. Bunch of jerk-offs. I don't associate with them any more than I absolutely have to. And George McDonald, he's been trying to force me into rehab."

She jammed a whole vial of crack into her stem, torched it, and took a blast. I noticed then that she had sores around her mouth, also one on her chin, almost like big zits that were infected. Also, there was still that twitch to her mouth, like she had a hook in her cheek that kept pulling up her lips. I wanted to tell her, Look, April, maybe George is right, maybe you should do what he says. But I knew if I said anything she didn't want to hear, she'd make me leave.

She handed me a pint of vodka. "You can have some," she said.

I almost said, No thanks. The sores around her mouth. That lump she showed me on her back last winter. But I took it, and we sat there for a while in the little cardboard nest, April smoking, me taking swigs of vodka. I thought of baby mice. It was a very warm night and April smelled of dirty clothes and sweat, because it was probably a long time since she got to shower. But there was another smell on top of that. Or, maybe, underneath. It was the smell of April, of her skin, the natural spicy-soap smell of her body coming through the dirt and sweat.

"So when are you going to California?"

"Soon," she said, "very soon. My father's gonna teach me to surf. Did you ever surf?"

"No."

"Of course you never surfed. That was a dumb-ass question." She took another blast off her stem. "My birthday was yesterday," she said. "So now I'm nineteen."

"I know. Happy birthday."

"Isn't life weird? I never thought I was supposed to live this long. Because Travis, he died when he was seventeen."

A long time passed. The vodka was almost gone and she was down to her last crack vial. "I think I've gotta go uptown now," she said. "You can't come."

"Okay."

We started pushing the cardboard off us. It was good to be out from under. I could feel a breeze. I started folding the pieces and stacking them on the step, just to be doing something, to maybe keep this going a little longer. April stood there watching me and I could see how her shorts hung on her. You could fit three of her legs through one of the openings.

"So I'll see you around," she said.

"Yeah."

"You know," she said, "when people start getting close to me, sometimes I hurt them to keep them at a distance. You understand about that, don't you?"

I nodded my head, yes.

"I knew you did, because you're the same way. That's why we're blood sisters." She started down the steps. I could feel tears coming to my eyes and I didn't know why.

"You weren't like that with Rio," I said. "You didn't try to keep Rio at a distance."

"His dope did that for me."

I wanted her to go fast, in case I started to really cry, so I didn't say anything else. Just watched her walk up the street toward the station. To catch the subway uptown, I guess.

I slept on the church steps that night. It made me feel close to April.


Maggy, when she got back the next day, had a meeting with my mom, and I know my mom told her I'd stayed out all night. Maggy could've turned me in then, but she didn't. She told me she understood this was a hard time, what with her leaving and things at home messed up, but she was giving me another chance because she wanted me to pass my GED exam so I could go to Brooklyn College. She told me she didn't want me to fuck it all up after I'd come this far. I told her I was really going to try, and I meant it.

The next day I took the first half of the GED exam. It was two and a half hours but it was easier than I expected. Afterwards, I told Maggy I thought I did pretty good and I was going home now to study for the second half, which was tomorrow.

It was a warm, sunny day. On the way home, I stopped off at Grand Central. There weren't many people in the waiting room because the weather was so nice, just Beverly and Micki and, over on the other side, some of the old people. I said hi to Beverly and Micki, they asked if I had any cigarettes and I gave them a couple, then started out. And going out the Lexington Avenue exit, bumped into Dwayne coming in.

I hadn't seen him in about six months. He looked paler even than he usually was, and thinner, and he'd let his hair grow almost to his shoulders. He had a pint of Häagen-Dazs ice cream he was eating with a little plastic spoon.

"Jesus," he said, "Tina. Where've you been? Jail?" He stuck the spoon between his teeth and shook my hand real hard.

"Probation," I told him. "But I've been around sometimes."

"Yeah? Well, we must've kept missing each other."

I went back into the station with him and we sat on the ledge over the stairwell, in the east corridor. "So," he said, "you look good."

"I've been going to school and I just took the first half of my GED exam today."

"No shit. Was it hard?"

"I think I did okay. Gotta go back for the second half tomorrow."

"Wow," he said, "you're going to get your diploma. I think you should celebrate. Have some ice cream." He shoved the pint at me. It looked like peach. I told him no thanks. He said, "Then how about a little blast?"


Dwayne and me, we went through five vials of crack and fell asleep at three in the morning in the little park on Forty-seventh Street. I didn't wake up until nine. When I realized there was no way I was going to make it downtown for the second half of the exam, I wanted to disappear forever. Or, at least, I wanted to never have to face Maggy Reilly again.

I went back to Grand Central and looked for April, but everyone said she was on a mission. She hadn't been around for a couple days, not since I was with her at the church. So I panhandled for some cash, smoked a little more crack with Beverly, then went down to Smokey's spot and slept all day.


Late that night, I went home. Everyone was sleeping. My mom, next morning, never said a word. I was pretty sure she'd talked to Maggy and Maggy'd told her to keep a lid on.

Walking into Maggy's office was one of the hardest things I ever did. She didn't say hello, just sat there at her desk when I walked into her cubicle. She didn't look mad, she looked way past mad. Cold, like a stranger.

I couldn't look at her, so I picked up a handful of paper clips, started arranging them across my palm. I said, "I guess you know I didn't take the test yesterday." She asked if I could tell her why and I said no, I couldn't. I didn't know, myself.

She asked where I was the night before last.

I told her, "With some friends." Still not looking at Maggy. Very busy with the paper clips.

"For God's sake, Tina, what's wrong with you?"

"There's nothing wrong with me. I missed my friends."

"It's like you *had* to fuck it all up. You know I have to report this, don't you?"

I didn't answer. I couldn't, because I was starting to cry. I dropped the clips back in their little plastic well and covered my face with my hands.

That happened once before with Maggy, that I cried, and she gave me paper so I could talk by writing. Now she slid over my diary and a pen and said, "Why did you fuck up, Tina? Write it for me."

So I wrote: "I fucked up because you care!" A tear dropped down on the paper and Maggy handed me a Kleenex.

"What's going on inside? Write down what you're feeling right now."

I wrote: "What's going on is the war between the good and the bad."

"Tina, why are you hiding your face?"

I wrote: "I don't want people to look at me and say I'm a worthless thief and a slut but that's what it looks like."

Maggy read my answer, waited while I wiped my eyes, said, "So what do you want people to say when they look at you?"

The tears wouldn't stop and I couldn't see to write anymore. I told Maggy, "I want people to look at me and see the real me, the good part. But it's so deep inside it's buried about fifteen feet."

She took the pen from my hand, closed my diary, put it back in the file drawer. She said, "I'll keep the diary safe for you." Then she got up and said, "I have to turn you in now."

In the elevator, on the way to the floor where the courts are, she put her arm around me and said, "You're a strong girl, Tina. You can dig down fifteen feet if you really put your mind to it."

The last time I ever saw April was in one of the holding cells on Rikers Island after Maggy turned me in. They put me and the other women from the bus into the first cell in the Receiving Area, and there was April, over in a corner, asleep on the floor. She was curled up in a ball, with an arm under her head for a pillow.

I went right over, sat down next to her, said, "Hey, April!" Said it a couple times, but she didn't move. She was really out, probably just now coming off the binge she was on when I saw her a few nights ago. She was wearing the same clothes and she looked really grubby. I was wondering why she had fallen asleep with her sneakers on, because they were Nikes and I knew she'd been here enough times to know better, but then I figured probably she was too messed up to care if they got stolen. Also I wondered why she'd been picked up and what the charges were. Maybe she was going to be here for a while, like me.

I stayed next to her the rest of the day, guarding her, except for when I got called out for intake and my picture. When they brought dinner I made sure they left a sandwich and tea for her, for when she woke up. Mine, I ate sitting on the floor next to her. One of the women, a prostitute about my mom's age with glitter in her hair, tried to take April's food, said she could see April didn't want it.

I told her get the fuck away, I'll decide if she wants it or not. Trying to sound as tough and bad as I could. Then this big black woman, who really did look tough and bad, told the prostitute if she knew what was good for her she better leave that poor, skinny little girl's food alone.

As long as I could, I stayed awake, watching over April. Making sure nobody bothered her or took her sneakers. I remembered how, the first time I saw her, she was also sleeping, curled up just like now on the futon in Vince's apartment. She was barefoot then, in jeans and a gray Garfield sweatshirt, she was about twenty pounds heavier, and I thought she was the most glamorous thing I ever saw.

Finally, when most of the other women were sleeping too, and I could hardly keep my eyes open, I lay down next to her. The last thing I remember was looking at her hair, which was just a few inches from my face, thinking how matted it was. I had a comb in my pocket, and maybe when we woke up I could try to comb out some of those tangles.

But when I woke up she was gone, moved to another cell or maybe released. Her sandwich was still there next to me. It was stale.


They give you a social worker if you're going to be on Rikers for any length of time, and mine was named Elaine. We were supposed to meet once a week, sit at a table in the dayroom and talk. She wanted me to talk about whatever was on my mind, so I told her about April and how much I missed her. I asked Elaine if she could find out if maybe April was still here on Rikers, or if she'd already been released.

The next week, Elaine showed up with a newspaper. She put it down on the table and opened it to the second page. There was a picture of April, and a story of how she committed suicide the day before yesterday by shooting herself in the head on the front steps of St. Agnes Church.

# PART FOUR

My first night living at Uncle Tony's we're up in his room, stretched across his bed, watching a movie on TV. And during a commercial he turns to me and says, "I know that you're gay."

I start to laugh. It's actually a nervous kind of giggle. Nobody ever said anything like that to me before, especially not someone in my family.

He tells me, "I had a real bad time when I was a kid. Maybe it's a little easier for you, now."

"Yeah," I say, "probably it is."

"Well, that's good."

The commercial ends, the movie comes back on. I sit there watching Uncle Tony watching the movie.

Where I'm living with Uncle Tony is his duplex apartment on Shell Road in Brooklyn, near Coney Island. It's a really nice place: kitchen, living room, half a bathroom, and a terrace downstairs, and two bedrooms, full bathroom, and a terrace upstairs. Oh, and a Jacuzzi. Wow, do I love that Jacuzzi. The building also has a doorman. I think it's neat, living in a place that pays a man just to hold the door for you.

Uncle Tony's duplex is furnished modern, with beige wall-to-wall carpets and a white and black sofa and love seat that's sort of zebra-ish except the stripes are wavy. There's a table with an all-glass top where he keeps his crystal collection—a whiskey decanter that was part of a set but one broke, and some ashtrays with bubbles inside the glass, plus a vase with twelve ceramic roses—and he dusts these things twice a week with a feather duster that has real feathers. There is no TV in the living room, only in the bedroom. Uncle Tony doesn't think TVs belong in the living room. The kitchen has all new appliances, because the building is new, and Uncle Tony even has a microwave oven.

Uncle Tony also owns a condo in Puerto Rico. His boyfriend, Freddie, is living there. Uncle Tony goes down there once every month or two, for about a week. "You'll come with me sometime," he says.

I can't imagine going all the way to Puerto Rico, and on an airplane too. I've never been on an airplane. In fact, the only time I've ever been out of New York State was when I was in New Jersey with April. The first time was when we got caught trying to hitchhike to Florida and the other time was with the football players.

Uncle Tony is around in his fifties, kind of thin, his hair is just starting to go gray, and there's a little circle of bald on top. Which you don't notice much because whenever he goes out he wears a white straw cowboy hat. It sounds like a corny thing to wear, but on him, somehow, it looks right.

He has long fingernails, for a man. He takes very good care of them. They always look manicured, but I think he does it himself.

Another thing Uncle Tony has is a dog named Freeway. It's a shih tzu, one of those little floppy dogs with long hair, and he actually bought it for Freddie. But somehow Freeway wound up living full-time with Uncle Tony. Freeway loves Uncle Tony and Uncle Tony loves Freeway. Spoils him rotten too. Freeway doesn't eat dog food. Whatever we're having for dinner is what Freeway has. Uncle Tony has no table for eating, only the glass one in the living room for his crystal. He eats on his bed, usually watching TV, and I eat on mine, unless we both happen to be eating at the same time. Then I sit in with Uncle Tony and Freeway, who has his dinner in a special bowl at the foot of the bed.

Uncle Tony has three or four dinner specialties and he makes them over and over. His favorite two things are hamburgers and a kind of chicken in spaghetti sauce. Once in a while he cooks pork chops or homemade chicken soup.

One night we're having chicken in spaghetti sauce and I remember something he used to make when I was twelve, when we were living with him. He'd put tuna fish on top of a hamburger and melted cheese on top of that, and we'd eat it on a roll or on bread. It was his own invention and he called them Toonska-burgers.

I ask Uncle Tony if he remembers Toonska-burgers and he says, Oh, wow, it's been a long time since he's made them. I ask could we have them sometime and he says sure, then he has to grab up his napkin, because Freeway just finished eating and his face and beard are full of spaghetti sauce. If you don't wipe the food off his face right away, Freeway will go downstairs and rub it off on the zebra furniture.

The next night Uncle Tony makes us Toonska-burgers for dinner and they're every bit as good as I remember.


Even though I finished the program at Ready, Willing & Able and moved to Uncle Tony's, I'm still working there. They told me I could stay on as a day worker. I get my full check now, two hundred and fifteen dollars. They put me on Gordon's crew, which is painting, because that's one of the things I do best.

Also, I've been accepted to college starting in September. Hard to believe. After blowing my chance to go to Brooklyn College a couple years ago, with Maggy, I didn't think I'd ever get another. But at the end of the nine-month program at Ready, Willing & Able you sit down with one of the counselors and they ask, "Where are you going from here?" I told them I didn't know, so the counselor suggested I think about college and Harriet also said that was a good idea. I had my GED now, but when I found out I had to take an admissions test I thought, "No way am I going to pass it."

I went anyway, and took the test at Kingsborough Community College, which is a two-year college in Brooklyn. When I was at Samaritan Village they had given us a career quiz where you answer a bunch of questions and then they tell you what kinds of careers you'd be good at. For me it was two things. One was physical therapy and I forget what the other was. So when I applied at Kingsborough I had physical therapy as my major.

A month or so later I got a letter from Kingsborough saying I was accepted for the September term. I couldn't believe it, I was jumping all around, waving the letter in everybody's face. I told my counselor and Harriet and Uncle Tony, then I called up my mom and Jamie. "Guess what," I told everybody, "I'm going to college!"


I don't spend weekends at my mom's now that I'm living with Uncle Tony, but we go there for dinner every Sunday. And sometimes I go grocery shopping with her on Saturdays so I can chip in a little money. But things are not good.

For a start, me and my mom are having a problem because I left my cats with her and they're driving her nuts. I have two now. A few months after I found Lucky, a guy on the crew gave me another kitten that someone found, a gray one I named Misty. I couldn't take them when I moved to Uncle

Tony's because he doesn't like cats. They might scratch his furniture, and anyway, Freeway doesn't get along with other animals.

So I asked my mom if she would take them, and she said okay. I think the kids like having them, but my Mom doesn't. Lucky likes to climb the curtains and he's making rips, and both of them are always knocking over stuff. Almost every Sunday, my mom tells me something bad the cats did that week. And she gets pissed off at me and then I get mad at her. I guess I feel guilty, but I don't know what else to do with the cats.

On top of that, Jessica is going through a lot of changes. She's wearing makeup to school when she thinks Mom won't catch her, and she's started hanging out with seventeen-year-old guys. One night after dinner I sit her down in the bedroom and tell her, "Jessica, you're only thirteen, you shouldn't be wearing makeup yet. And hanging out with older guys, what's wrong with boys your own age?"

Jessica is holding my cat Misty, trying to pet him, but he keeps squirming like he wants to get free. She looks closed off. It's a new look for her.

"I'm just telling you this because I care about you. Don't mess up like me. You're smart and you need to get a good education. But you keep hanging with these guys, you're going to wind up pregnant, then you'll be a welfare mom with three kids by the time you're my age."

"Don't want to hear it," she says. "Okay? I get enough shit from Ma." She lets Misty jump off her lap and he goes streaking out. Jessica looks so young, but I can see the teenager in her too. She is getting very pretty.


I've been in touch with Matt, my friend at Samaritan. We were writing to each other, and after he got out he went to his mom's, in Queens. So now we get together sometimes. It's good to have a friend again. I haven't had one in a long time.

Me and Matt, we go to a movie or just hang out, and once in a while we play pool. That's something I've been doing a lot with Uncle Tony. Uncle Tony loves pool, even has his own set of cue sticks, and he's good at it too. Nearly always beats me. But I can nearly always beat Matt.

One night I come home late because Matt and I were playing pool and then we went for a few beers, only I had more than a few. By the time I get home I'm not exactly sober. Plus it's two or three in the morning. I've never come home this late before.

All the downstairs lights are out except for the one in the hall. I'm starting up the stairs when Uncle Tony's voice booms out of the dark living room and nearly scares the shit out of me: "Do you know what time it is?"

For a minute I'm ready to run, until I realize it's just Uncle Tony sitting there in the dark living room like some weird version of a TV sitcom mom. "Well," I say, "I know it's late . . ."

"Don't you ever do this again, Tina. If you're going to be so late, call and tell me. You understand?" I can't really see him, just his shape at the far end of the zebra couch sitting very, very straight. But from the sound of his voice I can tell he's pissed. I'm getting pissed too.

"I'm not on probation. It's my business when I come home, not yours."

"Wrong. As long as you're living here, it's my business too."

"Hey, I pay rent and I'm over twenty-one, so don't pull this daddy shit on me."

Uncle Tony gets up then, kind of slow, like it's uncomfortable for him. Lately I've been noticing he's moving more slowly. And sometimes he seems stiff, like an old man. He starts walking up the stairs holding on to the banister, which is another new thing. "In my house we do things my way. And if you don't like it, you'd better leave."

"Fine," I tell him, "I'm outta here." And I'm through the door before he even gets to the top of the stairs.

If I wasn't pretty drunk, what happened next probably wouldn't have happened. But even if I'd been sober, just hearing Uncle Tony tell me I'd better leave would've made me a little crazy. I don't think there's anything he could have said that would have hurt as much as that.

I take the elevator downstairs, push the lobby door open myself without waiting for the doorman. I'm in a rage, but I have no idea what I'm doing or where I'm going until I see the Batmobile in the front row of the building's parking lot.

Uncle Tony never locks it because it's such an old car, who would want to steal it? I yank the door open, start pounding the dashboard with my bare fists. The dashboard is jiggling, and the more I pound, the more it jiggles. For some reason, it's loose. I grab the edge, give a pull, and the whole damn thing comes off in my hands. Radio included. The radio was new, Uncle Tony just put it in last month.

Suddenly I'm tired. Not tired—exhausted. And my hands hurt. I leave the bent-up dashboard on the seat, with the radio, and stumble back into the building. Uncle Tony left the door unlocked, which is a good thing because I didn't have my keys when I ran out. And all I want to do now is go to bed and sleep forever.


Freddie is visiting this week from Puerto Rico, and he's the one who discovered the damage in the Batmobile when he went to get a haircut. He told Uncle Tony, I guess, and Uncle Tony comes barging into my room without even knocking. I'm groggy, just waking up, but the minute I see him standing there by my bed practically snorting fire, I remember what happened last night. "Did you do that to my car?" he shouts. I never heard Uncle Tony shout before.

"Yeah," I tell him, and jump out of bed. I start opening drawers and throwing my clothes into Uncle Tony's shopping cart, which I keep folded under my bed for when I get groceries.

"Tina, what the hell are you doing?"

"I'm packing. I'm leaving." I just noticed I'm still fully dressed from last night. I was so out of it I never got undressed.

"You're not going anywhere," he says.

I empty the last drawer into the cart, take my money from the dresser, and try to get around Uncle Tony and out the door. But he grabs me hard by the arm.

"Damn it, let go!"

"I *said,* you're not leaving, Tina. This is where you live."

"You don't want me now. I trashed your car." All of a sudden it feels like I'm going to cry. Damn, I hate that.

"But you're going to pay to have it fixed, aren't you?" He lets go of my arm and I sit down hard on the bed. "New dashboard, new radio, that's going to cost at least a couple hundred dollars."

I can't answer because now I am crying, so I shake my head yes. He stands there a minute looking down at me. He says, "Man, are you ever lucky I take Valium."

After he's gone I put all my clothes back.

Uncle Tony wants me here.

Uncle Tony wants me.

Somebody, I forget who, told me, "If you ever have to do time on Rikers, make them put you in the psych ward. It's the best place, especially if you never did time before." I asked how do I make them put me there and the person told me it was easy. In the Receiving Area, when you see the psychiatrist and he asks do you have suicidal thoughts, just tell him yes.

So that's what I did after Maggy turned me in, and I got to do my thirty-four days in the pysch ward, which is actually called Mental Observation. Although at the time I thought it really sucked, I found out a year later that compared to General Population, MO was a pretty easy way to serve your sentence.

There were twelve other females in Four Upper, which was my block in MO. I had my own cell and it was only a little smaller than the room we all shared at home—if anyone could call the Prince George Hotel home. I wasn't used to so much space just for me alone.

But that was the only good thing about being in jail. Every minute felt like hours, the hours felt like days, and there was nothing to do but wait around for time to go by. You spent most of your waking hours in the dayroom, watching soap operas on TV or playing cards. I tried to keep to myself, which wasn't hard, because everyone was on medication and very laidback. I read a lot. My first week I read three books, mysteries, from the library cart.

The second week was when my social worker came and told me about April. It's weird, because at the time I didn't feel much. We were at a table in the dayroom, and I tried to read the newspaper article but the words wouldn't make sense. The social worker, Elaine, said, "You can keep the paper if you want."

After she left I went back and sat there on my cot for hours, staring at April's picture, waiting to feel something.

That night, after lights out, I stood at the window in my cell for a long time looking at the sky and telling myself over and over that April was dead. And suddenly it was like she was right there in my cell next to me. I started talking to her then, told her, listen, April, I just found out you died, and if you can hear me could you please, please send some kind of sign so I know you're okay?

And that's when I saw the shooting star. It was big and bright and very clear, and it streaked all the way across the sky. I whispered, "Thank you, April."


That night I had a nightmare. April and I were on the roof of a tall building, it might have been her grandma's in Coney Island, and I was trying to keep her from jumping. I grabbed her around the waist and held on tight, but just then a big wind, like a hurricane, came and blew her out of my arms. I heard her screaming, "Help me, Tina, help me!" all the while she was falling, but it was too late. There was nothing I could do.


I got out of Rikers the second day of September and went back to live with my mom. Nothing had changed. We were still crowded into that little room, my mom and Robert were fighting all the time, Robert resented me and I resented him. My mom, I guess, was stuck in the middle. Plus, she was disappointed in me for getting sent to jail. We never really talked about it, but it was there between us all the time.

I stayed out of the house as much as I could.

My new probation officer was the lady who had been Maggy's supervisor in the Intensive Supervision Program, before Maggy left to be a parole officer. I had met her a few times. Her name was Yolanda and she was nothing like Maggy, a big black woman with a no-nonsense attitude. Kind, I guess, but firm.

I had just two meetings with Yolanda before she went away on vacation. I told her I wasn't going to be able to stand living with my family very long.

She said she'd start working on getting me into a halfway house as soon as she got back from vacation.


The minute I set foot in Grand Central, everything felt different. Looked the same, but I knew it wasn't. And that's when I started to know, inside of me, that April was gone. It wasn't real for me on Rikers, but here, where April was so much a part of this station and the people in it, here I couldn't help facing it.

I found Smokey, I found Beverly, I found Micki, I found Dwayne, I found Corey and Francisco. Everybody had an opinion, you could tell they'd all done a lot of talking about it. Beverly and Micki told me, "That girl didn't shoot herself, she was murdered. I don't care what the cops say." I asked why they thought April was murdered and Beverly said it was because no one would want to die if they could get high on crack instead.

There was somebody on the steps with her when she died; I had read that in the papers. He was a guy I knew, called Santos, one of April's robbing partners. Corey thought maybe Santos killed her and so did a few others, but Santos got picked up by the cops right after the shooting and he had no gunpowder on his hands. The only gunpowder was on April's hands so the cops let him go. Two weeks after April died, Santos got sent to jail for breaking into an apartment on the Upper East Side. It was in the *Post*, that's how everyone found out. The newspaper called him "the East Side Cat Burglar."

Most everyone else thought April shot herself. Dwayne said she'd been on a four-day binge and was probably so bugged out she didn't know what she was doing. Then he asked if I wanted to get high. I told him no, thanks.

I asked Corey if he knew where she got the gun from. Corey didn't, but Francisco told me it was stolen from a van and April was trying to sell it.

Everybody I talked to, it seemed they already got through the shocked part and the sad part. For them it had happened three weeks ago, but for me it was happening now.


Smokey was the only one who still seemed messed up about April. He didn't look good. He was always small and skinny but he'd lost more weight while I was away, and I think a couple more teeth. His beard was growing wild, like gray Brillo.

"There was nobody could have saved that girl," he said. "Nobody." He shook his head back and forth, back and forth, like the movement was part of his sadness. It was a hot day, more like summer than September, and we were sitting in Bryant Park with a couple beers and some reefer.

I told him, "I should've been there. I would have taken the gun away and talked to her. She'd still be alive if I was there."

"You think she would've listened to you? You know April, she didn't listen to nobody."

"Well," I said, "her father. If she went to California, that could have saved her. She was waiting for him to come get her."

"She told you that bullshit story too? That her daddy's coming for her?"

"He wasn't?"

"Hell, no, he wasn't. He let her call collect whenever she wanted, but Daddy sure as hell wasn't about to let her move in and tangle up his life."

I popped open another Budweiser. Even if April made up the story about her father coming for her, I don't think she was lying to me. I think the lie was for her.


While Yolanda was away I started drinking a lot. Panhandling for cash, getting someone to buy me vodka or brandy when I could afford it, beer when I couldn't. I was trying to stop the pain, but I wasn't sure exactly where the pain was coming from.

Sometimes I came home drunk. If Robert wasn't there, my mom would just ignore me, which was one of her ways of showing how mad she was. I'd crawl into Robby's bunk and go to sleep. But if Robert was there, it was fight night. I did my best to keep my mouth shut because I knew I'd just make it worse. But he'd tell my mom, "Christ, look at her, coming home drunk, aren't you going to do anything?" He'd go on and on until my mother let loose, until she screamed and yelled and called me names.

Robby would be crying, Jessica would be comforting him and trying not to cry herself, and I'd be under Robby's covers trying to shut out the madhouse.


I went over to St. Agnes Church a few times. I heard it was three steps down from the top that she shot herself, so that's where I sat.

There was a bouquet of flowers on the step each time I went. A different one every day. Daisies once, pink flowers another time, and the third time there was a bouquet of six roses.

I asked at Grand Central did anybody know who was putting the flowers there. Everybody had seen them, but nobody knew who was doing it.


We were all in the waiting room. I was flat out on a bench, drifting in and out. There was this special place inside me where everything was calm and peaceful, and I could get there sometimes if I drank the right amount. So I was lying there floating, and sometimes I heard the singing and sometimes

I didn't. Hershey and his trio were practicing "This Little Light of Mine." Over and over they sang it, because Hershey was telling one of the guys he wasn't coming in at the right places. I drifted off again. When I came back, Beverly was sitting down at the end of the bench near my feet, eating a doughnut and listening, and Hershey had gone on to a different song.

I sat up. This song they were doing now, it was about April, even though the words didn't say so. I knew it was, but I didn't know why. Who did they think they were, singing about April like that?

I said, "Who do you think you are, singing about April like that?"

Hershey didn't hear me, but Beverly did. She said, "You're full of drink, go back to sleep."

She didn't care, either.

Nobody cared.

"Nobody cares," I said. "Nobody cares!" I hollered at Hershey. This time he heard. He stopped singing and so did Lester and Sam.

That's when I realized what the song was: "Under the Boardwalk," the one April used to sing sometimes with Hershey's trio. She was dead but they were just going on singing it like it wasn't connected to her anymore. They had no right to be singing that song when April was dead.

"You people," I hollered, "don't understand anything!"

They were looking at me like I was crazy, and maybe I was. "Tina," Hershey said, "what don't we understand?"

"She's dead and I loved her, and everybody just goes on like nothing happened!" I was on my feet now, screaming.

I ran out of the waiting room, walked for hours all around Manhattan. Across Central Park and back again, down to the Village, back uptown, over to the East River, back to Central Park. I was crying and people were looking and I didn't give a shit.

Just pushed my way through crowds, crossed at red lights, walked in front of buses, didn't look what direction I was going in. Needed to keep on moving, needed to keep on crying.


My mom told me if I came home drunk one more time I had to move out. I know Robert put her up to that.

Yolanda came back from vacation, told me to sit tight and hang in at my mom's and she'd have a spot for me soon in a place called Project Greenhope. It was a halfway house up on 119th Street. I told her, great, it couldn't be soon enough for me.

I went into Greenhope at the end of September. It wasn't a bad place and at first I really did try. There were twelve other females there, mostly in their thirties and forties, all people who were off the drugs and on the wagon, trying to set up their lives.

I was happier there than at my mom's. But then Yolanda started putting pressure on me. She was going to get me into a short night course for my GED, since I only needed review in order to take the exam again, and during the day I had to have a job. Like in McDonald's or Woolworth's or something shitty like that. And save up money so that before winter was over I could get my own apartment.

Whoa. Hold on a minute. *Please.*

I was starting to feel strangled. Depressing job, night school, get my own apartment—help! I'm eighteen years old, I'm still a kid, I want to stay a kid a little longer.

And who says I even wanted my own apartment yet? On the streets, the only responsibility I had was to stay alive. Responsibility is okay, but I needed to work up to it little by little. You don't start a five-year-old in high school.


Project Greenhope was in Harlem. There are probably more drugs on every block of Harlem than in all of midtown Manhattan. And every day when I went out, even if I was just going to the corner deli for cigarettes, I had my choice of anything you could think of. They were selling crack on the corners, heroin in the doorways, and reefer, angel dust, and mescaline in between. I tried to ignore them, but it wasn't easy because I was starting to feel stressed out. Yolanda was putting so much pressure on me, I needed a little escape.


Beverly had started selling crack. She went uptown to buy it so she could afford to sell it cheap, five bucks a vial. I bought just one vial, didn't slam-dunk or anything, just took a little hit every hour or so. It lasted most of the day. I figured that almost didn't count.

But by the beginning of November I was back at Grand Central full-time. Sleeping in the Clubhouse, which was still up on the ledge and still in just as good shape as when they took me to jail last winter. Shiv had done a great job.

I started hanging around with Harley sometimes, but he was always hassling me because I went AWOL. I hung out with Corey once in a while, but he wasn't around much. I don't know what he was doing, but I think he had forgotten about saving money for Georgia.

Then I got together with Jackie again and started staying with him at night. He was doing pretty much the same thing as last year, breaking into cars and sleeping in the Roosevelt Hotel bathroom, except now he was always complaining he was sick. He'd tell me, "My hair's falling out, look," and he'd pull out a handful to prove it. He wore a blue knit cap to hide all the bald patches, even slept in it. Once he told me he threw up blood. I told him to go to the clinic at Bellevue but he just said, "Are you crazy? They'll find out I'm doing drugs and arrest me."

Jackie didn't come around Grand Central a lot and I didn't want to be around the station much, either. Yolanda had a warrant out on me for violating probation and the cops had started telling me I better turn myself in or they'd have to pick me up.

Jackie didn't want to talk about April. I brought it up once and right away he changed the subject.


Robby's birthday was at the end of November. He was going to be four. I didn't want to go see him, didn't have the nerve to face my mom, so I bought a card with a red clown pin that said "4 Years Old," stuck a five-dollar bill in and left it at the hotel desk for Robby. Just hoping Robert wouldn't be the one to pick it up.

Also, right before Thanksgiving, I called Yolanda from a pay phone. I wasn't high, but I'd been drinking a lot that day.

She said, "Tina, where are you?"

I said, "I can't tell you."

She was quiet a minute like she was waiting for me to say more, then she asked, "When are you coming in to report?"

"I can't. If I do you're going to arrest me."

"So I don't understand why you're calling."

"Well, I just want you to know I'm alive, that's all. Because you're nice, and I thought maybe you might be a little worried."

"You're right. I was very worried. Tina, come on in and we'll try to work a deal."

"What kind of deal?"

"Not over the phone. Come in and we'll talk about it."

I said, "Happy Thanksgiving, Yolanda," and hung up.


April's ex-boyfriend, Rio, was around Grand Central again. He quit shooting heroin because he was scared of AIDS. Started smoking crack but then, after April died, he decided he wanted to get off crack too. He spent a few weeks upstate with his family and now he was on the list for a bed in a rehab place.

We went to the Salvation Army together for Thanksgiving dinner and he talked about April the whole time. He said, "April, man, I told her a hundred times, get out of here, this is a dead end. If she'd listened to me this never would've happened." He told me I should get out too, because if you don't have money or drugs nobody here gives a shit about you. He said, "Don't wind up like April."

I told him, "I can think of worse things." We finished eating, went back to Grand Central, down to the tunnels to get warm, have a little smoke. Rio took a couple hits, but mostly he was talking about April.

"You know what her ambition was? To be a mother. Have eight or ten kids. I think she would've made a good mother, if she would've grown up."

I emptied a whole vial into my stem. Slam-dunked it. I figured I needed it, what with all this talk about April. But Rio wasn't smoking anymore.

"You know what my ambition is now? To get free of all these fuckin' drugs, get a job, make my family proud of me. Live a normal life. Because people told me the most beautiful high is just being normal."

I think he meant it too. But last I heard he got picked up on a robbery charge and sent upstate for three to seven years.


Thanksgiving night, sleeping with Jackie in the Roosevelt bathroom, I had another dream about April. It was just as real as the last one, on Rikers, after she died.

We were in that abandoned building, the one where we were staying with Lorenzo a couple years ago, and it was Halloween. April said, "Let's go trick-or-treating on Forty-second Street," and I asked her why and she said because she was hungry and we could get some candy and food. It was very weird because, up to a point, it was like reliving what had really happened. When I said we didn't have costumes she said sure we did, we could wear our own dirty stuff and go as bums. Except we switched clothes.

Everything was exactly the way it had actually happened until we went down to the subway. And then, while we were standing on the platform waiting for the train, I suddenly remembered that April was going to die in less than two years. I thought, Okay, this all happened before and it ended with her dying, so maybe if I just do something different I can change the ending.

The train came rushing into the station. I said, "April, no, don't get on it."

"Why not? It's the express."

"No, please, just don't get on it. Let's not go trick-or-treating. I decided I don't want to go."

"Fuck you, you said you would and I'm not going alone." The doors of the train rolled open. April grabbed my arm and started pulling me inside.

"No," I told her. "No, let's do something else. Anything you want, I'll do anything you want. *Please.*"

We were both inside the train now. She was looking at me like I'd flipped out. The doors rolled shut, the train started, and she said, "What the hell is wrong with you?"

I was crying now. In front of all the people on the train, I was crying. I told her, "I was trying to make a different ending!" but the train was so noisy she never heard.


Jerry, in the deli, when I went to get cigarettes, told me, "I thought you got out, Tina. Why are you back?"

I shouldn't have gone in there. I should've gone to the newsstand. "Just give me my cigarettes, okay?"

He put a pack of Newports on the counter and rang up the cash register. "You look like hell."

"Thanks."

"You can do better, kid. You don't belong here."

I put the cigarettes in my pocket, told him, "Later," and I was out the door.

Other people who worked in the station were starting to hassle me too. One of the janitors, this old gray-haired Hispanic guy who knew me since I first came, he was pushing his cleaning cart across the main concourse when I was panhandling one night and he stopped to tell me, "I thought you went back home when your friend died. It makes me sad to see you here again."

I told him, "Hey, I'm doing fine."

"Pretty girl like you shouldn't be here. I have four daughters, did I ever tell you? If you were one of mine I would never let you live like this. I would come pronto, I would take you right home."

I wanted to tell him if I was one of his daughters I probably wouldn't be here in the first place, but I just said, "Don't worry about me, okay?"

Before he pushed his cart away he gave me three dollars. Told me, "Now, this is for food, you understand? Not for something else." I promised to buy pizza with it and stuck it in my jacket pocket so it wouldn't get mixed up with the crack money, which was in my jeans.


I was drinking as much as I was smoking so I could at least stay drunk when I wasn't high, because it was the only way to try not to notice that Christmas was coming.

I called Yolanda again. She sounded glad to hear me. Not pissed at all. "Tina, are you okay?"

"Yeah. I'm fine."

"You don't sound fine."

"I've been drinking a little."

"Tina, I want you to come to my office. I want to see for my own eyes that you're okay."

"No way. I'm not going back to Rikers."

"I told you, we'll work a deal."

"What kind of deal?"

"Turn yourself in, I'll see that you get put in Bellevue for observation. Otherwise, if I have to have you picked up, you'll do time again."

"Let me think about it."

"Don't think too long, Tina, because I'm going to have you picked up soon. And I really don't want to do that."

"Give me until after the holidays. Okay?"

"And then?"

"Then I'll turn myself in. When the holidays are over."

Yolanda didn't say anything for a minute. Then I heard her sigh. "Take care of yourself, Tina. Please be careful. I'll see you in January."

The cuts I had weren't healing like they used to. I'd have a cut on my finger and it wouldn't go away, it would get all red, sometimes even swollen.

I tried washing with soap and water, but it didn't help. Anyway, my hands would be dirty again in an hour. There was no way to keep them clean the way I was living. Last time I'd had a shower was five or six weeks ago when I was still at Project Greenhope.

I tried pouring vodka on some of the cuts. It stung, but they still didn't heal.

Jamie, the writer, got me a tube of antibiotic ointment, called Bacitracin, and a little box of Band-Aids. Told me to go in the ladies' room, wash the cuts good, then put the ointment and Band-Aids on. I told her, My throat hurts too, and I've got these swollen glands in my neck. I asked her, What do you think it might be?

She said, Maybe strep. She said I should go to Bellevue and have them check me over.

I didn't, though. I couldn't. Because what if it was AIDS?

Jerry, the old janitor, a couple of the conductors, and even one or two cops, like Korsoff, were all saying the same thing: you're young and cute and smart, you have potential, you have a future. What are you doing here?

Sometimes I wondered that too. I used to be here because of April, but now she was gone. So why was I still here? If it was true what they were telling me, that I was pretty and smart, that I had potential and a future, then there must be something wrong with me to get stuck here. I wasn't normal. A normal person would never live like this.

If I wasn't normal, then I was a weirdo. A freak. A misfit.

So, then, didn't I belong here?

I rolled up my sleeves and jammed a lit cigarette into my bare arm. Jammed it and grinded it so hard the cigarette went out. I whispered, "Take that, and that, and that!"

It didn't hurt. Not enough, anyway. Not enough to punish myself for living like a bum. Not enough to punish myself for being a weirdo and a freak and a misfit. Not enough to punish myself for letting the only person in the world I truly loved die.

I meant what I said to Yolanda about turning myself in. But I was high the week after New Year's, and then it was my birthday and I wasn't going to turn myself in on my birthday. Then I kept putting it off because whenever I thought about it, I panicked. Told myself, I'm not going to do it today—tomorrow, tomorrow, tomorrow. And tomorrow never came.

But the warrant squad did. Yolanda waited until the twelfth, and then she sent them after me.

It wasn't so bad this time, being on Rikers. I knew the routine, I was almost comfortable with it. On the jail bus there was a girl sitting next to me, she asked if I'd ever been to Rikers before. I told her yeah. She told me this was her first time. She looked as scared as I felt the first time I was on this bus.

I told her, Listen, if you think you're going to be here a while, tell the psychiatrist you're suicidal and they'll put you in Mental Observation, because that's the easiest place. She told me, Oh, I will, thanks a lot. I told her, That's okay, I'm glad to help out a new girl.

THE BEACHES IN PUERTO RICO are like nothing you'll ever see in New York: the sand is clean and white, the water is warm and so clear you can see right down to the bottom, and there is no seaweed or trash. Everywhere there are palm trees and bright flowers. It looks just like a postcard.

I spend most days on the beach working on my tan. I have my headphones, I have a book, and when I get too hot lying in the sun I go into the warm blue water, swim around a little, then come out and bake some more.

Uncle Tony and Freddie's apartment is on the seventh floor of a condo near the beach. There's just one bedroom, so I have to sleep on the pull-out in the living room and that's not too comfortable because only the bedroom is air-conditioned. And it's hot at night, sometimes too hot to sleep. I have to get up and go soak my head in cold water.

I flew to Puerto Rico alone because Uncle Tony was already down there. Freeway went to stay with my mom.

I was so nervous. My first plane trip and I have to go alone. Taking off was scary, and it didn't help to see some of the Spanish people on the plane holding rosary beads and praying. But once we were up in the sky everyone seemed to relax, so I did too.

I was the only person sitting in my row, so I had the window seat. I thought if I looked out the window I could see all the places we were flying over, but we were way up in the clouds. When you're in the clouds they don't look thick and cottony like you'd expect, it's more like being in the middle of a fog.

And it's a long way to fall.

I moved away from the window, put my feet up, turned on my headphones. Tried to doze but couldn't. When they told us to put our seat belts on because we were landing in San Juan, out came all the rosary beads and the praying started again. When we landed, everyone clapped. I almost clapped, myself. I looked out the window, saw the runway underneath us and thought, Thank God!

Uncle Tony was at the airport waiting for me. He hugged me, he asked if I had a window seat and I told him yes, but there wasn't anything to see except when we were taking off and landing.

It's funny, because when we took off from New York we flew right over a little island. I could see it down there clearly. Even though it was tiny it was jammed with buildings, and there were streets winding through it and a little bridge that connected it to the mainland. We passed completely over it before I realized that was Rikers Island. I guess I didn't recognize it at first because I never saw it from up above.

Besides getting in a lot of beach time, we also get in some sightseeing. Uncle Tony takes me to Old San Juan, which is the part of the city where the historic buildings are, and also the fort.

Uncle Tony and Freddie take me to the rain forest too. Freddie is from Puerto Rico, so he knows the names of most of the flowers and plants and trees. But all the walking is hard for Uncle Tony. He's been carrying a cane around the whole time I've lived with him, but he told me it was just for show. It's a polished wooden cane and he said he liked the image. Only now, in the rain forest, I notice he's using it the whole time, and still he can't keep up with Freddie and me. He has to keep stopping to catch his breath.

That night Freddie asks if I want to go out to one of the clubs. I ask Uncle Tony, "Are you coming, too?" and he says no, he's beat. I ask him, "Are you okay?" and he says sure.

Because I know that a couple years ago he had an operation. He had kidney stones. I'm wondering if maybe he's having a problem with that again.

The day before Uncle Tony and I leave, Freddie's family has a big dinner for us. They live in a small house up in the mountains. There are lots of little kids and three or four adults and when we get there they have a whole pig roasting over an open fire in the yard. I mean the *whole* pig—head, feet, tail, and everything.

They all speak only Spanish, so Freddie has to translate for me. When it comes time for dinner we eat outside in the yard, on paper plates. They just cut off pieces of pig and fill up everyone's plate. Sounds gross, but that pig is great. Everything is. There's also rice and beans, and sweet fried bananas they call "platanos," and other things I've never had before. I don't understand the names of everything, but there is nothing I don't like. Just tasting all those different things is fun.

The next day I fly back to New York with Uncle Tony. It's early September, and school is going to be starting soon.

I go over to pick up Freeway and my mom tells me she got rid of my cats. I say, "What do you mean, you got rid of my cats?"

"It's too hard for me, I can't take it, they're climbing on my curtains all the time. And the kids don't clean the litter box."

"What do you mean, 'got rid of'?"

"Then Tony gives me Freeway too."

"And you couldn't tell me first? You couldn't give me a chance to do something with them?"

"How, Tina? You were in Puerto Rico. And don't holler." I'm not hollering. I'm crying. I don't understand how a person could just get rid of a couple of animals. Not even give me a chance to do something about it. I grab Freeway's leash. "So I'll see you and Tony on Sunday?"

"You won't see me," I tell her, and slam out the door with the dog.

I've left their presents in a bag on the kitchen table, the things I brought back from Puerto Rico. There's T-shirts for Jessica and Robby, with a parrot and the name "San Juan" across the top. For my mom, there's a blouse with flowers on it.

The reason I didn't ask my mom what she did with Lucky and Misty is because I don't want to know.

I quit work at Ready, Willing & Able at the beginning of September, before I went to Puerto Rico. I told Uncle Tony I'd get a night job, because I'll be in school during the day.

Leaving Ready, Willing & Able makes me realize how important it's been to me. I learned how to work there, to take pride in my work and in earning a real paycheck. And also, I think I'm beginning to see how important Samaritan Village was, too, even though at the time I didn't know it. Ready, Willing & Able has been my transition from living as a homeless person to living in normal society, but Samaritan Village, even though I kept fucking up when I was there, got me clean and ready to start making that transition. I think they both came along in my life at exactly the right time.


Kingsborough Community College is in Brooklyn, and it's an enormous place. The first couple of weeks I'm getting lost at least twice a day.

These are my classes: math, English, biology, and Introduction to Psychology. Math and English I have to take, my adviser told me biology would be easy, and the psychology course is because I thought it would be interesting.

It's a cool feeling to be in college. This is one place I didn't think I'd ever see the inside of. But it's also kind of intimidating because most of the students in my classes are younger than me, eighteen or nineteen, right out of high school, and they all seem so sure of themselves. Like they fit in and they know it. I look like I fit in too, and I'm trying hard not to let anybody see that I don't.

I'm also trying hard to do well in my schoolwork. Math is hardest, even though it's just basic math. English isn't easy, either, because the teacher has us reading poems and we have to explain what they mean. Even though I'm good at reading, understanding poetry is difficult. It's not at all like reading a story. In a story, what they say is what they mean. In poems, sometimes you have no idea what the hell they're talking about.

I like biology. The teacher is nice. He doesn't just stand there and lecture, he has us discussing things. If there's something you don't understand he'll go over it until you do. We spend the first part of the course learning about food and vitamins and how they affect your health and your aging.

My favorite class is psychology. We study about basic human needs, and also behavior conditioning. It's so interesting that sometimes I read more than we're assigned, just keep reading until I'm two or three chapters ahead. When the teacher asks the class a question I usually know the answer.


When I come home, Uncle Tony always asks what I learned today. I tell him about psychology and the basic human needs and Pavlov's dog experiments, and I tell him a lot about the biology course too. I give him advice about what he should and shouldn't do. Like, since he smokes a lot, and smoking kills beta-carotene, he should start taking vitamin C to replace it.

One night he's made hamburgers and we're eating together on his bed, watching a special on ancient Egypt. During a commercial I tell him, "Another thing, you've gotta start broiling hamburgers, not frying them, because you eat too much fat and fat is very bad for you."

"Oh," he says, "that's really interesting."

"Yeah. And, you know, I learned today you shouldn't eat the skin from chicken either because that's *really* fatty."

"No kidding," Uncle Tony says. "I'm going to try to remember that. What else did they teach you?"

So then I tell him how we talked about exercising, how that can slow the aging process and help keep you healthy because it strengthens your heart and lungs and muscles. "Maybe if you got some exercise every day it might help you not be so tired and short-winded. Like you could start slow, maybe walk around the block once a day, and do a little more every week."

"That's not a bad idea," he says, and reaches down to pick a piece of hamburger out of Freeway's beard. Uncle Tony always seems interested in what I tell him about school, but I'm beginning to get the feeling he already knows it all. That he's only putting on an act for me, to keep *me* interested. Because nothing ever changes. He never does buy vitamin C, he keeps on frying hamburgers and eating the skin off his chicken, and he never walks anywhere he can drive, even if it's only a block.

The only part I don't like about school is, I have no real friends. I get along fine with the others, but mostly I stick to myself. I have one friend outside of school, Matt, from Samaritan Village, but we don't spend much time together. He's always pulling jokes and acting silly. I'd rather sit out on the terrace alone with a six-pack of Corona. Which is how I spend most evenings, when I'm not inside watching movies with Uncle Tony.

At school I see groups of kids eating lunch together, working on their homework, sitting outside on nice days. It's like they all belong to one gigantic club but I'm not a member and I don't know what it takes to join.

One day I get into a conversation with a girl from English class, and out of nowhere she asks if I want to go to the mall on Saturday with her and her cousin. I tell her, "Sure." This is on a Thursday and I have two whole days to chew up my nails and worry about whether I'm going to make an ass of myself. Good thing she didn't ask on a Monday, I would have chewed down all my fingers too.

Her name is Imani, and I don't make an ass out of myself at the mall. In fact, once I stop feeling nervous, I actually have a good time.

Imani is a black girl, a year older than me, and she's from Africa. Her parents are an interracial couple who adopted her when they were in Africa with the Peace Corps. She's smart and really nice, she wants to be a gym teacher, and for almost two months she is my friend.

"It's just too hard to be with you," she tells me at the end. "You don't ever want to go anywhere, you don't ever want to be with other people. You're too damned shy."

I'm more than shy, I'm terrified. Imani is always wanting to go to clubs, or to someone's party, and I'm too scared. If I go to her house and she's got more than one other person there I freeze up. Can't talk, can't move, just sit there like a bump on a log.

"I can't help it," is what I tell her. Because I don't want to explain that when I'm in a social situation with people my age, normal people, I don't have a clue how to act. I don't even know how to have a simple conversation. All I know how to do is wonder if they're pointing me out and making fun of me because they can tell I'm different.

"That's bullshit, that you can't help it," she says. She's trying to get me to meet some of her friends tonight, at a club. "All you have to do is relax and stop thinking how shy you are and you'll have a good time."

"It's not that simple."

Maybe I'm not being fair, expecting her to understand. I've told Imani a little about my background, but not much. Mainly just that I had a drug problem, and I went into rehab, and now I'm clean. Not enough so she can get some idea about where I'm really coming from.

"Yeah, it is simple. You just go and have fun. That sounds pretty simple to me."

But I don't go. I can't go. This is a phone conversation and Imani slams the receiver down. On Monday, in English, she won't even talk to me.


As if it's not bad enough losing the only friend I have, Uncle Tony is bugging me about getting a job. Every night he asks if I have any possibilities, and every night I have to tell him no. "Then you're not trying hard enough," he says. "Make a little effort, will you?"

I know he's worried because the money I have from Ready, Willing & Able is almost gone and he depends on my rent. He doesn't work regularly at interior decorating anymore. I'm not sure why and he doesn't talk about it. But I know he doesn't have much money.

Trouble is, it's hard to find night jobs, especially if you don't have many skills. I called a few places I saw in newspaper ads but they all wanted experience: waitress jobs, salesclerk in a men's store, selling tickets at a movie theater. I even called one lady who needed someone to take care of her baby while she worked a night shift. I told her I had experience baby-sitting, which isn't a total lie because I've taken care of my little brother and sister plenty, but she wanted references. I can hammer down walls, put up Sheetrock, and paint your ceiling, lady, but I can't prove I'm qualified to diaper your baby.

One night Uncle Tony comes home with a bag of groceries and tells me Pathmark has a HELP WANTED sign in the window.

"I don't have any experience working in supermarkets."

"The sign didn't say anything about experience. So get over there tonight after dinner and see about it."

Guess what—they hire me. As a *cashier*. Can you believe it? They don't care if I have no experience, they give you two days' training. Shit. I really didn't want that damn job.

At Pathmark you can wear your own clothes, you just have to wear a blue smock over them. So I don't have to change to go to work but sometimes, if I shower or take a Jacuzzi, I do anyway. One night I stay too long in the Jacuzzi and I'm almost late for work. Uncle Tony has company. He's downstairs talking with his lawyer, but he left me a pork chop for dinner.

I know why the lawyer is here. Uncle Tony is suing the hospital where he had the kidney operation. Why he's suing, I'm not sure, but he's had this lawsuit going for at least as long as I've been living with him. I'm rushing to my room to get dressed so I'll have time to eat, and I hear part of the conversation downstairs. "You know," the lawyer is saying, "if the judge or anyone asks, you have to tell them you're HIV positive."

I stop right there in the hall.

"Look, I don't want to tell them. I shouldn't have to." That's my uncle now.

"You're paying for my advice, Tony. You better take it." That's the lawyer again.

Then Uncle Tony says something more about not wanting to talk about it to anyone and the lawyer says something more about how he has to, and that's all they're saying now, just going back and forth, so I go into my room and start rushing around getting dressed.

We had Seminars at Samaritan Village about AIDS, and they showed us pictures of people who had it. They all looked really, really sick, they had sores and rashes and weighed about fifty pounds. But Uncle Tony doesn't look sick. He uses the cane now and he gets tired easy, but that's because he's getting older and doesn't take care of himself or eat right. Also, he's had kidney problems.

So what I just heard downstairs, I don't fully understand. In the Seminars they never said a person could have AIDS but *look* healthy.

I eat my dinner in the kitchen standing up, grab my coat, and say good night.

Uncle Tony is sitting on the couch with Freeway on his lap. He looks tired, or maybe it's because the light from the floor lamp is making dark shadows under his eyes and around his mouth. The lawyer—his name is Mel—is on the love seat with a bunch of papers spread on the coffee table in front of him. There is also a half-empty glass of something, probably Pepsi.

"Got your keys, Tina?" Uncle Tony always asks that.

"Yep."

"Because I'll probably be asleep when you come home." He always says that too, but usually he's up, watching TV.

"Okay." I wait a second, because he's got one last thing he always says.

"Don't take any wooden nickels."

"I won't, Uncle Tony." That one, I don't understand. I've never seen a wooden nickel. Don't think there is such a thing.

I lock the door behind me. I can hear them start up talking again, but I can't hear what they're saying.

I'm not going to tell him what I heard. He told his lawyer he doesn't what to talk about it, and I guess I don't, either.

THE JUDGE GAVE ME FOUR months on Rikers, I did less than three. Eighty-one days, if you want to be exact.

In Receiving, I told the psychiatrist I thought about suicide sometimes and he got me sent back to Mental Observation. They put me in Four Upper, the same block I was in last August. The girl from the bus also wound up there. I guess she took my advice.

MO was a comfortable place to be, and this time I was pretty run-down when I got there. The sores on my hands were healing from using Bacitracin, but I still had the swollen glands and I'd lost a lot of weight in the past couple months. To be honest, I didn't mind landing in a safe warm place where you got three meals a day, and a cot with clean sheets, and antidepressants to make you feel not-so-shitty. There was also a doctor to give me penicillin for my throat, and there was structure to my days. They told you what to do and when to do it, and they also told you what you couldn't do. It was nice to have everything taken out of my hands again for a while.

And now that I was here, I could stop worrying all the time about being arrested.

So the eighty-one days went by. I slept, ate, read, watched TV. Also they put me in the Inmate Education Program and I went to class every day for my GED. They tested me, and my reading level was tenth grade, third month, and my math level was eighth grade, sixth month. They said that was good, but my scores in summer school last year were higher.

The view from my cell window was a little dirt road leading away from the jail, along the water. I spent a lot of time at the window daydreaming about walking down that road. But where it led to, I could never picture.

I got released on April Fools' Day. My probation was finished because the judge decided I served enough time instead. No one to report to anymore. I was totally free.


I went straight back to Grand Central, of course. Because where else was there? I didn't give a shit about anything, anyway, except for getting high. And that's what I did the first three days, went on a nice long binge with Smokey. I had eighty-one days to make up for.


He was another middle-aged business guy—they all looked pretty much the same—and he had me staked out. Kept walking back and forth, trying to be inconspicuous, but he was eyeing me. I was just wanting to be alone, sitting on the ledge by Jerry's deli drinking blackberry brandy, and he was wanting me to be his whore.

Well, I'd been in jail a couple times, so that made me a full-fledged criminal. Might as well live up to the part. Maggy wasn't in my life anymore. There was nobody in my life I had to be on good behavior for.

I finished the whole bottle of brandy and thought, "Okay, mister businessman, come around one more time, I'm gonna get you."

And I would've tried to pull it off myself, but then Francisco came over to see if I had any smoke. He'd been in jail, too, but for much longer than me. He looked older somehow, and he'd grown a beard.

The commuter was over by the newsstand flipping through a magazine. I pointed him out to Francisco, I said, "If that bastard comes around again I'm going to take him down to Track 105. You meet us there."

The guy came around again, of course. I gave him a nod, he asked if I had a place, and I said, "What do you want?" He told me a blow job. That's something I learned on Rikers, that you've got to get him to say something first. Otherwise, if he's a cop, you could get arrested for soliciting.

I got him down to the platform, behind the staircase. Francisco was waiting until I had his pants down, because that's when they're most vulnerable, and then he was there yelling, "What're you doing with my sister!"

The guy said, "I'm sorry, I'm sorry, I didn't know it was your sister," but Francisco yoked him up and I started digging in his pants for his wallet, which wasn't easy since they were down around his ankles.

I don't think Francisco would've hurt the guy if he hadn't grabbed me, but even though Francisco had him yoked up the guy got my arm and wouldn't let go. I fought and cursed and tried to kick him, and he kneed me in the stomach, and that's when Francisco pulled out his butterfly knife and used it, closed, to hit the guy on the head. Had to hit him hard a couple times before he loosened his grip and I could get away.

We spent the night in the little plaza on Forty-seventh Street. There was seventy-five dollars in the guy's wallet, and we had gone uptown so we could get cheap bundles. We each smoked around fifteen vials that night. I went back to Grand Central the next day, sat there drinking beer on the ledge by Jerry's deli, and when I saw the same guy walk by—only now his head was bandaged—I didn't move. I remember when he looked at me I thought, Oh, shit, and then, when he walked away, I thought, I really should leave. But my mind and body were so fucked up from all that crack I just sat there like an idiot.

He came back ten minutes later with three cops. One came from the stairs, one came from behind, another came up beside me. I knew them all. They said, "Let's go, Tina." I didn't say anything. Just went.

The charges were assault and robbery. I was back on Rikers a week after my release.


What is there to tell about eight months in jail? There are three or four main things that happen, and they happen over and over again, and then over and over after that. Sometimes you want to scream, like you're stuck in a sort of bad dream and it keeps repeating. But there's a certain comfort in it, too, especially if you're coming from the streets. If you're coming from the streets, being bored is actually kind of relaxing.


They put me in General Population. I asked to go back to Mental Observation but this time they didn't listen to me.

General Population was a zoo, and one of the worst parts, if you're new, is the cafeteria. My first meal there was dinner, and the cafeteria was so crowded and noisy I would've run back to my cell if I wasn't so hungry. You had to get in line. They give you your food on a plastic tray through a little slot, with a plastic knife and fork and spoon wrapped up like in fast-food places, and then you have to find a place to sit.

There were thirty or forty tables, each one almost full, everyone shouting and yelling back and forth. I stood there with my tray looking around for an empty place, but as soon as I found one and sat down the women started hollering at me to move my white ass. I wasn't about to argue with them.

I found a seat at another table, and they didn't make me move but they must've known I was new. I ate my peas and one of them said, loud, "Lookit her, she's eating those nasty mushy peas." There was some kind of scalloped potatoes and someone else hollered, "Man, that girl is eating those disgusting potatoes, don't those potatoes look like throw-up?" Then they started talking about all the other gross things the potatoes looked like.

Me, I kept my head low, kept shoveling in the food, tried not to look at anybody or let them know I heard anything. I felt really nervous and self-conscious, though. Also embarrassed. Because to me, the food was good.

After that, I always tried to find places to sit where there were other women from my cell block. They weren't real friendly, but at least nobody bothered me. I saw women get beat up a couple times just for sitting down at the wrong table.


My cell in General Population was exactly like the one in MO. The sliding door had a small glass panel with bars, and inside was a cot, a chair, a desk, a locker, a toilet, and sink. From the window I could see part of La Guardia Airport and also the Bulova clock factory, which faces the airport.

Here's what you do each day: wake up, eat breakfast, sit in the dayroom and watch TV or play cards, eat lunch, go out to the rec yard for one hour, sit in the dayroom and watch TV or play cards, eat dinner, sit in the dayroom and watch TV or play cards, and get locked up in your cell for the night.

After the first week it got easier. One of the women from my block asked me, "You want to play cards?" They were playing Spades and somebody was short a partner. Spades was the big thing at Rikers. Everyone played, and you played for cigarettes, but you needed four people to make up the two teams. I said, yeah, sure. I already knew how to play from MO.

You start playing Spades every day in General Population and little by little you get to know the other people. After a while you just blend in.


There was one hour a day when you could use the phone, but everyone bum-rushed it and the line was twenty or thirty people long. Usually I didn't bother. I did call Stan in Staten Island a couple times to ask him to send money for the commissary, because he had sent me money when I was in Bellevue, but there wasn't anybody else I wanted to call.

Maggy was working as a parole officer upstate and I think Yolanda told her what happened and where I was. We were writing sometimes, but she made it clear how much I'd disappointed her. Jamie wrote too, and sent me paperback books and stationery. My mom didn't know where I was. I was too ashamed to tell her.

In the summer on Rikers you can die from the heat. There's no air-conditioning, which wouldn't be so bad except that in jail you can't throw open a couple windows or a door when you want to catch a breeze. In jail, you're sealed in, and so is all the hot air. On really hot days, especially when it's also humid, your skin is wet, your hair is sticky, your scalp itches, and you can forget about sleeping at night because in ten minutes your sheets and pillow are soaked too.

The heat made everybody cranky. There were fights every day. Look at somebody cross-eyed and she'd get a couple friends together and jump you.

Around the end of July they transferred me to a new part of the jail, the Rose M. Singer Center. I was in a cell in the top tier, and everything was new and clean. I had a couple of friends by then and they were transferred, too. Lisa was a tall blonde, about my age, and Vera looked about nineteen but was almost thirty. They got arrested together doing a robbery.

It's important in a place like Rikers to make friends and stick together. Because a lot of women go around trying to start fights, and they usually won't bother you if they see you're not alone.

Did I say what the days were like, now that I was in Singer? You wake up, eat breakfast, sit in the dayroom and watch TV or play cards, eat lunch, go out to the rec yard for one hour, sit in the dayroom and watch TV or play cards, eat dinner, sit in the dayroom and watch TV or play cards, and get locked up in your cell for the night.

I'd been on the job list for months, and finally one of the COs came and told me they were putting me on Sanitation. It was the midnight to five A.M. shift, stripping and waxing floors. One of us stripped the old wax off, another came behind and mopped it up, and then a third person mopped on the fresh wax. There'd be five or six of us working different corridors. I really liked the job, and it broke the monotony. Plus, we got paid five dollars a night, which went into our accounts.

I'd go to bed around six in the morning, sleep until afternoon. I missed a lot of meals, which was another good thing. I was getting a complex about my weight, because I'd gained twenty pounds so far.

I was going to still be in jail for my mom's birthday in September. I wanted to send her a card, maybe even call, but I was nervous about getting in touch with her. So I sent her phone number to Jamie, asked Jamie to please call and tell her she was in touch with Tina and Tina was okay. I told her not to say I was in jail unless my mom asked, but if she did, tell the truth. And then please, please write back right away and tell me how she acted.

When I finally heard my name at mail call my legs started shaking. At first I couldn't even open Jamie's letter, just sat there on my cot staring at the envelope and wishing I had X-ray vision so I could know what was in it before I opened it. Then I took a deep breath and ripped it open.

My mom *did not* ask where I was, so Jamie didn't tell her. My mom just told Jamie she was glad to hear Tina was okay, and to please let Tina know that her mom and her little sister and brother loved her and they always would, and they missed her very much and hoped Tina would get in touch with them soon.

I read the letter four or five times. And over again at least once a day the rest of the time I was on Rikers. Except toward the end it was almost impossible to read because my tears had smudged the ink and it was all wrinkled from sleeping with it under my pillow every night.


My other friend, besides Lisa and Vera, was a woman named Nilda. She was a Spanish lady in her thirties with plenty of connections. Which meant she had drugs, usually reefer. Her friends outside would smuggle it in during visits. Visitors have to get searched—not a full body search, but they pat you down, check your mouth and clothes and shoes—so how they snuck drugs through, I don't know. But I know it was possible.

Nilda's friend would pass it to her under the table in the visitors' room in a little plastic bag or a condom, and somehow, without the COs seeing, Nilda would stuff it up inside her body. Prisoners have to get a body search after visits, but the COs don't stick their fingers up there, so Nilda never got caught. I heard of other women getting caught and going to Solitary, but during the time I knew Nilda it never happened to her.

She'd tap the tobacco out of a cigarette and pack it up with grass. You could smoke reefer in the rec yard without the COs noticing because it looked like an ordinary cigarette.

One afternoon I was playing Spades in the dayroom and Nilda came and said she had a special present for me. I followed her back to her cell, and she opened her locker, took out a plastic cup. There was some orange liquid at the bottom and I knew what it was right away—methadone. Nilda was a heroin addict, and heroin addicts get methadone every day to help them withdraw. But the COs make you drink it in front of them. I asked Nilda, "Where the hell did you get this?"

She told me, real proud, "It's spit-back."

I held the cup, looked at the orange stuff. It was in her *mouth*. She'd carried it back to the block in her *mouth*. I thought, yuk, I don't want to drink spit-back.

But you don't turn down favors in jail. It's disrespectful.

I never had methadone before, and I liked it. It's a nice, relaxed high, like heroin. Everything goes into slow motion and you feel like you're in outer space, floating. I went back to the dayroom and played cards a while longer, then I nodded out and missed dinner.

I wrote to my mom. Kept it short. Told her where I was, gave her my address, told her to give the kids a big hug and kiss for me. When she actually wrote back I was so excited I called her instead of writing again. Stood in line thirty minutes to get to the phone.

She was nice. Said it was good to hear my voice. She put Robby on, and he was so excited about starting kindergarten next month he forgot to be shy. He told me, "I'm gonna ride the school bus!"

After that I called a couple times a week, except for when two women had a fight and yanked the phone out of the wall. It was ten days before it was fixed and we could make calls again.

I asked my mom if she'd come visit me. She said at the end of August, when Jessica got home from Fresh Air camp, they'd all come.

My mom's visit, it was so painful. Not just for me, for all of us. We sat at one of the tables, Robby on my mom's lap. Jessica was tanned from camp, but she was almost as skinny as Robby. My mom was wearing a bright flowered dress with lots of pinks and yellows and greens. I recognized it—it was the one she wore when she had to go someplace important, like the welfare office or to get on the waiting list for city housing or sign Jessica up for summer camp. I had a lump in my throat seeing her in it that day. Because she'd put it on to come visit me in jail.

She tried to get Jessica to tell me about camp but Jessica didn't want to talk. It was noisy and crowded, and the woman at the next table was having a fight with her boyfriend. He was threatening her and they were calling each other dirty names, and I could tell it was making Jessica uncomfortable. Maybe scared, too. I felt bad that my family had to be here, in this place, just because they wanted to see me.

Now that we were together there wasn't much to say, we just sat and looked at each other a lot. My mom never asked how come I was in jail. It wasn't the kind of thing she wanted to know. I asked if she'd heard about an apartment yet, because last spring she signed up for public housing but the waiting list was one to three years. She told me no, they were still waiting.

Robby started squirming on my mom's lap, jiggling and kicking his sneakers against her legs. I told my mom, "You should go soon. The kids."

She said yeah, she guessed she should. She said, "So when are you getting out?" I told her, the end of October, two more months. I asked could I maybe stay with them again. She said, well, for a little while, but it would be hard. She said, "You know how it is when we're all jammed in there."

I told her yeah, I knew how it was.

"And Robert's there and everything."

"That's okay, Ma," I told her. "Really." I didn't want to be cramped up in that room, anyway. Not when I could be on the streets and have my freedom.

Robby made his whole body go stiff so my mom couldn't hold him. She pushed him off her lap and he started whining to get back on. I just wanted this visit to be over. The lump in my throat was getting bigger every second.

When my mom got up to leave I gave her a quick hug, gave the kids hugs. Told my mom, "So have a happy birthday. I'm going to send you a card. They have some in the commissary."

They went out the visitors' door and I went out the opposite way, where the COs wait to search you. I turned just before the door slammed shut behind me, just in time to see my mom's flowered dress disappear behind two of the guards.

On October 31, Halloween, I got on the blue-and-white jail bus for the trip back to the city. I had eighty-eight dollars in my pocket from my working account, which was what was left after my weekly trips to the commissary, and I had my freedom.

Look out, New York, Tina's coming home.

THE FIRST MONTH BACK AT Grand Central I was smoking more crack than I ever did before, slam-dunking ten vials a night easy if I could get them. And when I couldn't buy crack, I was drinking: blackberry brandy, vodka, sometimes Johnnie Walker. People were telling me I was getting to be just like April. I told them, "Yeah? Well, good."

I needed to know where April was at before she died, needed to feel what April felt. So I had to do the same things she did, the same way she did them. I had to get to the point where *I* didn't care about anything anymore, either.


I was keeping to myself. Corey didn't come around much. Jackie was gone, I don't know where. They said Francisco was in jail, and Smokey was laying low because the cops were after him for stealing a hunk of brass railing off the main staircase. When I did hang out with someone it was usually Harley or, once in a while, Shiv. Shiv was out of prison but he was different. Prison had changed him, made him angry. Sometimes he scared me.

I spent a lot of time panhandling, always trying to get enough money to go on a mission. It was near the holidays, when people always gave more, but I wasn't making as much as I used to. And I was noticing that the commuters weren't as friendly as they used to be, either. I didn't want to think about why. Didn't want to think it was maybe because I didn't look as young and cute and out of place as I used to, or that there was any chance I was starting to look even *a little, little bit* like all the other panhandlers.

I called my mom the week before Christmas. I had stayed with her the first week I was out of Rikers, but we were fighting so much I left.

She sounded surprised to hear from me. We talked a little while, she asked if I was going to be home for Christmas. I told her sure, of course, then hung up fast.

Gave some money to one of the old guys who hung around the waiting room, told him to go into the liquor store and get me a pint of Johnny Walker. Drank it down so fast I had an upset stomach. Officer Korsoff was on duty by the ticket windows and he called me over, said it looked like I was boozing it up. "Got the Christmas spirit?"

I told him no, I just talked to my mom and I missed her and my sister and brother. I started to cry. He said, "Aaah, you'll be okay, you just need to sleep it off."

Sleep it off. I slept a lot. Smoking, drinking, sleeping—that was my life now.

I slept through most of Christmas Day down in the tunnels. That was fine with me, I wanted to be unconscious on Christmas.

Around seven o'clock I came upstairs, saw one of the older bums I knew, who always panhandled by the Lexington Avenue entrance. I sat with him and we panhandled until we had change for some beers, enough to get a little buzz on, keep us from feeling too bad.

He started telling me about his family and how much he missed them. He was from someplace like St. Louis. By then I was on my second beer and I started telling him about my family too, and also about April. Christmas music was playing on the PA system and the people today weren't commuters, they were dressed up and rushing around in a holiday way. You knew that everyone but you was in the middle of having a real Christmas.

Of the four Christmases I spent in Grand Central, that's the one I remember most. Panhandling with that old guy, drinking beer, listening to Christmas songs, and talking about our families.

By around nine o'clock the beers were gone, the old guy was dozing off, and I just wanted to go down to the tunnels where it was dark and sleep for a year. But before I could make myself move, two volunteers I knew from the food line came rushing over.

They told me, "We've been handing out gifts in the waiting room and there's a few left." They had a couple of presents wrapped in red and green tissue paper. From the shapes, they were either scarves or gloves or socks. I said thanks, I got one already. They said, "Well, Merry Christmas."

"The same right back to you," I told them.

I woke up in the tunnels, all groggy, had to come upstairs to find out what time of day it was. Turned out to be afternoon. My head hurt. I put my hand up there, felt a bump, and then, oh my God, I remembered what happened last night.

I was sleeping in one of the spots on a big slab of cardboard, and someone was pulling at my pants, trying to get them off. That's what woke me. It was so dark I couldn't see who it was, only knew it was a guy and his breath smelled rotten and he was big and strong and he was trying to rape me. I screamed, "Leave me alone!" I kicked and fought. He said, "I got a knife, bitch," and ripped at my pants some more until they were almost off. I yelled, "Leave me alone!" again and he slammed my head against the wall.

Then there were two more guys in there, and one was Shiv and the other was Shiv's friend who he met upstate in prison, and they grabbed the guy off me. I couldn't see much in the dark, just heard the punches and kicks and curses and knew Shiv and his friend were beating the guy up. I pulled my pants back on.

They left him unconscious, took his money and a bunch of crack vials he had in his pocket. I didn't get any of it, money or crack, but at least I didn't get raped.

Talking to myself helped when I was coming down off a high. Because my mind was getting so messed up, it was playing tricks on me. Sometimes I was almost delusional. I needed something to focus on in order to get back to reality, something solid like the sound of my own voice. My voice, it was like a light I could steer my mind toward.

January sixth was my twentieth birthday. Twenty, oh wow, that was really scary. I didn't want to get old, I wanted to stay a kid. Old was a bag lady with swollen legs.

In January I did the *48 Hours* program, but they told me it wasn't going to be on TV until February. I only did it because Harley wanted me to get the money. I didn't have many friends anymore so Harley was pretty important to me.

———— • ————

I was smoking so much crack I was starting to hear things sometimes: walkie-talkies, cops telling each other, "Okay, we have her in sight now, yeah, she's smoking all right, she's got her stem in her jeans zipper, she's proceeding east on Forty-third Street."

So real quick I'd cross the street and head west.

I had to keep moving because the voices might catch up to me if I stood still, only sometimes I felt too paranoid to go out in the streets. Grand Central was safer. So I'd spend the day walking the terminal in big circles, going in one door and out the other, just to keep the motion going. That's how I got to know Mary. She was always sitting at the east entrance panhandling, and I started saying, "Hey, Mary, what's up?" when I passed.

Mary hung by herself like a lot of the older ones, only she wasn't old, maybe thirty. Nobody wanted to be around her because she was one of the people whose mind wasn't all there. Mary always wore the same dirty trench coat, with baggy jeans and sneakers that didn't match. She was thin, dark-skinned, had long wiry hair that stuck up like she'd just jammed her finger in an electric socket.

Sometimes we'd share cigarettes and beers together. I felt sorry for her, because every week or two she had a story about how some guy had raped her. I knew it was mostly the truth, because Mary was someone people took advantage of a lot.

Other times she was way off, talking about how she had more powers when it was raining, or that today everything she was thinking was orange. So I didn't hang around with her on those days. On those days, I'd just keep circling the terminal.


Jerry saw me sitting by the deli with my bottle of brandy, called me inside, gave me a container of clam chowder and a sour pickle from the barrel. The soup was good, hot and thick. The last time I ate was yesterday. He said, "You look like something the cat dragged in."

I told him, "You wouldn't win any beauty contests, either."

Two conductors came in and ordered sandwiches from Jerry. "How you doing, Tina?" one of them asked. His name was Moe.

"Doing good. How you doing?"

"Oh," he said, "getting old."

"Nah, you're not old."

"But I'm getting there," he said. "And I want you to get old someday too."

I told Moe, "Ahhh, don't worry, we'll get old together."

"You're going to wind up like April. You got to start taking care of yourself."

"I am, I am," I told him. "Look. I'm eating."

"What's in there?"

"Soup. See? Soup is good for you."

"And pickles?" the other conductor asked. "Pickles are good for you?"

Jerry said, "Well, it's a vegetable."

Moe started talking about me to Jerry then, like I wasn't there. "This kid's got a lot on the ball," he said. "I wish to hell she'd straighten out before it's too late." He said to me, "Tina, this is the wrong place. You hear me, Tina? It's the wrong place for you."

I told him, "Guess what? I'm going to be on TV this month. On *48 Hours.*"

*A* is for "April." I spent half an hour carving an *A* into the back of my hand with a Budweiser pop-top.

When the blood came I stopped. I thought if it bled it would leave a scar, but it healed up in a week or two. You couldn't even tell where it had been.

Harley figured out I was pregnant. I never told him, he just knew. Said he'd seen pregnant women before, knew how their bodies started to change.

Harley said I had to start eating right. No more drugs, not even reefer. He said now I had to think of the baby.

I said, Fuck you, Harley, what baby? You promised you were being careful, you promised there wasn't going to be any baby. So believe me, Harley, there won't be.

There was this one matron in the ladies' room who was always screaming, "No smoking in here!" whenever I walked in. But if it was a different matron on duty I could sneak into the toilet and take a couple hits.

Then I'd come out and stand and look in the mirror at my eyebrows. In my eyebrows, well, in my eyebrows I thought there were bugs. Because if you rub your eyebrows the wrong way with your finger, you hear this little crackling sound. And I thought maybe that was the bug eggs.

The matron, she was wiping out the sinks and watching me rub my eyebrows. "What's the matter, sugar?"

"This," I told her, "is the wrong place for me."

Went out onto Forty-second Street, walked down Lexington. "This is the wrong place for me," I told myself. "I'm not like the other people in the station. It's the wrong place, the wrong place." People were looking at me. Maybe I was talking out loud again. Well, who gives a fuck. They didn't have to listen if they didn't like it.

"It's not that I'm better or anything," I told myself. "I don't think I'm better. Just that I don't belong here."

I ducked into the doorway of a closed hardware store. Took a good blast. Uh-oh, walkie-talkies. The plainclothesmen were coming. I got out of that doorway quick, started walking uptown fast as I could. Walked all night, until dawn, until my feet were swollen and sore and my legs ached. But I stayed ahead of the plainclothesmen.

I crashed in Harley's spot for a few days. Needed a rest from the last binge. In between sleeping I lay listening to the trains pulling in and out, the people up on the platform. Sometimes, when it was very quiet, I could hear rats. Once I woke up and saw one sitting near me chewing on a Burger King wrapper.

Sometimes I could see myself like I'm up above, looking down. Me in my dirty clothes, no shower in I don't know how long, sleeping on a stinky blanket in a dark hole under a train platform.

This was the wrong place for me.

I felt feverish. Harley was nice, bringing me hamburgers and sandwiches and hot soup from Jerry's. I could tell he was worried. Beverly came down with coffee and a bottle of aspirin she stole from Rite-Aid. The second or third day my arm started waking me up. It hurt so much I couldn't sleep on it. First I didn't know why, then I remembered that I cut it on the stairs a few days ago in a fight with this girl, Michelle.

Next day I couldn't move my arm at all. Even crack didn't take the pain away, so I knew it was serious. I got myself up to the waiting room and called Jamie, collect, and she told me to get over to the emergency room at Bellevue Hospital, then she called George McDonald.

WORKING AT PATHMARK IS JUST as much of a boring drag as I thought it would be, but it's where I met Sinead, so I wouldn't change getting that job for anything.

Sinead is the night manager, but I didn't really get to know her until I'd been there about six months. We didn't work too many of the same nights, and on weekends, when I didn't have classes, I worked days. There's something about Sinead that makes me feel comfortable right away. She's a warm person, very easy to be with. And she laughs a lot.

The first time she comes over, Uncle Tony makes dinner, chicken in spaghetti sauce. Afterwards I make coffee, and we sit around the living room for an hour or two while Sinead and Uncle Tony talk. Me, I just listen. Sinead is from Ireland, and she tells Uncle Tony what it was like growing up there, and he tells her about some of the places he's been to, like Egypt. They seem to have a lot to talk about, and I'm proud I have a friend who can have smart conversations with Uncle Tony. After Sinead leaves, he can't stop talking about how nice she is.

Uncle Tony is getting thinner. He's doesn't go out much anymore, except for walking Freeway and sometimes going to my mom's for Sunday dinner. He doesn't even work on the Batmobile anymore, just spends most of his time lying on the couch downstairs listening to the stereo, or in bed watching TV or videos. His hair is almost all gray now, and his bald spot has spread so it covers the top of his head. He looks old. Fragile too, like he might break.

I bring him home groceries from Pathmark so he doesn't have to go shopping, and when I'm not rushing to class at night I cook too. I try to make stuff he likes, like the chicken with spaghetti sauce, but it never comes out as good as his. I make us hamburgers a lot, and a stew he showed me, and soups.

Because he's tired so much, I'm doing a lot of the cleaning now. I vacuum and mop the kitchen floor once a week, but the bathroom I do almost every night. I clean the shower, sink, and toilet with a solution of bleach, because I looked it up in the school library and I know bleach is one thing that kills HIV.

Uncle Tony knows I'm always scrubbing out the bathroom with bleach. He has his own glass and fork and spoon that he uses and he keeps them in a special place in the kitchen. We never talk about him being HIV positive but I guess he's figured out, by now, that I know.


Sinead came to this country in 1987, the same year April died. She talks with an Irish accent, which sounds neat, and she grew up on a farm, in a family with five kids, in a part of Ireland called Limerick. She's the oldest, and she told me she was cooking and cleaning and helping take care of the others before she was big enough to see over the kitchen table.

She's different from anybody I ever met before. She has a cute round face, brown hair that's about shoulder length, and big round eyes that always make her look surprised. She's six years older than me and she went to college in Ireland and got her bachelor's degree in marketing management. I never thought anybody who is a college graduate, and who has as much class as Sinead, would choose to be friends with someone like me.

But I figure, well, she doesn't really know me. When she does, then we'll see if she still likes me.

So I'm going to do this little by little. The second week, we go see a movie, and in her car on the way back to Uncle Tony's I mention that I didn't go to college sooner because I ran away from home and had a drug problem and was in rehab. She's kind of interested in that. She wants to know what drugs I took. So I tell her crack, mostly, but also heroin and angel dust and marijuana.

She's heard of those drugs, but she doesn't know anything about them. Like, what they look like, how you take them, why you take them. So I tell her.

Then she wants to know what rehab is like, so I tell her about Samaritan Village. That really interests her and she asks a lot of questions. Then she says, "Well, I really admire you for having the strength to go through all that and stay off drugs."

So far, so good.

It's one of the first warm nights of early spring and I'm out on the terrace with a can of beer feeling sorry for myself. Sinead went to a party with her friend Eve. She tried to get me to come, but even though I like Eve, I couldn't face a party.

I hear Uncle Tony come up behind me. I thought he was in his room, watching TV or sleeping. "Tina?" he says. "Are you okay?"

I tell him, "Nope."

Uncle Tony is wearing a pair of blue silk pajamas that Freddie got him, and over that a thick pullover sweater. He sits down in the plastic deck chair beside me. He does it slow, like old people do, kind of eases himself down like he's sore all over. He says, "Look how clear you can see the stars. Wish we had a telescope."

"Wish I had a life."

"You do. You just don't know it yet."

"No shit."

"Things'll get better. You're so young and you have so much to look forward to. Me, I'm at the end." He leans over, stubs out his cigarette in the ashtray, then lights another. I notice he's shivering, even though it's warm and he's wearing a sweater.

"Don't say that," I tell him.

"It's okay, Tina. I've had a full life."

For a while we sit there, not talking. The elevated is only blocks away, and every time a train passes it sounds like it's going right through the living room. But I got used to it right away from living in a train station so long.

A couple trains go by while I finish my beer, then it's quiet again. "Uncle Tony, could you do me a big favor?"

"That depends."

"When you die, if somehow there's a way, could you come back and contact me? Or give me a sign so I know you're okay?"

He reaches over, puts an arm around my shoulder. "If I can. But even if I can't, you know I'll still be with you."

Sometime in the spring my brother Frankie moved back up from Florida. Sinead got him a job at Pathmark, sweeping and stuff. I can't remember the last time I saw him, but it was around six years ago. He's almost twenty-two now and it's weird to see a grown-up man instead of my little brother. For years we were writing and talking on the phone long distance, but now that he's here we don't know what to say to each other.

Around the time Frankie came back, Robert moved completely out of my mom's house. I don't know exactly when or how it happened because I wasn't around a lot, but I know he'd been spending less and less time there and finally he just stopped coming altogether. Nobody minded much, not my mom or Jessica or even Robby, who is his son.

Now my mom is seeing Walt. Walt is the first guy my mom was involved with, since my father, who is older than she is. He's a retired cop, and she's known him a couple years because he drives the school bus for handicapped kids that she works on. He's divorced, and even though he's not the greatest, because he criticizes my mom a lot, he's a big step up from the other men she's been with.


Without really noticing it, I've been putting together a life for myself. It's been sneaking up on me when I wasn't looking.

Every Saturday, Sinead and I bring home groceries for her place and for Uncle Tony's. As we're carrying the bags out to her car I see this old man hanging around the parking lot. He was in the store a while ago, cashing in a bag full of cans. Sinead is up ahead unlocking the car trunk, but he catches up with me. "Excuse me, miss," he says, "you need some help?"

He's wearing scruffy clothes, a heavy jacket even though it's about seventy degrees, and he has one blind eye. I tell him, "Yeah, sure." He takes the two bags out of my arms and carries them to the car.

This guy, he looks a little like the bum I spent my last Christmas in Grand Central with. He'd never believe that where he is, I was too, and not long ago. But I don't really believe it, either.

I give the man with the blind eye a dollar. I guess he didn't expect that much because he thanks me about six times. But, you know, what's a dollar to me now?


Sinead lives in Brooklyn not far from us. One night I go over for dinner and to watch a movie. After we eat, I take my video of the *48 Hours* program out of my backpack and tell her, "Let's watch this first."

She has no idea what the hell it is and I don't tell her. I just sit there while she pops the video in the VCR and watch her face during the first part, which shows the tunnels of Grand Central, the filth and darkness, and some of the drugged-out people who live down there. She looks a little confused. Like, why is Tina showing me this?

Then I come on. Close up, my face big as the TV screen, cigarette dangling from my mouth, doing my Tina the Tough Guy bit. Sinead's eyes get even bigger and rounder, she looks over at me quick like she has to make sure I'm still in the room with her, and the Tina on the screen is the fake one. She says something I can't quite hear, it sounds like "Oh my God."

She watches the whole interview sitting on the edge of her futon. I'm on the floor by the TV, but I'm watching her face, not the screen.

The end of the interview is where I tell Harold Dow, "I'm through talking to you," and get up and walk away, because Harley is waiting for me with the crack. But I leave it on a minute longer, long enough to show George McDonald telling Harold Dow, "Tina's just waiting to die." Then I reach over to the VCR, click it off, eject the tape.

"So," I say. Holding the tape in my hands. Waiting.

Sinead is still staring at the TV screen, even though it's blank now. "I didn't know," she says.

"Now you do."

Finally she looks at me. I think maybe there are tears in her eyes, because they're so shiny. "Oh, Tina," she says, "you looked like such a brave little kid."

UNCLE TONY DIED IN 1992, in October. My mom and
Walt came to Pathmark to tell me. She'd been calling him all day and got
worried when there was no answer, so she and Walt went over there. Walt's
the one who went upstairs and found him on the bedroom floor.

They took me back to Uncle Tony's, and I made myself go upstairs to see
him. I was terrified. I never saw a dead person before, but the people from
the morgue were coming to pick him up and I had to make sure he was
really dead and it wasn't all a crazy mistake.

I had known Sinead for ten months. She was on her way out of town
when this happened, or at least I thought she was. She was supposed to be
going to the Poconos for the weekend with Eve, and she tried to get me to
come but I wouldn't. They kept having car trouble, though, like a flat tire
and then a clogged fuel pump, and then they got lost. Finally they stopped
in a McDonald's for hamburgers and fries and directions, and when the girl
rang up the cash register Sinead took one look at the numbers in the total
and told Eve this was the last straw, they were going home. Eve didn't understand, so Sinead had to explain that "666" meant Satan and it stood for
everything evil, and if you were raised in a religious Catholic family, like
Sinead was, you took that seriously.

So they turned around and came back to New York, and when Sinead
went into Pathmark to surprise me they told her I'd gone home early
because my uncle had died. And that's how she happened to walk into Uncle

Tony's bedroom just as I was about to kneel down by his body. I was either going to kiss him good-bye or try to wake him up, I'm not exactly sure which, but then I turned and saw Sinead.

I never even wondered how or why she got there at that very moment, it just seemed right that she did. For once in my life I didn't try to stop crying. Because in her arms, it felt okay.

A few weeks after that, Frankie went back to Florida and took the kids with him, and my mom moved in with Walt. The kids were staying with me at Uncle Tony's the last week, and the night they left we all went over to the old apartment so Jessica could get some things she forgot.

The place was a mess. The four of us, me and Frankie and Jessica and Robby, just stood there in the doorway a minute because no one wanted to go in. It looked like my mom dumped everything out of the drawers, took what she wanted, and left the rest all over the floor: the kids' old toys and clothes, some of her clothes and makeup, hair curlers, and a bunch of mail, most of it never opened. Robert's bead curtains were still hanging in the doorway, and most of the furniture was there too.

"All our pictures and everything," Frankie said, and bent over to pick up a photo. "This is my third birthday. And look, Tina, over there, that's a picture of our dad."

"Why did she leave the pictures?" Robby asked. "Doesn't she want to remember us?"

"She could've at least saved them for us, even if she didn't want them," Jessica said.

Frankie had talked my mom into letting the kids go with him to Florida. He said the schools were better and Florida was safer and healthier for kids than New York. And since Walt was after my mom to move in with him, I guess it was the best thing for my mom, too. Because I don't think Walt would've taken the kids. Jessica was fourteen and Robby was almost nine, but Walt had already raised two kids and probably didn't want someone else's.

While Jessica was digging through a pile of clothes for her tank tops and her bathing suit and Robby was looking to see if he could find his Matchbox cars, Frankie and I waded through the mess looking for things we might want. But I didn't have the heart to go through it all. It was too sad to see the place this way. Like my mom wasn't just throwing out everything in the apartment, she was throwing out our lives together too.

Frankie took the picture of him on his third birthday, and the one of our father, and I took one of my father and mother and me together when I was just born. Also, I took the baby pictures of Robby and Jessica off the wall, so they would at least have that, and the one of my fifth-grade graduation.

The oil painting of Jessica was also still on the wall, the one with the weird-looking thumb. On the way out I asked Jessica if she wanted me to take it for her. She said no, just leave it there with everything else.

Today I'm sorry I did. I should've tried to save more.

Sinead gave up her apartment and moved in with me at Uncle Tony's after he died. Just before Christmas she brought home Einstein. She'd already asked if I wanted a puppy, because a friend of hers had a dog who had a litter, but I told her I didn't want any animals. We didn't even have Freeway. My mom had kept him after Uncle Tony died, and when she moved in with Walt she gave him to a neighbor.

I told Sinead having animals doesn't work out for me because I start to love them and then they're gone. I wasn't going to get hurt again. Next day Sinead walked in the house and she had the dog, anyway. "Look," she said, and held it up: a fat, fluffy little ball of puppy. "This is Einstein. He's part Lab, part shepherd."

I didn't look at him for hours. I knew if I did, I was going to get attached. But he climbed into my lap while I was watching TV, then tried to climb up my chest to lick my face. He was making little puppy noises, he smelled sweet and milky, and he wiggled all over.

Before Sinead and I were hanging out together, she used to go out a lot. There was this one bar her friends always went to on Friday nights. Once in a while, in the beginning, Sinead tried to talk me into coming to meet her friends, but I always said no. So we'd go to a movie instead, or rent a video.

But after a while she started talking to me about things like "compromising" and "being more flexible." Meaning, I should stop being so stubborn. Meaning, sometimes I do what she wants, then sometimes she does what I want.

I tried. I went out once in a while. But whenever she asked me to go somewhere with a lot of people, like to the bar or a party, I'd tell her, "I'll make an ass out of myself. Go without me." Because I couldn't explain that this was not about me wanting it all my way, this was about terror.

So a couple times a month, she did go without me. I'd spend those nights sitting home with the puppy, drinking beer, hating her for being able to have fun without me, and hating myself for not being able to be there too. And drinking beer wasn't a good thing for me to be doing alone. It made me think too much about the past. And if I let myself think too much about the past, all the pain and guilt came crashing down because I was still here and April wasn't.

Sinead was always correcting me about stuff like my grammar and, especially, my manners. "Don't lick your knife, Tina," she told me the first time we were in a restaurant together. She wasn't sounding nasty, just looking at me like sometimes I amazed her.

We were having pancakes. I told her, "Okay, okay, okay," and put the knife down, even though there was still syrup on it.

"But didn't anybody ever tell you that before?"

"I never used a knife to eat with."

"And how ever do you cut your meat?" she asked in that funny Irish accent of hers.

"I don't. I just pick the whole goddamn piece up on the fork and take bites."

That wasn't the whole truth, actually. The whole truth was that sometimes I just picked food up with my fingers. Unless it was spaghetti. We never had meat that often, anyway, and when we did it was usually chicken wings or hamburger. My mom never cared if we used our fingers, but I didn't want to tell Sinead that.

"Well," she said, "that's not very ladylike."

I swear, a couple years ago if anybody tried to tell me I wasn't being "ladylike," I would've called them a stupid asshole motherfucker. But I'd changed a lot, I guess, and also there was something about Sinead, and the way she said these things to me, that made me know she was doing this because she cared.

She was also on my case about putting my napkin on my lap at the table, and saying please and thank you to people. Also stuff like not saying "ax" when I meant ask, and never, ever saying ain't. Even the way I walked wasn't right. She said I bopped. She made me copy the way she did it—keep your body straight, put one foot in front of the other.

One day we were in a little restaurant having ice cream, and I was in the middle of telling her about something that happened at work when I noticed she was just staring at me like, well, like I was *amazing* her again. "What?" I asked her. "What?"

She said, "You don't even notice it, do you?"

"Notice what?"

"The burping."

I hadn't noticed. What's there to notice about burping? It happens when you eat, and you get used to it. "Don't tell me," I said. "It's not ladylike, right?"

Sinead explained that if you do have to burp, do it quietly. And you should also try to cover your mouth and say excuse me afterwards.

"Well, fuck you," I told her. "If you don't like my manners or my grammar and you don't like my walking and you don't like my burping, you can go hang out with someone who's a little more ladylike. Like maybe the Queen of goddamn England."

And I got up and walked out.


It bugged the hell out of me, having her on my case all the time. Sometimes I'd try to do things right when I was with her, but when I was alone I'd burp as loud as I wanted and bop all over the place when I walked.

Except, a funny thing started happening: after a while, when I was alone, I'd forget to switch back to my way of doing things. The ways Sinead showed me, little by little, were getting to be my ways.

I started realizing that knowing how to do things right made me a little more confident about going places. The more I learned the rules of the game, the less I had to worry about doing something so dumb that everyone would know I was an outcast. I started thinking, well, maybe Grand Central wasn't the only place I could ever fit in.

WE MOVED HERE TO THE apartment in Bensonhurst, Brooklyn, in January 1996. It's in a three-family house in a quiet neighborhood. We have the whole basement floor and the yard, which is great for us and our animals. Because we not only have Einstein, there's Minnie now too. She's part pit bull, and one of Sinead's friends rescued her after she got thrown out of a car during a hurricane. We also have a little black cat named Rubbish. One of the construction-crew guys found her in a garbage can a couple years ago, when I went back to work at Ready, Willing & Able for a while as a cook.

My sister, Jessica, is eighteen, and she lives with us too. She was going through a rough time in Florida, so we told her to come back to New York. Now she's working at a Pizza Hut and going to classes for her general equivalency diploma.

Robby also had some problems. The State of Florida was going to put him in a foster home, because I guess they felt he wasn't getting enough supervision with Frankie. Instead, my mom sent him to Boys Town, in Nebraska, because she felt that would be better for him. He calls me every couple weeks and he seems to be doing okay.

I've been working as a salesperson at Macy's, in the domestics department, for more than two years. I had to drop out of school for a while because working full-time and carrying a full class load was getting to be too much. But I'm planning to go back, because I want to become a drug counselor. I have a pretty good life now and sometimes, when I see a homeless person, I feel guilty. Being a drug counselor would be a way to give something back. I think I owe that.

Sinead is a manager at Office Max, and by the time we both come home at night we're tired. Weekends are mostly for grocery shopping and cleaning and all the shit stuff that doesn't get done during the week, so we don't go out a lot. We have a couple of friends we see once in a while, but mostly we stay home and watch TV or rent a video. Once or twice a year we go camping on Cape Cod or in the Poconos.

I still have nightmares. A lot are about crack. I'm in the tunnels, I've just taken a blast, and I wake up in the middle of an adrenaline rush. There's also the dream about the man who raped me. And the ones about April. Sometimes, if it's an April dream, I wake up crying and holding my pillow, because I'm dreaming the pillow is April and if I don't keep holding tight she'll die.

Sinead knows about the nightmares because they wake her up too. She tries to get me to talk about them, but I won't. I can't. There's so much I haven't told her.

Now I'm like one of the people I used to pass in the streets when I was cracked out, people going to work, coming from work, going home, normal people having safe, ordinary lives. But only on the surface. Inside of me, nothing feels normal. I've learned that just because you have a home and a job and a car and two dogs and a cat and a MasterCard, and you know your table manners and remember to say please and thank you and you don't burp loud in public or bop when you walk, it doesn't mean you're not still a misfit. All it means is now you can fool everybody.


It was a big fight we had that night, me and Sinead, an ugly one. Over nothing important, like most fights. But this was something that didn't usually happen, because Sinead is the one who taught me it's not the end of the world when two people fight. That never dawned on me before. With my mom and Robert it was slap, bang, boom and he's out the door. And my mom would be left by herself for a day or a week or maybe two weeks to go on from there and take care of herself. Sinead showed me that arguing and even fighting can be a way of working things out. If you do it right.

But we didn't always do it right. This time we both said stuff we shouldn't have. I yelled shitty things about her middle-class thinking and her perfect manners and tight-ass religious Irish background, and she yelled shitty things about where I came from and told me maybe I ought to go back there, see if I liked it better.

So I am. That's just where I'm going. I slammed out of the house, I'm in the car on the Belt Parkway heading toward Manhattan at sixty-five miles an hour.

It's after eleven o'clock when I get to Grand Central, and the station is almost empty. I walk from one end to the other, and it really creeps me out because not only are most of the homeless people gone, so is the waiting room. I mean, the room is still there, but they've taken out all the benches and filled the place with potted trees and about twenty food carts with striped awnings and signs advertising stuff like pastries and coffees and fresh fruit and bagels. Most of the carts are either closed for the night, or closing now.

This is like one of those weird dreams where you go back home after being away for a long time and everything has totally changed. It makes me feel a little better to see Jerry's deli is still there. But it's closed too.

There's a couple of cops around, but none of them look familiar. A janitor is sweeping up the main concourse. I don't know him, either. But the ladies' room looks exactly the same and the same old matron is there, the one who was always screaming, "No smoking in here!" when me and April tried to sneak a hit in the stalls. I go in and wash my hands at the sink, then stand at the mirror a minute or two, combing my hair. Just to see if she's going to recognize me. But she's reading a newspaper the whole time and never once looks up.

I walk through Grand Central again, do an even bigger loop. There isn't a corner that doesn't make me remember something, or someone. It's like going back to a house where you grew up and seeing it for the first time with the eyes of an adult.

And what I'm seeing now is a railroad station.

Right outside one of the Lexington Avenue entrances is Mary. She's sitting on the sidewalk panhandling, she's in exactly the same spot and she looks exactly the same as the day I left. Not a day older. Her hair is just as wild, she's just as dirty, I swear it even looks like she's wearing the same clothes.

I sit down next to her and right away she says, "Hey, Tina! You got any change?" Like six years haven't gone by, like it's the most natural thing in the world to see me sitting there.

She smells of urine, but I don't mind. I give her a five-dollar bill, enough for a couple beers, and maybe she'll get a sandwich too. She thanks me and stuffs it in her pocket without looking at it. Later she'll notice she's got a fiver, or maybe she won't, maybe she'll give it to the guy in the liquor store thinking it's a one. He won't tell her, either.


St. Agnes Church is less than half a block from Grand Central, and when I get there I can't believe my eyes. All that's there is an empty shell, just the outside walls and the front steps. I knew they had a fire last year, only I didn't know it was so bad. There's some scaffolding along one side of the church where they're starting to rebuild.

I sit down on the step like I used to after April died, when I was missing her so much. The pain comes as strong and fresh as if it was yesterday. And the questions are still there: What was she going through when she did it? And why couldn't she hold on just a little bit longer? If only she could've gotten through that moment, whatever that moment was, she might have made it. April deserved life as much as me. Why did I make it and not her?

And worst of all: Why wasn't I there? If I had been there with her instead of locked up in jail, maybe I could have kept it from happening.

I want to sit right here on this step, the place that was the last April ever knew of life, and if I sit here long enough—like forever or a hundred times forever—maybe I can understand what it was like.


Francisco told me he knew April had the gun. She showed it to him in Bryant Park. Said she and Jackie found it under the seat of a delivery van they broke into, and she pulled it out from her jeans waistband for him to see. It was a small gun, a .25 caliber. Maybe, she said, he might want to buy it? She'd let him have it for twenty dollars. "Hell, no, I don't want a gun," Francisco told her, "and you better get rid of it. Guns are nothing but trouble, and besides, that one looks like a piece of shit."

April told him it's just that the clip was broken, but it still worked okay. She told him, Fifteen dollars. I'll give you the gun for fifteen dollars. And for a minute Francisco almost bought it, just to get it out of April's hands. She'd been bingeing for days, she was just coming down, and nobody in her state should be walking around with a gun even if it did have a busted clip.

But before he could say anything, April told him, Ahhh, don't worry, I can unload this easy. I know someone who'll give me twenty-five, but I just wanted to give you a break at a discount price. She stuffed the gun back in her jeans and was gone before Francisco ever got a word in.

Beverly told me that a few hours later, at around five o'clock, her and Micki were sitting on a bench in the waiting room eating Chinese take-out when April came rushing through. Beverly hollered, "Hey, April, you want some shrimp fried rice?" But April kept going like she didn't even hear. Beverly told me she looked out of it, like a zombie.

280

About the same time, Francisco was going into the terminal through a Lexington Avenue door when he saw April fly out. He only got a glimpse of her face, but he told me he was sure she was crying.

"April," he called, "hey, wait." She hollered back, "Bye!" and kept going, heading down Forty-third Street in the direction of St. Agnes Church. Francisco could see Santos sitting there alone on one of the lower steps. He wanted to go after her, but he knew better. When April wanted to be left alone, you left April alone.

Santos was an Hispanic guy in his thirties, had a long smoky-colored beard that made him look like a Bible picture. I never liked him, but he was April's main robbery partner around this time, even more than Jackie. Right after she died he got sent to jail for being a cat burglar, but I cornered him when he got out and made him tell me what he knew.

He was sitting on the fourth step of St. Agnes Church, drinking a Budweiser out of a paper bag and eyeballing a silver Audi across the street, trying to figure his chances of breaking in and getting away safe. It was a quiet Sunday afternoon, hardly any people on the street. There were services going on inside the church and Santos could hear hymns being sung. He knew, from hanging around the neighborhood, that it would be almost an hour before services ended and the people came out. He was thinking, well, maybe he would go for the Audi.

He started to take another swig, saw out of the corner of his eye that someone was coming, and shoved the can down in the bag. Then he realized it was April. She was running down the middle of the street, but she looked spazzed out and unsteady on her legs, and her arms were flopping around in a way that would have been funny if she was doing it on purpose.

April nodded hi to Santos and started up the stairs. He held up the can, meaning, You want some? but she just waved her hand at him and sat down on one of the top steps. Santos was raising the beer to his lips again when he heard, just behind him, a sudden sharp *bang,* like a firecracker. He turned around, started to say to April, "What the fuck was that?" But never got the whole sentence out.

April was lying on her side, curled up, her right hand hanging over the step holding the gun. Her eyes and mouth were wide open, like in amazement, her left hand was reaching up clawing the air like she was trying to grab hold of something. "Oh shit, April," Santos said, "oh shit, oh shit."

He reached out to touch her, then pulled back. Ran up the church steps, banged on the double doors yelling, "She shot herself, she shot herself!" but no one answered, so he figured maybe they couldn't hear him over the singing.

There was a car stopped half a block away, at a red light. Santos took off after it yelling, "Help, she shot herself!" He was aware that someone, maybe a priest, had come and opened the church door just as he was running down the steps, but he couldn't make himself go back.

An ambulance and two police cars were there in five minutes. Everyone in Grand Central heard the sirens, and some came to see what happened. Francisco said the cops told him she shot herself in the right temple and the bullet went clear through and out the other side. She was still alive when they took her away, but she was unconscious, twitching and kicking, having seizures. One really spooky thing Francisco told me: her right hand was curved like she was still holding the gun, and her trigger finger kept jerking, repeating over and over the last conscious thing she ever did.

All that was left on the step was one of her sneakers and the stuff the EMS workers had taken from her pockets: a screwdriver, pocket knife, Bic lighter, pack of Marlboros, and two unwrapped squares of Double Bubble gum. There was a small bloodstain on the concrete where her head had been.

George McDonald called her mom, who sat with her all night in Bellevue Hospital. April died at nine-thirty the next morning without ever regaining consciousness.

It's like, *wham,* holy shit, I just got hit in the stomach with a sledgehammer. I'm sitting on April's step doubled over with pain, my head is pounding, I'm crying and sobbing and shaking and I don't even give a damn that I'm doing it right in the middle of East Forty-third Street. It was that real. It was like it happened all over again, and I saw it.

Then I start noticing a warm feeling in my middle spreading out all through me, and somehow I understand that I don't have to look for April in the sky anymore. She's right here inside me.

And so, I talk to the inside of me. April, I say, I'll never know if there was one reason you did it, or if it was just because all the shit was piling up too high and too heavy. And maybe I'm not supposed to know. But I think even if I *was* there, I couldn't have stopped you. I just might have put it off a day or a week. Because you always did what you wanted and you would never listen to anybody. That's one of the reasons I loved you.

It's after midnight. My eyes are swollen and puffy from crying, I've smoked most of my cigarettes, and my butt is starting to ache from sitting on the concrete step so long. I'm about to light my next to last cigarette when I have the feeling I'm being watched.

Up the street, by the door of Grand Central, three guys are hanging out. Two are black, one is Hispanic, and even though I can tell from here that they're strangers, they look like half the guys I knew when I lived in the station. And five years on the street tells me they've got me targeted.

I realize in a flash that I'm not safe here, not anymore and not ever again.

Because these guys, when they look at me, they're not seeing one of their own. They're seeing a young white chick alone on the street in the middle of the night.

I get up from the step real casual, check that I'm not being followed, and walk very quickly away from the burned-out shell that was St. Agnes Church. My car is on Third Avenue, only half a block away. I lock the doors, start the ignition, turn the radio up way loud, and head on home.